You can taste the ma... bobwhites...

Once upon a department store, Gable's was the place to shop, eat, meet, and be seen in downtown Altoona, Pennsylvania. Now, the classic store has come back to life in the pages of this one-of-a-kind book. For the first time, the whole true story of Gable's, its leaders, its employees, and the shoppers who loved it has been told, complete with secrets and inside stories from those who knew it best. You'll never forget this trip through a century of retail history, from the store's humble beginnings to its glory days to the thrilling fight to save it from going out of business. Hundreds of rare photos and images, never before gathered in one place, will take you back to the people and moments that made Gable's great, then carry you forward to a modern-day reunion of Gable's employees and a VIP tour inside the Gable's buildings as they stand today, complete with yesterday's treasures. Discover mysteries and surprises that have never been revealed to the general public until now. Relive the story of a lifetime on a magical journey straight out of your favorite memories and dreams. If you've ever longed to return to the department store where you always felt at home, or you just crave a simpler, sweeter place where the malts are always delicious and the customer is always right, step inside. You're invited to the grand reopening of the store that comes to life every time we remember...

The Glory of Gable's

The Glory of Gable's

By Robert Jeschonek

pie press publishing

Other Pennsylvania books by
Robert Jeschonek

Christmas at Glosser's
Easter at Glosser's
Halloween at Glosser's
Long Live Glosser's
Death by Polka
Fear of Rain
Penn Traffic Forever
The Masked Family

DEDICATION

To the people of the William F. Gable department store, whether they are with us in body or in our hearts. Without them, there would be no store and no story. Thanks to them, we will never forget.

Introduction

What if you could shop at Gable's department store in downtown Altoona just one more time? What if you could get incredible bargains on quality merchandise at one of Gable's famous sales, then meet old friends for lunch in the restaurant? What if, just for one day, you could enjoy shopping the way it used to be, when the customer was king, and people were happy to be there?

If you're like me, you would seize the opportunity in a heartbeat. Once you've had that kind of magical shopping experience, you never forget it. There is a longing in your heart, always, to go back to it...even if the store you loved so well is gone forever, closed since 1980.

After 96 years in business, Gable's left its mark in a big way. Generations of people in Altoona and the surrounding region did most of their shopping in that store; every milestone and special occasion in their lives was marked by a visit to Gable's. For many, it also was a place of employment and a stepping stone to bigger and better things.

And for everyone who ever shopped there, it was a place where necessities, dreams, and desires were all within reach. Where the vision of one man, founder William F. Gable, became the shared vision of thousands of shoppers.

That vision inspired this book, even 36 years after the store's closing, in an era when those who remember the store are being slowly outnumbered by those who don't...by those who weren't even alive when it closed its doors forever.

The fact is, the love of Gable's—and the longing for this book—are still strong. They motivated local collectors and historians to preserve precious photos, relics, and knowledge about the store long after its closing. They inspired members of the Gable's family, whatever their job or connection to the company, to save up their special stories, priceless artifacts, and inside information.

And they encouraged everyone who had a piece of the puzzle to come forward in a spirit of generosity and add it to the mix for posterity's sake. This book could not have succeeded without them, without their love of Gable's and willingness to help me tell (and show) the story in full.

Photos by Robert Jeschonek

Courtesy Jeffery Holland

They've made it possible for you to read and remember the glories of Gable's—or discover them for the first time. Maybe you're not old enough to remember the store, but you've heard about it and wondered what was so special about it. Now, thanks to this book and the people who helped make it possible, you can finally understand what made Gable's so special.

You can find out about the incredible display windows that became a holiday wonderland each year...the innovative sales techniques of William F. Gable and those who followed in his footsteps...the pet department, hair salon, million-dollar china department, and all the departments within the four walls of the two Gable's buildings...and the radio station, WFBG, that broadcast from studios within the store (and later became local TV station WTAJ).

Photo by Gelon V. Smith

Nothing short of being there can convey the full glory of Gable's, but at least you'll get some idea of what it was like. For the rest of it, ask someone who shopped at the store.

Ask them what was so great about Gable's merchandise and prices. Ask them if it's true that Gable's employees were the most qualified and courteous you could ever meet. Ask them if the food in the restaurant was really as good as they say, and if they've ever found any food better.

Courtesy Altoona Mirror

And ask them if they've ever shopped at a store so wonderful in every way, or ever expect to do so again.

Those of you who remember Gable's know the answer to that one loud and clear. The sights, sounds, tastes, smells, and textures of Gable's are etched forever in your memory, telling a story of a perfect place that makes every modern store pale in comparison.

It's a story that begins in 1884, with one man who had a dream, and continues through decades of expansion and success...through the sale to an out-of-town company, the enclosure of the building's grand architecture behind a brick façade...and, finally, the store's going out of business in 1980. But the story doesn't end there.

It continues to the present day with dedicated keepers of the flame who reunited to bring the store alive again the best way they could: By sharing their memories and treasures and laughter and tears.

And, in so doing, helping ensure it will *never* be lost or forgotten, no matter how many more years may pass or how different the shopping experiences of future generations might be from the glories of good old Gable's.

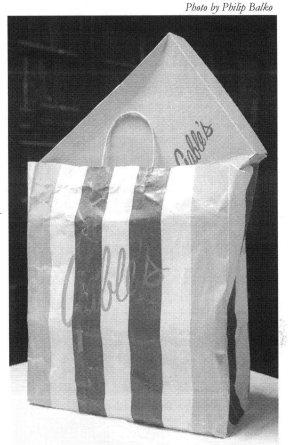

Photo by Philip Balko

Photo by Philip Balko

Photo by Matthew Germann

Courtesy Jim Shannon

Photo by Gelon V. Smith

Courtesy Jennifer Snyder

Courtesy Frank Barry

Courtesy Helen Hildebrand

4

Chapter One

A Miracle on Eleventh Avenue

2016

It started as a slow trickle, a little before 10 a.m. on a Saturday morning in June. As organizers watched nervously, a handful of people made their way along Eleventh Avenue in downtown Altoona. They gathered across the street from what had once been the main Gable's building,

greeting each other with friendly hellos as if no time had passed since their last meeting at Gable's.

They had come in response to invitations published in the local newspaper

the *Altoona Mirror*, posted online on local-interest Facebook groups, featured on local TV station WTAJ, and talked about on five local radio stations courtesy of Forever Broadcasting. They had come because this was a reunion, and anyone who had worked or shopped at Gable's was welcome to join the fun.

Still, no one really knew how many people would show up.

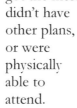

After all, it had been 36 years since the store had closed for good. In all that time, plenty of Gable's notables had moved on in one way or another. There might not be that many left, and of that number, there might not be that many who got the message, or didn't have other plans, or were physically able to attend.

As the minutes dragged by, the trickle continued. It was starting to look like there wouldn't be many folks attending at all. Perhaps, the organizers would have to try again on another day and hope for a better turnout.

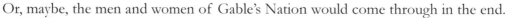

Or, maybe, the men and women of Gable's Nation would come through in the end.

Reporting for Duty, One Last Time

Soon, the slow trickle became a steady tide. Attendees came out of the woodwork, pouring toward the Gable's building from all directions.

Every one of them was smiling. They came together like family, hugging and laughing and catching up on news and gossip. Without being prompted or missing a beat, they reminisced about the times they'd shared when the store was still open for business.

Photos by Philip Balko

Some had been shoppers and supporters of Gable's, like Frank Berry, Linda Emery, Linda Hudkins, and Steve McKnight. They came to remember spending time in the center of excitement in Altoona, the place where people gathered to dine and socialize as much as to shop for quality merchandise at bargain prices.

Most of the guests had worked at Gable's at one time or another, however. For example, Deborah Huffman (maiden name Kimberly) was head cashier in the credit department from 1968 to 1975. Jim Dixon worked in the paint and shoe departments from 1964 to 1968 (and met his future wife on the job as well).

World War II veteran Earl Pattillo worked at Gable's in high school, and his father worked there from 1926 to 1970. Then there was Rose Marlett, a clerk in the foundations department on the third floor from 1964 until the store's closing in 1980.

Nadine Shade had an especially long Gable's career, having worked in the receiving room from 1947 until the store went out of business 33 years later. "It was wonderful," she remembers. "I had a wonderful boss. We didn't make much money, but they treated us like family."

The oldest former employee at the reunion was 103-year-old Beatrice Mannion, who worked in the bargain basement from 1935 to 1940 and directed Gable's choir in holiday performances.

Gable's In Her Blood

Dozens of supporters and former employees came together that morning to celebrate the place they'd loved for so many years. But the reunion was truly complete when a member of the Gable family that had once owned the store joined the festivities.

Virginia Gable Brantner, great-granddaughter of store founder William F. Gable, drove in especially to mark the occasion. Virginia, who worked in the store during her high school years in the early 1960s, reminisced about the good times she spent in the store as a child, immersed in the family legacy that became an Altoona institution.

Photos by Philip Balko

"I have good memories of my granddad bringing us in sometimes on Sunday afternoons and letting us play in the toy department," said Virginia. "He would let us run all over the store. It was great fun."

Does Gable's Still Matter?

As the reunion continued, employees and supporters posed for photos and told their stories to local TV and newspaper reporters. Folks exchanged contact information and made plans to stay in touch and get together in times to come. Some guests even pulled out photos and treasures like store name tags and gift boxes.

Meanwhile, the Gable's building on Eleventh Avenue towered over them, the place where they'd spent so many happy hours and lived so many memories. Being there, in its presence, made the reunion seem so much more meaningful and real. Even closed for the day, its grand original architecture hidden behind a brick façade bearing the name "M&T Bank" instead of "Gable's," the building made everyone feel at home again.

After all, the spirit of a great department store doesn't go away when it goes out of business, does it? Whatever the sign outside, that building will always be Gable's to the people who worked and shopped there.

Photos by Philip Balko

It was there so long, for 96 years, that it became ingrained in our lives, dreams, and imaginations; its bond with the people of Altoona, Hollidaysburg, Duncansville, Cresson, Bedford, and all the surrounding area will never be broken.

Gable's still *matters*. If it didn't, those dozens of people would never have come to the reunion. They wouldn't have kept coming right up to the very end, straggling in even at the last minute with memories and memorabilia.

Does it matter as much as it did in its heyday, when Gable's was the king of Blair County retail? When everyone, but everyone, did their shopping at Gable's, and planned their calendars around the store's annual schedule of sales? When you could get your hair done in the beauty shop, find a perfect deal in the bargain basement, and top it off with a Bobwhite at the snack bar? Probably not.

Or maybe Gable's matters more than ever now. In an era when shopping has become much more of a hit-and-run affair, and it can seem that corporate profits—not the

customer—are always right, perhaps looking back to a different, time-tested approach would do us some good. Yes, there was a place where shopping was an *event*, shoppers and employees were treated as *family*, and quality, fairness, and honesty were seen as *necessary*, not *optional*.

Photos by Philip Balko

9

There was a time when people weren't in so much of a hurry, and weren't glued to their electronic devices or detached from the world and people around them.

There was a store that embodied the best qualities of democracy, the free market, and America, back when we took such things to heart.

And that place was Gable's. And remembering it is the first step we must take if we ever hope to bring back the best parts of it that were lost.

So consider this book a map as well as a reminiscence. Maybe it will show us the way back to that legendary place, or at least point us in the right direction.

And all of it starts 132 years ago, at the end of a century that in some ways feels more like a thousand years in the past.

MEMORY DEPARTMENT

There will never be another department store like Gable's. It didn't matter who you were, Gable's had something for everyone!

Debbie Maitland Burgan

I will always remember going there with my grandmother to purchase books. She would always buy me a Nancy Drew mystery or Bobbsey Twins book. Later, when my interest turned to nursing, it was the Cherry Ames series. I remember eating in the dining room in the basement and also getting lunch in the eating area just inside the Twelfth Avenue entrance, where we would get off the bus from Gallitzin. On the sidewalk in front of Gable's was our favorite place to view the annual Christmas parade; then, we would go inside and get in line to visit Santa and have our picture taken with him. My favorite things were browsing in the book gallery, where you could look down at the main floor, and choosing

Photo by Gelon V. Smith

candy from the bins that the clerk would scoop out, weigh, and put into little bags for us to take home. My dad would always buy warm, salted, and roasted cashews, too. It was also the best place to purchase Brownie and Girl Scout uniforms, handbooks, and badges. What great memories!

Karen Marlett

I remember feeling like I was in *Miracle on 34th Street* during Christmas season when going to Gable's with my mother. Long Live Gable's!

Carol Gioiosa Martino

I met my husband of 42 years working at Gable's. I was in accounting, and he was the assistant manager of men's furnishings. I can still remember a lot of the department numbers and department managers.

Barb Nycum Koehle

11

I used to work at Gable's down in the bargain basement. I remember the restaurant. My favorite was the chocolate malt. Mom used to meet me for lunch, and the food was great. Mom and I used to shop together at Gable's. We would spend all day just walking around the store and sometimes come home with nothing. I so miss those wonderful times with mom and Gable's.

Marie Andrews Jenner

I grew up in Bellwood in the 1950s and 60s, when Gable's was central to any trip to Altoona. Mother always checked the Arcade for special bargains—and a stop in the ladies room located near the Arcade. The shoe department (2nd floor by the stairs?) was the best place for shoes in Altoona (in my opinion). Churning through the crowded aisles on the first floor, the air redolent of perfume, past the cases of chocolates and roasted nuts to get to the exit on Eleventh Avenue. The spacious (and quieter) fabrics and needlework department on the third floor. And perhaps best of all, the book department on the mezzanine, where I bought my first new book, *The Observer's Guide to Cactus*, printed in England (and therefore exotic) for $2.00. Gable's in Altoona, Where Quality and Fashion Still Prevailed.

Elizabeth Kurtz Lynch

Photo by Philip Balko

Photo by Gelon V. Smith

Chapter Two

In the Beginning, There Was...Sprecher's?

1884-1909

If William Francis Gable had never come to Altoona, you might have done your downtown shopping at a store called *Sprecher's* instead of *Gable's* for all those years.

It's true. The store that became Gable's started out as a dry goods firm under the ownership of John A. Sprecher. Would that firm, with John Sprecher running it alone, have become the same great success that Gable's someday did? We'll never know.

Courtesy Jamie Powers

But the fact is, everything changed on February 12, 1884, when William Gable came to town. Less than a month later, he and Sprecher were partners, opening the doors of their co-owned store at 1300 Eleventh Ave., also known as Virginia Street at the time, in downtown Altoona. And six months after that, well...Sprecher was out. William had new partners, and the name on the door wasn't Sprecher and Gable anymore.

It was William F. Gable and Co.

About the "and Co."

William F. Gable was a young man, just 28, when he showed up on Sprecher's doorstep with $800, looking to make a deal.

13

He had just spent six years working as a bookkeeper for the Dives, Pomeroy, and Stewart dry goods store in Reading, Pennsylvania, and that job became a stepping stone for his big new challenge. It was his former employer, Mr. Pomeroy, in fact, who tipped him off to Sprecher's firm and encouraged him to try to buy into it.

Dives, Pomeroy, and Stewart stepped into the picture again later, buying out Sprecher's interest in the company. They became William's new business partners, the "and Co." in "William F. Gable and Co."

It was the start of a beautiful relationship. William had big ideas and plans, and Dives, Pomeroy, and Stewart gave him the freedom and backing to make them a reality. The result was a steady stream of growth and success that eventually culminated in the giant store we came to know and love so well.

Courtesy Altoona Mirror

One-Room Store, One-Horse Town

The first store, the one that William opened with Sprecher, was anything but giant, however. Just imagine: the grand Gable's empire started as a single 20- x 40-foot room at 1300 Eleventh Ave./Virginia St., rented for just $75 from a man named Clement Jaggard.

Altoona itself wasn't exactly enormous or opulent then, either. According to the store historian of that era, William B. Parker, a Gable's department manager for more than 30 years, the little town had only one paved street at the time—a block of Eleventh Avenue/Virginia Street between Twelfth and Thirteenth Streets. All other public thoroughfares were mud, navigated by horse-drawn wagons. "It was no uncommon sight, even on Eleventh Avenue, to see wagons stalled hub deep in the mud," remembered Parker.

According to Parker, the only public transportation came in the form of horse carts that followed a route from Chestnut Avenue and First Street over the Seventeenth Street Bridge to Eighth Avenue and down to Fourth Street. Hours were limited, as the last ride from the west side of town to the east came at 9:30 p.m.

Walking across town was no joy after dark, as dim gasoline lamps were the only light source, and a sparse one at that. Electric lights didn't arrive on downtown streets until years later. Electric service in the city started on March 6, 1887, courtesy of Edison Electric Light and Illuminating Co.

The town had a long way to go to become a thriving, modern city. Its destiny, and that of Gable and Co., would be forever connected, beginning with that one-room store in that muddy-street town.

Opening Day

When the store first opened, all its contents put together would not have filled a single average department in the expanded store just a few decades later. According to a list from the company's original cash book, the total cost of all merchandise delivered to the store—purchased from Dives, Pomeroy, and Stewart on February 6, 1884—was $4,612.75. Items from that first stock included the following:

27 dozen spools of thread, $14.04
5 gross of horse buttons, $1.25
5 dozen of children's hose, $4.50

16 boxes of paper collars, $2.24
3 gross of red handkerchiefs, $1.35

The selection of items aligned well with customer demand. Sales on the first day of business totaled $266.50...not bad, considering it was a cold and blustery day, and the store only opened at 11:00 a.m.

The handkerchiefs were the first items to sell, in fact. The store's first customer, Samuel A. Hamilton, bought some when he dropped in just after the doors opened. He was a passenger train director for the Pennsylvania Railroad and, after working the night shift, had a habit of going for a walk after breakfast, before going to bed.

"As I was about to start out, my aunt, Mrs. Theodore M. Beam, reminded me that I needed some handkerchiefs and that a new store was about to open that day and that I might get a bargain there. When the store opened, I entered and made a purchase of handkerchiefs amounting to $10," remembered Hamilton.

It was a humble start, but it kicked off a busy day for William, Sprecher, and their small sales staff. According to entries in the cash book, that first staff, and their salaries for the day, were as follows:

Davidson Long, cash boy, $.25	Thomas Drass, $1
Charles Weaver, cash boy, $.25	E. Lytle, $.53
Fanny Wilson, $1.34	E. Ingram, $.57
J. Stanley, $2.92	William Wilson, $2.67
Mrs. Roop, $2.30	Mr. McCaster, $1.25

Movin' On Up...the Street

As small as that first store was, its appeal was strong. William put his ideas about retail to work, and customers responded with enthusiastic support. Business increased so much and so quickly, that a bigger location was needed after a few short months.

In the fall of 1884, William and his team packed up their goods and fixtures and moved to bigger digs up the street. This new location, a rental at 1402 Eleventh Ave./Virginia St., gave the firm multiple rooms to work with, enabling William to stock more goods and present them more attractively to potential shoppers.

Courtesy George Rowles

15

Courtesy William Burket

But the new store didn't leave room for everything, especially during the holiday shopping season. In late 1889, Gable and Co. rented nearby space and opened temporary satellite stores in them. The Gable and Co. Coat Store at 1500 Eleventh Ave. featured "Everything in Ladies' and Children's Coats." The Gable and Co. Toy Store at 1106 Fourteenth St. carried "Everything in Holiday Goods."

The multiple-room main store and satellite locations led to more business, and the cycle of success continued. Business got so good that Gable and Co. moved again just three years later—and this time, for the first time, they would own, not rent, the space.

Courtesy Jeffery Holland

MEMORY DEPARTMENT

I well remember the store's opening day. On my way home from the Miller school, I stopped at the new store and made some purchases.

The store became a halfway house between my home and the school, where I was a teacher, and I became almost a daily customer.

Mr. Gable was a man worth knowing. A congenial soul, who liked books and knew his authors in a familiar way. I always enjoyed a chat with him, and if he were not busy with customers, always came to chat about a favorite author or to point out new beauty in some book he could recommend.

In looking over my present library, I find almost fifty volumes bought at the Gable store. Among them all, the one I think I prize the most is a beautifully illustrated volume of Tennyson's poems. Many a delightful evening my "boyfriend" and I passed, reading his poems. I think our favorites were: "Dora," "Enoch Arden," "In Memoriam," and "Locksley Hall." The girls then did not meet their "boyfriends" with hat on and say, "Where are you going to take me tonight?" but often found enjoyment in the home circle. Yes, "I love my books as drinkers love their wine, the more I drink, the more they seem divine." And Mr. Gable was a great help to develop my love for books and good literature. His passing was a great loss to the literary world.

Viola Patterson Walter

The personnel of the store, as I remember them in 1887, was: Mr. Gable, as the guiding hand and advertising manager; Miss Anna Gable, bookkeeper; Miss Amanda Thompson, cashier; George Curtis, floor manager; Miss Annie Hill, Fred Eisenberg, and Homer Kerr, notions; Misses Lizzie Settle, and Ida Bobletts, ribbons; Misses Anna Plank, and Nettie Kolley, dress trimmings; Misses Ella Drass and Clarenden Lewis, hosiery; Misses Sadie McCloskey and John Nicodemes, underwear; Harry Newman, men's furnishings; Jesse Fay and Michael Delvin, linens; William R. Hotchkins and Clare Plummer, domestics; Harvey Schubert, cotton dress goods; Miss Lizzie Evans, gloves; Miss Katharine McCullough, Theo. Rupley and William B. Parker, dress goods; George

The Best Dry Goods Store in Altoona.

Courtesy Frank Barry

McFarlane, H. King McFarlane and John Newman, cash boys.

In addition to his duties in the linen department, Michael Devlin also was window trimmer. W.R. Hotchkins wrote the show cards, and the three cash boys swept the store and delivered packages after store hours.

John Nicodemes, a Civil War veteran, was one of the kindliest men I ever knew.

William F. Gable set many precedents in Altoona. He was the first intensive advertiser; first in windows and interior displays, and I believe the first in the country to have anniversary sales; which now, all over the country, are established customs.

One ad I remember for its pulling power was one written for the last sale in the old store, just before we moved. It read: "Be There!" And after each article advertised the same "Be There!" was written. Another, a display card in a window where men's higher priced ties were marked down to 25¢, read: "'Tis true; 'tis true, 'tis pity, and pity 'tis, 'tis true; but we must sell these fine ties at 25¢."

Many amusing incidents occurred over the years. One of the best was when a lady came in to buy muslin. Mr. Anspach was then domestic buyer. A young man, Alonzo Gill, was waiting on her. She asked, "What would the price be if I took a full piece?" Mr. Anspach was in a little office just off the department. Alonzo stepped into the office to ask Mr. Anspach what the price would be just as Mr. Anspach put his head out of the office to call for a cash boy. He called "Cash!" The lady, thinking he was speaking to her, replied rather sharply, "Certainly it will be cash."

Another one which happened back in the 1880s: A lady had come in a buggy to do some shopping and asked if someone could watch her horse and buggy while she was shopping. Homer Kerr, whose father was the first pastor of the Millville Lutheran Church, was given the job of watching her horse. In the meantime, King MacFarlane, then a cash boy, came out of the store with a package to be delivered to Eighth Avenue and Seventeenth Street. Homer said, "Jump in the buggy, King, and I'll drive you over. Before they got back, the lady, having concluded her shopping, came out to go home and not finding her rig where she left it concluded that her team had been stolen and promptly fainted. She was revived in a few minutes when the boys returned.

The same Homer Kerr, who could get in more scrapes due to his sense of humor than any boy I knew, one day opened the door of the west window, and seeing a pair of feet, and thinking it was one of the boys, grabbed hold of them crying, "a dead man, a dead man in the window," and began to pull him out. A voice said, "What do you want?" Kerr paid no attention to this, but pulled away. Imagine his surprise when he pulled him out to find it was Mr. Curtiss, the floor manager. Anyone who remembers Mr. Curtiss as a very dignified man can appreciate how Homer felt when he saw who it was. Mr. Curtiss had been adjusting something in the window and nothing could be seen but his feet.

William B. Parker, Store Historian and Department Manager

Courtesy Frank Barry

Chapter Three

The Bigger They Are, The Bigger They Get

1892-1902

While the money rolled in at the 1402 Eleventh Ave. location, William and his partners erected a brand new building that spanned 1320-1322 Eleventh Ave. By late 1892, the structure, which included three stories and a basement, was finished and ready for occupancy.

William and his staff moved the contents of the store overnight, hauling goods down the street on baggage trucks. They opened the doors to the public the next morning, December 8th...though store historian William B. Parker remembered the new location was not exactly finished in every way.

"'The doors were opened' is hardly correct," wrote Parker, "as there were no doors there.

"The building was far from being completed, the heating plant just started, no electric lights were installed and the counters were in the course of construction."

As incomplete as the new store was, steps were quickly taken to make it ready for business. "Temporary doors were put on, gas heaters were installed, and plain boards were used for counters. Electric lights were strung the length of the store," remembered Parker.

Half a Million Bricks and 90 Tons of Iron

Gable and Co. customers had no problem with the inconvenience and stopgap measures. They poured into the new store to spend their money...and the new building, when completed, turned out to be spectacular.

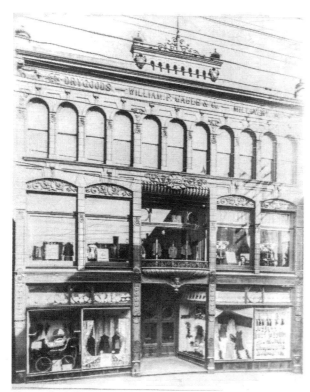

Courtesy Jamie Powers

"Upon this lot has been reared a magnificent three-story high dry goods palace," wrote a reporter for the *Sunday Graphic News* on Oct. 21, 1892. "The building is constructed of brick, iron, copper and wood. The foundation walls are of brick laid in cement and are 30 inches thick.

"The walls are also of brick and are 22 inches thick. The floors are supported throughout by iron columns, over 90 tons of iron being used in the building. Over half a million bricks were used in the building of the foundation and walls.

"The front ornamentation is of carved wood and pressed copper and presents a magnificent appearance. The entrance will be twelve feet wide and the sides of the vestibule will have show windows, while the floor will be covered with vault lights, thus admitting light to the basement. Two large show windows, each sixteen and one-half feet wide and eight feet deep, each containing movable partitions, divide the window into three separate sections."

In addition to the structural elements, the new store included some cutting edge technology for the day—a newly patented electric cash carrier system traversing the various departments. It was the first of its kind installed in a commercial establishment in the U.S.

The Utmost Courtesy

Gable and Co. kept providing customers with the kind of goods they wanted, at prices they could afford. It all evolved from William's personal philosophy of retail, one the company remained faithful to for much of its history.

Courtesy Frank Barry

From the beginning, William vowed to handle only honest, high-grade merchandise, for which he would always charge a fair price. He would always have the latest designs, models, and fashions in his store. And he would treat all customers with the utmost courtesy.

William also implemented innovative marketing techniques to boost interest in the store. On March 1, 1894, for example, he held a big sale to commemorate the tenth anniversary of the opening of the store. The response was so good, he made the anniversary sale an annual event that lasted throughout the store's lifetime. It was the first such anniversary sale in the retail world and was a true game-changer, copied by other major department stores, such as Wanamaker's in Philadelphia.

According to Parker, William F. Gable also came up with a plan to bring in more customers from outlying areas for special events. "One of the big events was the spring opening of 1895," recalled Parker. "We had made great preparations for this. Then to get the greatest number of people in the store, Mr. Gable hit on the idea of free carfare for persons living as far east as Tyrone, as far west as Cresson, and on the railroad branch from Martinsburg and

Williamsburg; also free trolley fare from Hollidaysburg and Bellwood. In addition, everyone, both customers and employees, were fed in the basement of the store. Long tables were erected the length of the store and everyone was fed by a corps of waiters. I might say there was no obligation on the part of anyone to buy. The only restriction was that all the special tickets which were given for free rides had to be countersigned at the store for the return trip."

Again and again, William's way of doing business paid off, in spades. Sales rose, word spread, and the store again outgrew its space. Approaching the turn of the century, even more expansion was in the cards.

Turning the Century

In 1898, Gable and Co. built an annex on the west side of the main building, adding 25 feet of frontage to the store. Another annex was added in 1900, this time on the eastern side of the main building. To make this addition, the company bought and demolished the property at 1318 Eleventh Ave., occupied until then by the residence of Dr. J.A. Rohrer and a grocery store owned by John A. Smith. With the completion of this annex, the store had a frontage of 100 feet and a depth of 120 feet.

Photos courtesy Dave Czuba

Two years later, in 1902, Gable and Co. bought and remodeled a property at 1326 Eleventh Ave., providing temporary space for several expanding departments. This remodeled structure came down in 1906, making way for another new annex that added 25 more feet to the store's frontage. At this point, the store had 125 feet of frontage along Eleventh Avenue. The place had so many windows, admitting so much natural light, it became known as "The Daylight Store."

Courtesy Frank Barry

And it wasn't anywhere near done growing yet. With William at the helm, and the backing of Dives, Pomeroy, and Stewart, the biggest expansions and most exciting times were yet to come.

Courtesy Frank Barry

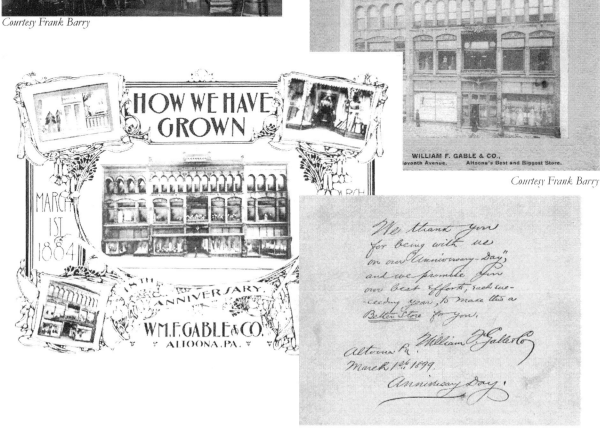

WILLIAM F. GABLE & CO.,
Eleventh Avenue.   Altoona's Best and Biggest Store.

Courtesy Frank Barry

Gable's VIP

WILLIAM F. GABLE
FOUNDER AND PRESIDENT
37 YEARS' SERVICE: 1884-1921

Did you know that William F. Gable once owned autographs of every president of the United States? Or that his personal library featured more than 35,000 books? Or that he bred Guernsey cattle on his 800-acre estate, Glen Gable Farms, each with its own special name?

It's all true. William went a long way from his humble beginnings in Chester County, Pennsylvania, to his days as a larger-than-life retail magnate in Altoona.

Roots of Greatness

William Francis Gable was born February 12, 1856 in Upper Uwchlan, Chester County. His father, Isaac, had German roots, while his mother, Hanna, could trace her lineage to the American colonial era. One of her ancestors, George Smedley, was a British Quaker who moved to America in 1682.

When William was 13, his family moved to Reading, PA, where he attended Reading High School. After graduating from Reading Commercial College, he went to work as a bookkeeper at the Reading lumber firm of Boas & Raudenbush. He put in five years there before moving on to a bookkeeping job at the Dives, Pomeroy, and Stewart dry goods firm in Reading. It was that job that laid the foundation for the retail success that would characterize the rest of his life.

Always alert to new opportunities, William paid attention when his bosses at Dives, Pomeroy, and Stewart suggested he consider partnering with John Sprecher for a dry goods operation in Altoona. By then, William had been a bookkeeper for

the firm for six years, and it was time to spread his wings. He and his wife, Kate Elizabeth, whom he'd married in 1879, agreed it was worth moving to Altoona to take a shot at the retail trade.

The risk he took paid off.

23

Paintings Courtesy Blair County Historical Society

Business at the original one-room store in March 1884 was brisk; gross receipts for the first month totaled a respectable $5,875.33. Soon, with backing from Dives, Pomeroy, and Stewart, William was able to buy out Sprecher and rename the firm William F. Gable and Co.

Courtesy Russ Stone

Site of the Gable House, 2016

Home and Family

As William got his new venture off the ground, he, Kate, and their daughter, Edna, moved into a house on Fourteenth Avenue in the 1st Ward in downtown Altoona. Five years and two more children (Bayard and Lowell) later, in 1889, the family moved into a big new mansion across the street, at 1221 Fourteenth Ave.

He and Kate had five more children while living in that house: Gertrude, Robert, Anna, George, and Mary Virginia. The three-story, 14-room home would be the heart of William's world for the rest of his life, a place where he could relax and spend time with family and friends. Neighborhood residents of the era remembered William as "a big man with a distinctive walk," who would stroll past their porches on summer evenings with his wife and sister, Anna.

But the department store still consumed much of his energy and attention. William wasn't exactly a hands-off kind of guy when it came to his business interests.

Type-A to the Max

As his company grew, William tirelessly pushed it to new heights. His type-A personality drove him to never let Gable and Co. rest on its laurels for even a little while. According to an entry on William in Jordan's *Encyclopedia of Pennsylvania Biography,* "there remains as the keynote of his achievement in many lines his limitless energy, his boundless capacity for unremitting toil, and his untiring industry."

William's personal philosophy of retail and his inventiveness in applying it also fueled the success of Gable and Co. He believed the customer was always right. To support that approach, he instituted a money-back guarantee policy in the store at a time when such policies were not commonplace.

He also put the One Price system in effect, eliminating haggling in the store. According to the March 1906 edition of Gable's newsletter, the *Store News,* "Ours is a One-Price store where everyone buys on an equal basis. The prices that you pay for goods are as low as anyone else would pay for the same goods, if purchased on the same day. There is no deviation whatever, in our prices—a rule that makes it entirely safe for even the smallest child to trade here." Customers knew what items cost and wouldn't have to waste time and effort dickering with salespeople, trying to get the best price they could. They also wouldn't have to worry about someone else getting a better deal than they did.

But customers weren't the only ones William insisted on treating fairly. He also showed equal respect to all members of his staff, no matter what their position. According to the *Encyclopedia of Pennsylvania Biography,* William said, "There is no line drawn in my mind or heart between employer and employee."

Courtesy Jeffery Holland

Store historian William B. Parker recalled that William F. Gable laid the foundation of the store "in honest dealing, courtesy, and kindness." According to Parker, William was a kind man to all. "To him all men were equal; he was not servile in the presence of the mighty; or haughty in the presence of the lowly. In business, the newest cash boy received just as much courtesy as the manager of the store. In fact, if there was any difference, the boy had the edge."

Another associate, W.R. Hotchkin, wrote of William, "He was a whole-souled believer in the Democracy of Man. Everybody to him was brother. He never had employees—he had fellow-workers, and any man or woman who was ever discharged by him was hopeless. They were there for life, if not totally unworthy."

A Future Without Profits?

William's philosophy of retail merchandising had a utopian component, to be sure. Though he had all the trappings of a first-rate capitalist, and his business was an example of great free enterprise success, he dreamed of different systems and means of fulfillment.

Twenty-five years after the store opened, at a banquet marking the company's silver anniversary, he expressed a vision that might be considered unorthodox for such a captain of commercialism.

"Just a word...about the ideal store, or 'the store beautiful,' that I often dream of. Present economic conditions interfere with this store being all we would like it to be. The mad, wild, greedy rush of competition forces us to use some methods that we would instantly dispense with were it not that we must protect ourselves under present conditions. One establishment cannot fight the battle alone.

"We do what we can to make things better and hope for the day when the competitive system will be no longer in the way of a higher and better civilization. Under a cooperative commonwealth we could get nearer the ideal store.

"With the passing of pay rolls and profits the real pleasure of work would begin. That time is coming with as much certainty and splendor as an Alleghany mountain sunrise."

We Almost Had a Gable Library

William's particular brand of retail management magic led to decades of great success for the store, which in turn enabled William to amass a vast personal fortune. A lover of knowledge and literature, he spent that fortune, in part, on building the largest personal collection of books in the region.

Over the years, he acquired more than 35,000 volumes for his library. According to his longtime friend and fellow book lover, H. Luther Frees, William's library had "hardly an ordinary book in it," and many editions were "of rare and costly character."

The books filled every corner of William's mansion on Fourteenth Avenue. The main library was located on the first floor, to the left of the main entrance. Rare and valuable books and manuscripts were stored in steel cabinets and cases on the second floor. Additional books were stored beside the servants' quarters on the third floor and on shelves lining every stairway in the house.

He hoped to someday share this extensive library with the public. Over the years, Frees wrote, it had been a dream of William's to "erect in the city of Altoona a fireproof library building in which to place his treasures, endow it with an amount sufficient for its proper maintenance, and then present the entire thing to the city of Altoona." But the Gable Library never quite came together, and the people of Altoona missed the chance to enjoy William's vast collection.

Courtesy Jeffery Holland

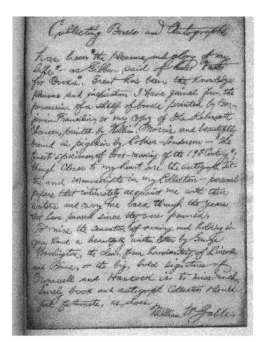

Treasures of the Autograph Hound

Books weren't William Gable's only great obsession, however. He was also an autograph hunter extraordinaire, with a collection that grew to encompass some of the rarest signed letters and manuscripts on the planet.

According to Frees, William owned original letters written by every signer of the Declaration of Independence except two. He also owned documents signed by every American president, starting with George Washington.

William's collection featured papers signed by a roll call of literary greats, including Elizabeth Barrett Browning, Robert Burns, Lord Byron, Charles Dickens, Nathaniel Hawthorne, Washington Irving, Rudyard Kipling, Milton, Edgar Allen Poe, William Shakespeare, Robert Louis Stevenson, and Oscar Wilde. A first edition of *Tom Sawyer* in the collection was signed by Mark Twain, who wrote, "Never put off till tomorrow what can be done day after tomorrow just as well." William also owned 400 original letters and manuscripts from Walt Whitman, including a first edition of *Leaves of Grass* that included an autographed manuscript related to the book.

It's hard to imagine what that collection would be worth today. A portion of it fetched over $100,000 when it was auctioned off in the early 1920s, but the number of famous names it included is staggering.

For example, Frees recalled exploring the collection with William one night until 3 a.m. Exhausted, Frees jokingly said he was going to have to leave unless William had a letter from "any real celebrity," such as Alexander the Great.

"Nothing doing," said William. "Alex was a little too previous for me, and besides, being of Quaker descent, I never cared especially for military heroes, but you old faultfinder, if it will do you any good to look at it, here is an authenticated signature of Napoleon Bonaparte."

Farmer Gable

Collecting books and autographs weren't William's only hobbies, though. He also bought an 800-acre estate near Elverson in Chester County that he called Glen Gable Farms, where he raised thoroughbred Guernsey cattle and trotting horses.

As its centerpiece, the estate featured a 100-square-foot barn with the space and facilities to house more than 200 head of cattle. The barn included three large offices; several bedrooms; a spacious sterilizing hall; a milk separating, sterilizing, and refrigeration plant; a boiler; and an engine room. Every stall had its own special drinking fountain for the use of its livestock occupants.

According to records of the livestock at the farm, Glen Gable cattle were given a host of fanciful names, everything from Bessie Bonnie of Hazelbrook to Juanita of the Pines.

There was even a Gibson Girl of Ballieu Place, a Primrose Goldie, and Bertha's Glen Gable Girl.

The animals and products from William's farm were ranked so highly that the *Altoona Mirror* wrote, "Mr. Gable is a gold medal business man, a gold medal collector of manuscripts and rare books, a gold medal friend, and now to these symbols of superiority has been added the gold medal as a farmer."

Managed by William's son, Lowell, Glen Gable Farms won the gold medal at the National Dairy Show in Chicago in 1913 for the finest milk produced in Pennsylvania, with a score of 96.75. That same year, Glen Gable Farms also won the gold medal and medal of honor in the market milk class at the Panama-Pacific International Exposition in San Francisco.

A Thing of Beauty Like a Gable

But William didn't spend all his wealth on collections and farming. He also put money back into the community that fed his success, donating to various philanthropic causes in the Altoona area. According to the *Encyclopedia of Pennsylvania Biography*, "No worthy object in his city has been long without his substantial aid, and the measure of the good he has accomplished cannot be told."

One of his favorite causes—and one with the most far-reaching impact—was tree-planting. Every year, he distributed thousands of tree saplings to local schoolchildren for planting on Arbor Day. These trees came to be known as "Gable trees" and were adopted as the symbol of the Gable department store.

Every year, William gave trees to every school pupil in Blair County, and every year, the trees were a different variety than those donated previously. They also were carefully chosen to thrive in the soil and climate of the area.

Courtesy Matthew Germann

In 1911 and 1912, for example, he donated 20,000 silver maples and catalpas. In 1913, he gave 25,000 elms, and in 1914, he provided 25,000 white ashes.

William went on to serve as parks commissioner in the city, where he continued to support tree-planting projects. Years later, it was written that, "there is not a spot of any considerable size in Blair County that does not have its elms, its catalpa, its mulberry, walnut, etc., a living monument to the generosity and foresightedness of William F. Gable." His efforts brought shade and beautification that continue to make Altoona a greener place to this day.

No Wonder Gable's Was Glorious

On top of everything else, William was a member of several literary societies, including the local Robert Burns Society. He was a lifetime member of the Blair County Historical Society and other local organizations.

By all accounts, he was a big man who made a big impression wherever he went. According to an article in the Sunday Graphic News from Oct. 21, 1892, "His intelligent enthusiasm, speculative boldness and his vice-like grip of details was manifest in his every movement."

After years of success in the business world, William was remembered by the directors of the Altoona Booster Association as building an institution "on the architecture of truth and fair dealing, never placing property values before human values, and treating with friendly courtesy both customer and employee.

"His strong personality, his benevolent disposition, his manifest civic pride, his wonderful love of nature, won for him an enviable place in this community.

"Those who knew him best loved him most."

Courtesy Matthew Germann

1884
CUSTOMERS
PLEASE
REGISTER HERE.

Photo by Gelon V. Smith

Courtesy Matthew Germann

Memory Department

The store was an institution. It was a part of our lives, like school, Sunday school, and church.

Author Unknown

The Gable store had baseball teams from time to time, but the team I remember is the one of 1891. We lined up as follows: Jesse Fay, catcher; Myers, pitcher; H. King MacFarlane, first base; Packer, second base; Schenfelder, third base; Wertzberger, shortstop; Gill, Summerville and J.G. Anspach in the outfield. Fay was star of the team and really a fine ball player; Anspach, a better store manager than a ball player, kind of evened things up. The rest of us were just "run of the mine."

In a newspaper write-up, the reporter gave Fay credit for playing a fine game, and had the following to say of your present manager, "Anspach did nothing in the field, and at the bat managed to miss the ball in great shape."

William B. Parker, Store Historian and Department Manager

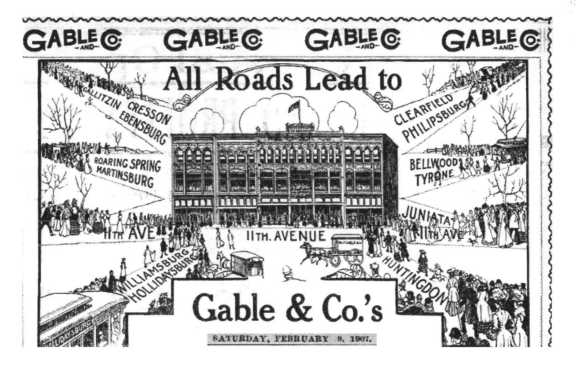

Gable's
Clip this coupon

It entitles you
to a 50¢ can of
BATHASWEET
for 25¢

⅛ ACTUAL SIZE

Bathasweet not only perfumes the bath, but it softens water magically and cleans the pores so thoroughly that the skin takes on a new, unblemished loveliness. Truly it is the maker of beautiful bodies. Also — it's a great help in shampooing, manicuring and shaving.

THIS VALUE CANNOT BE PURCHASED WITHOUT THE COUPON

Easter Candies

Ready Now
In Three
Convenient
Locations

ARCADE   MAIN FLOOR   BASEMENT

Cassidy's Fruit-and-Nut Eggs . . . . 19¢
Pound size of these delicious eggs

Hardie's Foil-Wrapped EGGS **3** for **10¢**
Maple, cocoanut and fruit-and-nut eggs

Fresh Jelly Eggs 25¢   **Cassidy's Cocoanut Eggs** 19¢
Assorted flavors   Pound size eggs
3 pounds   Each at only

Wunderle's
Butter Creams 29¢   **Easter Novelties** 75¢
Rabbits, hens and   For Baskets at
other figures, pound   5c and up to

Chocolate Covered Cocoanut Cream Novelties, 5c each, 6 for 25¢
Chocolate-Covered Eggs, Various Centers, 5c each, 6 for 25¢

1884   **GABLE'S**   1934

Easter Special!

Three 8x10
Portraits
And one Van Dyke
Miniature

$2.45

Four Proofs to
Select From
No Appointment
Necessary

Gable's
11th AVENUE BUILDING
FOURTH FLOOR

Only **15¢** *a day*
ON OUR
METER-ATOR PLAN

* The METER-ATOR can be placed anywhere near the refrigerator, out of sight and out of the way.

NOW ON DISPLAY
20th Anniversary
KELVINATOR

BEFORE you buy any electric refrigerator, see the new Kelvinator and let us show you how easy it is to own a Kelvinator on our METER-ATOR plan.

With a Kelvinator, you can actually save enough money to cover the 15 cents a day you put in the METER-ATOR.

Come in to-morrow and get the facts. There is no obligation to buy.

GABLE'S
12th AVENUE ARCADE

IS YOUR WATCH **BROKEN?**
OUR MODERN
Watch Repair
DEPARTMENT
Offers for
DOLLAR DAY ONLY
Mainspring $1.00
or Cleaning

EXPERT WORK   YEAR'S GUARANTEE
Genuine Cowhide Straps 12c

CRYSTALS
ROUND   FANCY
12¢   24¢

GABLE'S
12th AVENUE ARCADE

Highest Quality Blood-Tested
Chicks, $8 and $9 hundred

Place your orders now for these high quality blood-tested Baby Chicks. Tested for B. W. D. (Pullorum disease) by the stained antigen method. All reactors removed from flocks. Delivered to your door.

GABLE'S
11th AVENUE BUILDING—BASEMENT

Chapter Four

The Crash Next Door

1906

The collapse happened on a Tuesday morning, with a mighty roar and clouds of dust. By the time it was over, people had been injured, lives had been heroically saved, and construction plans had been forever altered. And it was all because Gable and Co. couldn't stop growing.

Courtesy George Rowles

Before the Fall

On the morning of Tuesday, Sept. 11, 1906, workmen were excavating a site next door to Gable's on Eleventh Avenue, preparing for the construction of the latest annex to the expanding store. Business at the store was just too good; more retail space was needed soon to keep up with customer demand. "The present quarters of the firm have become entirely inadequate to keep pace with the demands upon them, making the extensive additions almost imperative," according to the *Altoona Tribune*.

Workers were digging in the basement area of what had once been the Casanave Building. They were preparing to construct the foundation for the new Gable's annex, adjacent to the McClain Building on the corner of Eleventh Avenue and Fourteenth Street. The annex would add 14,000 square feet of floor space, bringing the store's total to 64,000 square feet. Elevators and other improvements would be installed in the new structure, aligning it with other modern retail establishments.

31

As the work unfolded that morning of Sept. 11, it seemed things were rolling along smoothly. But signs of trouble had been cropping up for some time. Businessman E.F. Miller had been worried since a week ago, when the wall of his hat shop in the adjacent McClain Building had cracked and slightly given way. Around 8 a.m. on Sept. 11, Miller noticed the wall trembling again, though chief contractor P.W. Finn had braced it. He went straight to Gable's and told the store manager, who ordered the contractor to take safety measures…but it was too little, too late.

Meanwhile, Alderman Banks Duncan walked out of Hurley's drug store in the McClain Building around 9 a.m. and noticed the wall trembling at the site. He saw dirt and sand rolling down over the bricks and told an engineer, "That wall will fall out inside of half an hour." His prediction came true.

Moments later, as Duncan walked to Bridge Street, the wall—and much of the McClain Building—suddenly collapsed.

Blood and Fear on Gable Street

According to eyewitness Harry Delano, a sign painter working on a nearby roof, one of the braces supporting the wall of the McClain Building slipped, and the foundation proceeded to crack and crumble. When enough of the foundation gave way, the entire wall collapsed into the hole with a roar, sending up a huge cloud of mortar dust.

When the wall fell, it took a sizeable chunk of the McClain Building with it. The roof split diagonally from the Eleventh Avenue corner to the rear corner of the inside wall, and part of every floor dropped suddenly.

Luckily, there were only ten occupants in the building when it partially collapsed. E.F. Miller and druggist D.G. Hurley ran out as soon as the cracking started…though Hurley soon ran back in to rescue Lizzie Adams on the second floor. The girl, daughter of Major Adams, was recovering from typhoid fever; the ceiling fell in directly above her, though the wall remained intact enough to hold back the worst of the debris and keep her from being crushed.

Lizzie's nurse, Miss Barr, and the building's owner, Mrs. McClain (widow of Frank McClain, who'd erected the structure 35 years earlier) weren't quite so lucky. They'd both been in a second floor hallway when the collapse struck, and the floor fell out from under them. Bricks, mortar, and timbers rained down around them as they dropped onto a landing between the first and second floors. According to the *Altoona Mirror* account, Mrs. McClain "crouched paralyzed with fear, expecting every minute to see the other half of the building descend on her head and bury her in the cellar." Instead, Hurley the druggist helped her get to her feet and escape just as the roof fell in behind them.

Meanwhile, janitor John O. Gonder had been sweeping up in the third-floor Odd Fellows Hall when the crash occurred. He thought he was done for when the place started falling apart around him. "I says to myself, 'Your time has come,' and ran into the corner and held my hands above my head to protect myself," said Gonder. "I got down the fire escape, but could not tell you how." Fortunately, though Gonder was covered with blood when he got outside, he was found to have no concussion or fracture.

Debris also bombarded workmen in Small's cobbler shop in the building behind the McClain Building. Wreckage crashed through Small's skylight and hit the busy workers, but no one was seriously injured.

A Hero Rushes In

Hurley the druggist wasn't the only hero that day. Edward "Happy" Hamilton also rushed in to save a life in the midst of chaos.

Hamilton, the African-American operator of a shoe-shining stand at the railroad passenger station, was walking up Eleventh Avenue when the McClain building started its collapse.

Alerted by the cracking noise from the crumbling structure, Hamilton headed toward it.

It was then that he saw William Alleman, son of Fire Chief Theodore Alleman, take a hit from a falling piece of wood in front of the building. Knocked out, William slumped to the sidewalk, right in the path of the toppling front wall.

Hamilton raced to his aid. Grabbing Alleman, he dragged him out of the way, just as the rest of the front wall smashed down on the spot where he'd been lying.

Courtesy George Rowles

Miracle in the Basement

As the dust cleared from the initial collapse, the scope of the damage became evident. The McClain Building looked about halfway gone; the rooms in the side that was still standing were filled with rubble and open to the elements. Onlookers braced themselves for the worst when it came to loss of human life.

But, miraculously, no one had died in the crash. The ten upstairs occupants all got out safely, though some were injured and required medical care.

Even the 50 workmen in the basement managed to survive, though they'd been directly in the path of the falling debris. Between the crumbling of the foundation and the fall of the wall, they'd had just enough time to run to the rear of the basement excavation. Since the weakened wall didn't extend all the way back to the alley, there had been just enough room for the men to get out of the way of the plunging mass of bricks, timbers, shingles, and tin.

Aftermath

But the danger at the site was far from over. Cleaning up the wreckage turned out to be a harrowing challenge.

When everyone who'd been inside during the crash had been accounted for, workmen started clearing debris. One of the men, carpenter George Glace, was nearly killed when a piece of timber fell while he was working atop a large piece of roof. The roof swung out toward the pavement just in time, and the timber only grazed his back on its way down.

Glace walked away with minor injuries, but the point was clear. The crash site was a risky place to be.

Responding to the threat, Altoona police arrived in force to keep away curiosity-seekers. Even the night shift cops were awakened and called in to cordon off the vicinity.

Physical danger wasn't the only reason to keep bystanders away. Some of the McClain Building's occupants had left behind valuables; police had to retrieve them before they could be stolen in the confusion after the collapse.

Mrs. McClain, for example, had $100 tucked away in her apartment, which Special Officer Bradley recovered for her. Bradley also brought out jewelry and clothing from residences in the structure.

In addition to the police presence, firefighters were summoned in case the ruins caught fire. When a fire didn't happen, the firemen joined efforts to tear off the broken roof of the downed building.

Who Brought Down the Building?

Soon after the fall of the McClain Building, Mayor Walker appointed a three-man commission to determine if the structure should be repaired or demolished. The commission included William Houseman, carpenter foreman at the Juniata railroad shops; contractor/builder J.A. Elder; and architect W.L. Plack. Their findings were unanimous: damaged sections of the building should be removed, including the remaining roof timbers and cornice on the Fourteenth Street side, and more modern building techniques should be employed if any parts of the building were used in reconstruction.

Another group was commissioned by the contractor, P.W. Finn, to determine whose fault the crash was. This group included architects Sholiar & Hersch, and Chas. M. Robinson of the architectural firm Robinson & Winkler. The result of their study? They determined that the McClain Building had been built improperly and had only stayed standing as long as it had because of the support of the Casanave Building. When the Casanave Building was knocked down for the new Gable's annex, the McClain Building was left unanchored and collapsed.

In other words, Gable and Co. and its contractors weren't to blame for the disaster. But in the end, it would still benefit the company.

Make Way for More Gable's!

The McClain Building was never rebuilt. Wreckage was cleared away to protect pedestrians, but the ruins of the old structure remained in place.

A year after the collapse, the building was bought at public sale by Attorney Robert Smith of Hollidaysburg, then sold to William F. Gable and Co. The purchase would enable Gable and Co. to expand the store's frontage to 175 feet and wrap around the high-traffic downtown block of Eleventh Ave. and Fourteenth Street.

A new building would encompass this property, containing 76,000 square feet of space. It would establish Gable and Co. as the biggest retailer in Altoona and that part of the state, setting the stage for more massive success.

And it would bring to life the main store building we would come to know and love in decades to come, the Eleventh Street structure that we still think of as the heart of Gable's.

Courtesy Jeffery Holland

MEMORY DEPARTMENT

Do you remember the Anniversary Sales, and the boxes of candy and/or plates which were distributed to the customers to mark the event? It was a special occasion and brought forth a special feeling of good will and camaraderie. Customers who couldn't get to the store found flowers and candy delivered to their homes.

Mary Catherine Mallon

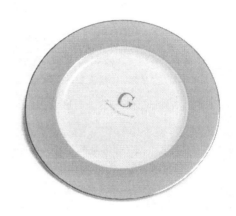

Buying a pair of leather gloves in the William F. Gable department store was quite a special occasion. Taking a walk down memory lane, I visualize the long, narrow counter, along a wall on the first floor. A customer would perch herself on one of the raised stools facing a wall of glass cases, filled with soft leather gloves, which were arranged and labeled precisely by color and size. The sales clerk, with a tape measure, would have you prop an elbow on the counter while she measured the widest part of your hand. Next, she would turn to study the cases, pause, then pull open the drawer with the exact type of glove you were looking for. The next step was rather unique. She pulled the glove over your hand, (elbow still propped on the counter) then worked each finger down into the tip of the glove. You would automatically spread your fingers and turn your wrist, to get the feel and admire the look of the glove! To this day, I'm not sure if it was the clerk, the gloves, or the way you were treated that made you feel like royalty when the purchase was complete.

Peggy Gutshall

My mother-in-law managed the book department, and my father-in-law managed the paint department at Gable's for many years.

Marie Andrews Jenner

I remember the great stairways just inside one of the Eleventh Avenue entrances with its swinging doors. The down stairway led to the grocery store where a great hogshead of dill pickles always stood beside one of the counters. I, as a child, would beg my mother to buy me some egg biscuits, which I like to nibble away, and after each nibble I would look to see the indentations of my two upper front teeth.

During World War I, the rumor would spread around town that Gable's had sugar for sale, and my brother and I would be dispatched to stand in line to buy whatever amount we could get—usually a pound—and often it was rainbow sugar with its colored crystals—not the best quality—but still sugar. Also during the war, my mother sometimes had to buy potato and other flours in order to buy a sack of wheat flour.

And the beautiful meat market to the right of the down stairway! My mother never bought much there because in those days, there were no

Courtesy Altoona Mirror

insulated bags, and in the summertime, meat could begin to spoil before we reached home—walking, of course. But I do remember seeing people lined two deep at those meat counters, especially on Saturdays.

Around the corner from the grocery department was the restaurant. Many a meal I ate there with my mother and sometimes an older sister. The restaurant was free of enclosures so that one could see and be seen...unlike the dimly lighted enclosure of later years. The food seemed delicious. Nearby was the soda fountain with its high stools and colored glass above the counter fixtures. A cool soda or dish of ice cream there was a treat for children weary of adult shopping.

Off to the left was the beautiful china and glassware department. When we could afford it and

Courtesy Altoona Mirror

the children were all past the dish breaking stage, my mother bought a set of hand-painted Bavarian china, a 12-piece set, not the 4 or 8 piece sets that one usually buys now. I know my father thought that the purchase was an extravagance, but he never really said so. I still have all of these dishes, now worth many times their original cost, and just as beautiful as when they were bought. They are now a precious family heirloom.

Returning to the first floor, who can forget the children's shoe department where small chairs were on an elevated platform, so the clerk didn't have to stoop so low for a fitting. Black patent bottoms with champagne kid tops were just the right thing for a pre-adolescent girl, and I proudly wore those shoes with my long shite cotton stockings until I decided that I was too big for them. And I'll never forget the long underwear that I desperately tried to fit inside those long stockings and high topped button shoes, so that no wrinkles would show. The effort was useless, and I usually wound up in tears.

I'm not sure where the children's hat department was, but I do remember the hats with luxurious beaver for winter wear, with grosgrain ribbon band and long streamers. I felt very rich in one of those. In summer, the hats were of Milan straw with grosgrain bands and streamers, or filmy gossamer bonnets with lace, black velvet, and flower trim. And in years when mother couldn't afford a new spring bonnet for me she would sometimes buy a bottle of Colorite and dye an old hat. Heavens, how that stuff smelled, especially if one got caught in a rainstorm. It not only dripped colored dye all over you, but left a never-to-be-forgotten odor.

Photo by Gelon V. Smith

An often visited counter on the first floor was the ribbon department. There a child with mother's approval could choose from the many bolts of gorgeous ribbons, and once the choice was made, Miss Heacox could so deftly twist that ribbon into a hair ribbon and a matching sash. It was sheer magic, and I was never more proud than when I could step out on Sunday morning with a new hair ribbon on my curls and a new sash around my waist.

The lace department was almost as enchanting, for I could help select from among the many bolts of delicate laces, the edging and trimming for my homemade slips, panties, and nightgowns.

The most luxurious department in the whole store, I thought, was the linen department, where Mr. Fay was the manager. An extra-wide counter was used to show the rich table linens, many of them imported, to a prospective customer. Large, full-sized dinner napkins, pure linens, and damasks sold for seemingly low prices. They never seemed to wear out, even with years and years of usage. Today, such purchases are impossible, especially for middle-class Americans.

The notions department always fascinated me. There, mother would take scrap material from a purchase made upstairs in the yard goods department and match it with the seemingly hundreds of spools of thread. Pins, buttons, needles, elastic, and many other small items were purchased here. My mother always wanted the same woman clerk to wait on her. For some reason, it was felt that she was more congenial.

Upstairs in the yard goods department, Miss Annie, a friend of the family, always had to wait on us. I can still see her measuring off yards and yards of material on a yardstick attached to the counter. As a young child, I envied Miss Annie her job, and I was certain that when I grew up I wanted the same occupation—measuring yard goods, or in a pinch, I'd settle for laces. And I remember, when mother was at the sewing machine, I loved to empty the drawers and measure and remeasure all of the scraps of lace, binding, and rick rack.

The balcony on the west side of the store was a popular place. There, the weary shopper could sit down to rest for a while before continuing the task. It was a good place to talk to strangers and a wonderful place for meeting people. Many times, my mother, sister, or both waited there for me on my way home from high school, and on Saturday evenings, I often used to meet a friend there and then go to the movies.

Progress did away with the little carrier baskets—cages that used to carry one's cash to the cashier's desks located on a balcony at the back of the store near the notions or linen department. Now, the charge-a-plate and cash register have taken over.

My memory of many other departments is slim, but I do remember the anniversary and Mill and Factory sales days. On anniversary days, everyone hurried to Gable's to register to get a souvenir plate, a flower, or whatever was being given away, and to shop for bargain special discounted items. Mill and Factory sale days were just as popular. A standing order from our house was 10 bars of Ivory soap for $1.00, ten rolls of toilet tissue for $1.00, one 24-pound bag of sugar, one 25-pound bag of pastry flour—all to be delivered.

Gable's was at one time known for quality merchandise, and it was always a pleasure to have the merchandise shown to you by friendly clerks, many of whom we knew by name and considered as friends. More merchandise was kept in enclosed glass cases, dresses behind sliding glass doors. The pace was rather relaxed, and customers usually waited their turns with cheerful patience.

Author Unknown

Courtesy Matthew Germann

Photo and Items Courtesy Jeffery Holland

Chapter Five

Expansion, Inspiration, Incorporation

1910-1919

What about the rear corner?

After the expansion of 1910, the Gable and Co. building was a big, perfect box...*almost*. The store included all the great frontage it had inherited from the McClain Building, spanning a significant stretch of Eleventh Avenue and wrapping around Fourteenth Street. But the rear corner of the big box was cut out, incomplete. Another structure occupied that space at 1106 Fourteenth Street, and Gable and Co. didn't own it.

Edison's Cameraman

The building on that 30- x 50-foot rear corner site was home to the photo studio of E.D. Bonine. Altoona native Bonine was the brother of well-known photographer and filmmaker Robert Kates (R.K.) Bonine, who had traveled the world shooting stills and films for companies including Edison Films and Biograph. R.K. Bonine had shot newsworthy events like the building of the Panama Canal and the aftermath of the Great San Francisco Earthquake of 1906.

R.K.'s father, R.A. Bonine, also was a photographer and original owner of the Altoona studio. By 1910, R.A. had stepped away because of illness, leaving E.D. in charge of the business. In E.D.'s hands, the place was still thriving, its services in demand.

But it was also still an obstacle to Gable and Co., preventing the completion of that perfect box of a store. After purchasing the McClain lot, William F. Gable made E.D. Bonine an offer for his property...but it was an offer that Bonine *could* refuse. He told William thanks, but no thanks. The studio would stand, and Gable's store would just have to build around it.

As long as the studio building stood, there would always be a corner missing from Gable's—and valuable frontage on Fourteenth Street that Gable's couldn't have. It just went to show that the Gable juggernaut, as mighty as it was becoming, could still be slowed in its relentless progress.

But not yet *stopped*.

Warehouse Raising

When William ran into a brick wall with his pursuit of the Bonine property, he turned his ambitions toward another expansion opportunity. Later in 1910, he bought property along the alley behind the Eleventh Avenue building and erected a warehouse on the site.

The new 50 x 90-foot building provided much-needed storage space for merchandise sold in the store. Though separated from the store by the alley, which had to remain open, the warehouse and store were connected by a walkway built over the alley. Gable and Co. employees wouldn't have to cross at alley level every time they wanted to bring in stock from the storage facility.

The warehouse also was linked to the store by a tunnel cut under the alley, providing another access way for employees moving merchandise for restocking. Meanwhile, the open alley continued to provide space for customer parking.

Bye Now, Bonine

Thanks to the new warehouse, Gable and Co. was better positioned for future growth and additional milestones...like the acquisition of the Bonine corner.

In 1912, E.D. Bonine finally folded his hand. For a while, it had looked like he might never give in; he even had plans drawn up to raise a new building on the photo studio site.

But before E.D. could hire contract builders, William came in with a new offer...and E.D. accepted. The Bonine studio building became the property of Gable and Co. Finally, it would be possible to add that one last piece to complete the box of the Gable building.

Before the Bonine site could be united with the rest of the store, however, it served as a holiday annex during the 1912 Christmas shopping season. The annex was stocked with fruits and sweets for holiday shopping and opened to the public.

Courtesy Jeffery Holland

"Gable & Co.'s Store," War Governors Celebration, Sept. 25, 1912.

Then, during the following year, the Bonine site was fully integrated into the Gable and Co. Department Store. The Gable building formed a four-sided, four-cornered box, extending all the way back from Eleventh Avenue to the alley, without any missing pieces. It now had a full 120 feet of frontage on Fourteenth Street to go with the 175 feet on Eleventh Avenue.

Finally, the store had attained the configuration that would be best-known by the most people for the longest period of time—the profile that would become instantly recognizable as "Gable's" for decades to come.

Courtesy Jeffery Holland

The Big Three-Oh!

By the time the store's 30th anniversary rolled around on March 1, 1914, Gable and Co. had become a real showplace.

Within its walls were 45 separate departments, manned by 375 to 500 employees, depending on the time of year. Counting warehouses, Gable and Co. included some 130,000 square feet of floor space—nearly three acres. Merchandise was artfully displayed in the 250 feet of show windows wrapping around the front of the building.

And the selection of that merchandise was considered excellent. "The goods we offer our patrons are gathered from every market of the world and are of the very best grades it is possible to secure," according to Gable and Co. "Buying, as we do, in large quantities in connection with fifteen other big stores, we secure advantage of many price concessions that mean savings for our patrons that other stores cannot offer. We have a permanent buying organization in New York City and connections in Paris and other Continental cities, which enable us to bring to our customers the new styles as soon as they appear."

A system of electric Cable Cash Carriers zipped money to cashiers and returned change to customers. An overhead sprinkler system kept the place fireproof, and steam heat kept it warm during the winter.

A new photographic studio was up and running—the largest between New York City and Chicago. Operated by William's son, Robert, the studio featured darkrooms and finishing rooms, all outfitted with the most up-to-date equipment. "The Commercial Photographic Department is equipped and ready to make pictures at a moment's notice," according to Gable and Co. "The equipment includes View, Banquet, Graflex and Cirkut cameras, and the latest smokeless flash light apparatus, so that pictures can be made 'any size, any place, any time.'"

Then there was the new kitchen for the restaurant, also tricked out with the latest equipment. Set up in the basement of the latest addition on Fourteenth Street, the kitchen featured a natural gas range and baking oven, a ten-foot steam table, a refrigerator with an ice capacity of 1,000 pounds, and a modern Blakeslee dish washer that could wash 4,000 pieces per hour. A dedicated elevator made it possible to have supplies delivered quickly from street level to the kitchen.

Courtesy Jeffery Holland

Special attention was paid to making the kitchen sanitary in every way. The walls and ceiling were finished with a heavy coating of white enamel; a special "mineral floor" was installed; a modern ventilating system carried away fumes; storage cabinets were made of galvanized iron; and an effort was made "to have every piece of equipment made of metal, in order to make it as sanitary as possible."

Taken together, these and other innovations gave Gable and Co. the look and feel of a thoroughly modern department store and enticed customers to continue to shop and spend there. More and more, Gable's was becoming a world unto itself, gathering more and more attractions under one roof...making it easier to get almost everything in one place instead of shopping around.

This strategy only gained momentum in years to come, and became more rewarding for William and his partners. The growth and improvement of the physical store were not the only ways they prepared to profit from the future.

Courtesy Jeffery Holland

Gable's, Inc.

In 1919, Gable and Co. became a corporation. The tax savings and legal protections that came with incorporation would position the company for future success.

It was funny what those three letters could do: Inc. Gable and Co., Inc., would be seen as a more serious business enterprise, one that made smart moves and was fit to compete with other top-tier companies. It would be seen as an organization that was in the retail game for the long haul.

In some ways, it was the ultimate achievement of William F. Gable. His project, which had started in a single room in 1884, had become a corporate entity with 45 departments, based in a big box building.

"What next?" he must have thought. What could he do for an encore? So many possibilities beckoned; which among them would do the most for the store and the city? Which would help raise Gable's department store to new heights, enhancing the brand and fueling further success?

As the decade that would come to be known as the Roaring Twenties opened before him, William must have been excited. His heart must have beat faster as he thought about how far he had come and how far he had yet to go.

Unfortunately, not long after the new decade started, that big heart of his stopped beating.

And William F. Gable, the visionary, the businessman, the philanthropist, the collector of books and autographs and cows, ended his time behind the wheel of his dream.

This Is the Big Store

you have helped us build, as it appears on its 34th birthday

March First 1918

Courtesy Frank Barry

Chapter Six

William F. Gable, R.I.P.

1921

For once, the crowd at William F. Gable's home was bigger than the one at his store.

People poured in from across the region, entering solemnly with hats in hand. Sadly, they paraded through the house and into William's precious inner sanctum: his first-floor library. They came from near and far to see him one last time, surrounded by bouquets of flowers.

He lay on a couch amid his beloved books and autographed papers, silent and still. The people who filed past him were customers; the money they'd spent in his store had helped pay for the books on the shelves. He'd brought them happiness in the form of his retail paradise, and they had given him happiness too.

They also had given him their respect and gratitude, their devotion and admiration. He had given Altoona something to be proud of, and the people were proud of him in return.

As the day wore on, they kept coming—1,000, 2,000, 3,000. They paid tribute to the man who'd made a difference, and they wondered.

What would happen to Gable's without him?

The Death of a Giant

Three nights earlier, his family had not suspected anything was wrong. Seemingly healthy as always, William had stayed up to work on his mail while the rest of the family turned in for the night.

But sometime in the early hours of the next morning, around 3 a.m. on Monday, Nov. 28, 1921, his condition had suddenly taken a turn for the worse. Something inside him had given way, and he had gone down.

His son, George, had found him later that morning, dead in a hallway leading to a first-floor washroom. Apparently, he'd been on his way to the washroom when he'd collapsed and expired.

Courtesy Blair County Genealogical Society

Later, the coroner had determined that William had suffered a severe stroke. He'd been struck down without warning, with no one else awake in the house to render assistance. His late nights of solo toil on work or hobbies had gotten him in the end.

Just like that, the retail titan was finished.

Ode to a Retailer

As word spread of William's passing, an avalanche of cards and letters bombarded his family. Condolence messages poured in from throughout the country. William was well-known across the U.S., not only for his prominence in the business world, but for his unwavering support of literature.

One tribute, in particular, spoke to that literary connection. Members of the Altoona Robert Burns Club, of which William was a longtime member, composed a poem in his memory and presented it to his family. The poem included the following verses:

O William, the man, the brother;
And art thou gone, and gone forever?
And has thou cros't that unknown river,
Life's dreary bound?
Like thee, where shall we find another
The world around.

An honest man here lies at rest,
As e'er God with His image blest;
The friend of man, the friend of truth,
The friend of age, and guide of youth.

Few hearts like his, with virtue warm'd,
Few hearts with knowledge so inform'd;
If there's another world, he lives in bliss,
If there is none, he made the best of this.

Courtesy Jamie Powers

5,000 Souls

Cards, letters, and telegrams continued to flood in as the Gable family prepared for the viewing according to William's instructions. Two days after his death, the house—and library—were opened to guests, who came from near and far to honor the great man and mark his passing. They trooped past his body all day—3,000, 4,000, and more—all too aware that they were witnessing the end of an era.

By the time the viewing ended at 5 p.m., and the family closed the doors of the house for the day, more than 5,000 souls had gone through it. How many of them would continue to shop at Gable and Co. now that the man who'd breathed life into it had breathed his last?

All of them, no doubt—but none of them until after the funeral.

Closing Gable and Co.

A private funeral service was held the next day—Thursday, December 1—from 10 to 11 a.m. During the hour of the funeral, Gable's store, warehouse, and offices would be closed out of respect for the departed founder.

William was placed in a bronze casket, only the second of its kind ever used in Altoona. He was laid to rest in the Gable family plot in Fairview Cemetery.

The future of his business interests remained to be seen. For that one day, at least, the public was more concerned about the memory of the man than the direction his legacy might take. As the Robert Burns club's poem said,

> *Once fondly loved and still remembered dear,*
> *He was the poor man's friend in need,*
> *The gentleman in word an' deed.*
>
> *But now his radiant course is run,*
> *For William's course was bright,*
> *His soul was like the glorious sun,*
> *A matchless, heavenly light.*

William's friend, H. Luther Frees, wrote his own poetic tribute, in which he attempted to sum up William's character in three verses:

> *I take my privilege of years and read this friend of mine,*
> *Read him as one whose scope of life looks past the dollar sign;*
> *Read him with earnest love of all that truth and right impart,*
> *For nature gave him ample form to hold the ampler heart.*
>
> *Read him as one for whom life holds an obligation strong,*
> *Of love, and gift, and grace of deed and stalwart hate of wrong.*
> *Read him as one who gives this creed its fullest, freest sway,*
> *That all you can hold in your cold dead hands is what you have given away.*
>
> *Read him as one who places worth beyond the mask of grace,*
> *Read him as one who holds the man above the pomp of place;*
> *Read him with scorn of cant and sham and outworn thought, and then*
> *In brightest text read him as one who loves his fellow men.*

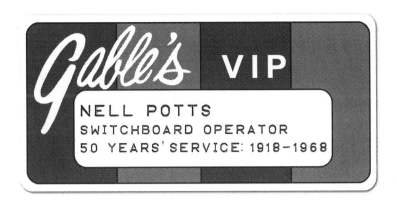

Nell Potts got hundreds of phone calls a day, but none of them were for her.

How many did she field, day in and day out? How many times did she patch an incoming call to a recipient in Gable's department store? Or connect someone from the store and its offices to someone in the world outside?

And how many times did she overhear important things said by William F. Gable, who had hired her, or Robert Gable or George Gable? How many times did she serve as the conduit between important people about to make history?

After which she went home, where she lived with her sister. And maybe there weren't many phone calls for her there, either…for a spinster who spent most of her time holed up behind a switchboard in a department store.

Or maybe there were. We just don't know.

Operator, Can You Help Me Place This Call?

William F. Gable didn't hire just *anybody* for his store. On Jan. 28, 1918, Nell Potts became one of the lucky few.

Back then, the switchboard was very different than in later years—bigger, clunkier, buggier. It was located in the cashier's office on the first floor…and therefore so was Nell, who was hired by William to operate it. With her years of experience working as a supervisor at Bell Telephone, she was the perfect candidate for the job. The perfect candidate for *lots* of jobs, probably, but that was the one she wanted, the one at Gable's.

That was the job she took, though it meant catching the train every morning at 7:03 from Tipton, where she lived. That was the job she kept for years to come, though it meant moving with the switchboard all over the store—to the third floor of the Eleventh Avenue building, then the second floor of that same building, then the fourth floor of the Twelfth Avenue building.

And as the years winked past like lights on a switchboard, Nell became a fixture. She joined Gable's Quarter Century Club in 1943, and never missed a meeting. She hardly ever missed a day of work either, other than a handful for surgery in '46. The calls came and went, came and went, and Nell stayed, her hands deftly weaving the switchboard cords like threads on a loom.

Her voice, when she got on the line to ask who was calling or whom they were trying to reach, always sounding so familiar. So *Gable's*.

Fifty Years on the Line

Nell was still there in 1968, after 50 years' service, plugging and unplugging, connecting, disconnecting. She moved to part-time hours for a while, working four days a week, sharing duties with Helen Halley.

And still, she was one of William's girls. She remembered how things were in 1918, and the 20s and the 30s and the 40s, which were like a million years ago to the people of 1968.

And as the calls kept coming in those waning years, they were for everyone else but her. There were never calls on the line for Nell Potts, offering to change her life for the better, to finally get her out from behind that blinking, beeping board and send her somewhere exotic, somewhere far away where she could live a different kind of life and be the one who *makes* the calls instead of connecting them, the one who has something to *say*.

Or maybe there were. We just don't know.

Courtesy Altoona Mirror

Chapter Seven

Here Come the Sons

1922-1924

What would Gable and Co. be like without a Gable in charge? Luckily, after the passing of William F. Gable, the store's customers did not have to find out.

"Robert B. Gable Heads Store Firm." Thus read the headline on the front page of the *Altoona Mirror* on Wednesday, Feb. 1, 1922. It was official: William's son, Robert Blair Gable, had been voted in as president at the annual corporate board meeting of Gable and Co. Robert's brother, George Pomeroy Gable, who was already general manager of the store, would serve as the organization's secretary.

A new era, led by a new generation of Gables, was about to begin.

From Head of Film to Head of Firm

Was Robert ready to lead Gable and Co.? He certainly knew the store well enough, having worked his way up through several departments in the ten years before his election to the presidency. He had set up and operated the in-store photo studio, which had become a successful venture for the company. He also had originated the gift shop department and managed the book shop.

In 1917, Robert had moved into the administrative offices, taking charge of the department of accounts and the business office. He did well enough there that when Gable and Co. incorporated in 1919, he was elected to the post of secretary-treasurer of the corporation.

The skills he developed helped him find success and recognition outside the store, as well. He served as a director of the Pennsylvania Retail Dry Goods Association, and was chosen as the organization's treasurer in the fall of 1921.

This all led up to his biggest promotion of all, his election to fill his father's shoes. He was just 29 years old when it happened—a young age, perhaps, to take over a thriving business enterprise like Gable's. But it wasn't like he wouldn't have trusted help to back him up.

His brother, George, would be right there with him. Younger than Robert by six years, George also was well-equipped to carry on in his father's absence. In addition to serving as general manager of the store since 1919, George had been a director of the Gable corporation for several years. Like his brother, he had learned from the best, soaking up all the wisdom he could from William before his death.

Also like his brother, George would be serving as a president of the company—a *de facto* co-president, according to a modern day source within the family. Though George's official titles were general manager and corporate secretary, and Robert was officially the sole president in the eyes of the outside world, George occupied an office adjacent to Robert and served, for all intents and purposes, as a fellow president with equal power and influence within the company.

Now it was time for the brothers to put what they'd learned to work. Would the moves they made be conservative or aggressive? Would they be content to leave the store largely as they'd found it, or would they feel compelled to push forward with major changes?

It did not take long for the answers to become evident.

Gambling on the Arcade

How's this for a major change? On May 15, 1922, Gable and Co. announced the store would expand to a second building on another street.

According to Robert Gable, the plan had been in the making for years. The new building, called the Arcade Annex, would span 1315-1321 Twelfth Ave. It would include 24,000 square feet of additional floor space and would be connected to the main building on Eleventh Avenue so shoppers could walk between them without going outside.

"This expansion has been made imperative by our steadily growing patronage and we believe there is no more opportune time to build than the present," said Robert. "Because we feel that Altoona is about to enter the greatest period of prosperity in its history and it is our aim to be prepared to give our patrons the best possible service."

Lavishly Appointed Rest Room

Parts of the Gable Arcade opened for business in a few months, though the full building would not be finished and open until the following year.

Designed by Frederick J. Shollar of Altoona firm Hersh and Shollar, the building was constructed chiefly with brick and copper trim meant to emulate the appearance of the Eleventh Avenue store. The floors were done with Terrazzi marble, and marble staircases provided access between levels of the place.

Like the Eleventh Avenue "daylight store," the Arcade was set up to make the most of natural light. Electric lighting also was plentiful, as the Arcade would be one of the first local shopping facilities with evening hours.

The structure extended back from Twelfth Avenue, bridging the alley behind it, and linked with the Eleventh Avenue building. Each floor of the Arcade was designed around a central corridor, with individual "shops," like departments, arranged on either side.

In addition to expanded furniture and drapery departments, the Arcade featured a ladies' hair and nail salon, a children's barber shop, a flower shop, a candy shop, a radio shop, an optical shop, toy shops, a soda grille, and a "lavishly appointed" rest room "for women and children."

Santa's Headquarters and the Christmas Service Bureau also opened in the Arcade, marking the 30th anniversary of the opening of the Eleventh Avenue building on Dec. 8th. The Christmas Service Bureau offered gift boxes, stamps, ribbons, cards, and free gift wrapping for customers' purchases.

Courtesy Altoona Mirror

"Every Person Is Welcome"

More changes and additions were made in months to come, as the Arcade Annex took shape. Finally, on Wednesday, Nov. 21, 1923, Gable and Co. held a formal opening and reception for the Arcade and the new shops in the main store.

The event ran from 7:30 to 10:30 p.m., and "every person" was welcome to attend. Free souvenirs were handed out, and live music was provided by the Bluebird Entertainers Orchestra and Gipprich's Symphony Orchestra.

"We want you to share in the comforts, the conveniences, and services at the new Arcade Annex as well as the various new shops and sections numbered among the Main Store's innovations." That was the text of the ad in the *Altoona Mirror*. "To give you ample opportunity to get acquainted with our employees and to enable you to familiarize yourself with all sections of the Store, the sales and all other forces will devote themselves entirely to you during the evening, but selling of any merchandise is not expected or desired."

Guests flooded the store that evening, chatting with employees and store executives, receiving their free souvenirs, and taking in the new surroundings. Gable's department store had become something new and greater, a two-building retail giant on a par with big city stores...and it wasn't done growing. Robert and George had more plans on the table, more ambitions still to pursue.

More additions to the Arcade were yet to come...including what was perhaps the most high-profile, high-tech venture of all for Gable and Co...one that would eventually become the most long-lasting and far-reaching legacy of the organization.

WFBG radio was about to go live on the air.

Formal Opening and Reception In Gable's Arcade
Annex and New Main Store Shops

7:30 to 10:00

WEDNESDAY EVENING, NOVEMBER 21st

7:30 to 10:00

Bluebird Entertainers Orchestra

NO SALES

Only the Arcade Candy Shop, the Flower Shop and Soda Grill, open every week-day evening, will cater to purchasers as usual.

NO ORDERS

Gippgich's Symphony Orchestra

These Employes Will Greet You at Their Respective Places

STORE EXECUTIVE RECEPTION COMMITTEE

ROBERT B. GABLE, President.   GEORGE P. GABLE, Secretary.   W. WALTER HENRY, Treasurer.   J. GEORGE ANSPACH, General Manager.   KARL S. ISENBERG, Advertising Director

MEMORY DEPARTMENT

My grandmother, Esther Ramsey, worked in the fine china department. That store was awesome and really made downtown Altoona great!

Geri George Selfridge

I had my senior photos done there. Had a relative, Phil Moreland, who was a buyer for them. He died many years ago.

Barb Quarry Richardson

My mother worked in the lamp department, and I remember the Arcade Restaurant and having a sundae and visiting the pet section. I bought my wedding dress there, which I still have today. I also have a Gable's plate, and I bought my dinnerware there, which I still have and use after 47 years.

Donna Sprow

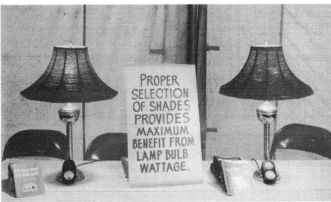

Photo by Gelon V. Smith

When I was about 8 years old, I found a $1 bill in Gables. That was a lot of money then. Mom said I could keep it. I bought a pencil sharpener like the ones in school. I still have it and use it. It is a Boston KS, made in the good old USA.

Betty Barroner

I loved shopping all day at Gable's with my maternal grandparents. Grandpa would take us to the Arcade Restaurant downstairs every time. Their food was so good, and their fries and milkshakes were the best! I also loved the Christmas animations in the big windows.

Tom Fedesco Sr.

My mother, Effie (Eamigh) Vance, worked in Gable's credit office for many years in the 1930s and 40s. She quit when I was born in 1943. She had many friends among the employees, including David Little (the Floor Walker), Margaret "Marg" Gordon (in the credit office), and Mr. Gable himself. She kept in touch by visiting with them when shopping. They all got to know me quite well this way. David Little used to call me "Little Effie." Any time I would wander away, a clerk would pick me up and set me on the counter and, if in talking distance (NEVER yelling) would call out, "Effie, Linda's over here."

Photo by Gelon V. Smith

Photo by Tom Lynam

I remember the credit office was on the second floor of the Twelfth Avenue building, along the Fourteenth Street side. It had huge windows on the two sides. When there was a parade in town, Mom would take me up to the credit office, where we would be welcomed by her friends still working there, and we could watch the parades above the crowds. This was especially good in the winter, because we could stay inside in the warmth.

Linda (Vance) Garman

Chapter Eight

You're Listening to Gable's Radio

1924

WFBG

The Staff And
Management
of
WFBG
Extend Their Felicitations
to the
Citizens Of Altoona
on this
Happy Occasion

"The Voice Of The Alleghenies"

Imagine it's Aug. 24, 1924. You're in the Altoona area, turning the tuner knob on your bare-bones radio set, searching for a station to listen to. These are early days in the world of radio, so there's not much out there—certainly not in the town of Altoona.

And then there *is*. Suddenly, as you turn past a frequency that has always been empty before, the crackling static gives way to a clear signal. You hear a *voice* over the airwaves, talking about a brand new station, the first of its kind in Altoona. "This is WFBG," says the announcer. "Broadcasting from the Crystal Studio in the Gable and Co. Department Store Arcade Annex in downtown Altoona, Pennsylvania."

And you smile. This is the start of something big, you just know it. The airwaves are a little less lonely tonight.

And they're going to *stay* that way.

Radio Station in a Department Store?

The new radio station had been part of Gable's Arcade Annex from the design phase, announced before construction on the Arcade began in 1922. It was meant to be the first radio station between Pittsburgh and Philadelphia, broadcasting over a 50-mile radius from a studio on the second floor of the Arcade Annex. The station's mission? To provide "the best in entertainment, enlightenment, and promotion of public welfare in the Central Pennsylvania area."

The station's call letters would be WFBG—including the initials of the company's founder, William Francis B. Gable. As for the programming, local shows would originate from the in-store "Crystal Studio."

Courtesy Altoona Mirror

Did it make any sense to set up a station in a department store like Gable's? In those days, absolutely. Big city stores like Wanamaker's in New York City had had radio stations for years. Broadcasting content encouraged consumers to buy radio receivers for home use, receivers sold at the same stores where the stations were based. Operating proprietary radio stations also gave those stores a way to control the means (and costs) of advertising to listeners.

So buying expensive broadcasting equipment looked like a good investment to Robert and George Gable. They ordered the installation of a Western Electric transmitter and antennae system on the highest part of the Gable complex—the roof of the Eleventh Avenue building. Microphones and other equipment were brought in for the Crystal Studio.

Setting everything up took time and money, but it all came together in the summer of 1924. The station team—director Walter S. Greevy, chief operator William K. Augenbaugh, and chief announcer Roy F. Thompson—had the studio and transmitter ready for launch by late August.

It was perfect timing. The perfect high-profile event to draw listeners to the first broadcast was scheduled to happen on Aug. 24.

Racing on the Radio

An annual 250-mile board track automobile race was held every August at the Altoona Speedway near Tipton. It was a big deal, attracting drivers from around the world to compete for $25,000 in prize money.

If race fans couldn't attend in person, they wouldn't know the results until the next edition of the local newspaper...but that changed in 1924. WFBG broadcast updates during the race and announced the winners and times afterward. Live sports coverage had come to Altoona.

The New Twin Radio Towers of WFBG

The roof of The William F. Gable store, showing new radio transmitting towers of WFBG.

And WFBG had made its mark. As word spread that the station was broadcasting race results, awareness of its existence got a huge boost. Curiosity about the Crystal Studio and the programming it hosted rose steadily, fueled by newspaper ads and promotional events in Gable's department store.

Under the leadership of Roy Thompson, who took over as station director after the untimely death of Walter Greevy, WFBG beamed news updates, music and comedy shows, educational programs, church services, children's entertainment, and more to its growing audience.

The station also supported community service organizations and aired emergency bulletins during disaster situations. After a killer tornado tore through the Midwest, for example, the station put out an on-air fundraising appeal that brought in thousands of dollars for relief work. When a blizzard shut down most communications and transportation in Central Pennsylvania in 1928, WFBG informed listeners about emergency measures and helped direct aid where it was needed most.

The station also was active in providing rescue service to Johnstown, Pa. during the Saint Patrick's Day Flood of 1936.

Roy Thompson

Photo by Gelon V. Smith

How's This for Happy?

As the ownership of home radio receivers expanded, WFBG's popularity increased. On-air hosts and entertainers became local celebrities, in demand for personal appearances and performances. In January 1925, for example, WFBG staged a live show called *Three Happy Hours* at the Mishler Theater, featuring members of the troupe of musicians, vocalists, and announcers who starred in the station's *The Happy Hour* program. Admission was just $1.

The Happy Hour itself showcased local musicians and included late night live broadcasts from venues like Rainbow Gardens on Eleventh Avenue at Bridge Street. The show piggybacked on informal dance events and ran till 2 in the morning.

Enter the Golden Trio

In the years that followed, WFBG filled its airwaves with popular shows and became a local broadcasting institution...but never stopped searching for new ways forward. Station management regularly bought new equipment, installing the latest microphones, antennae, and updated transmitter components.

The Amateur Hour ready for broadcast from WFBG's studios. ... the end of the table with his young daughter Jenny is J. E. At the piano, left, Norman Boland; Roy Thompson, emcee of Blatchford. the weekly program is center, beneath clock, and seated at

THE AMATEUR PROGRAM

The winners of the Sunday radio contests are chosen by Contest on the stage of the Mishler Theatre. At the time of telephone votes, and at the end of each twelve week period publication, the Amateur Hour had been on the air about the twelve weekly winners meet for the Grand Final Amateur 32 weeks.

The WFBG team was always seeking improvements in the content it provided, as well. In 1933, the station launched a daily show starring the Gable Golden Trio—three musicians who performed a repertoire of classical pieces.

The show ran weekdays at 10:45 a.m. and Saturdays at 10:30 a.m. The theme song was the Brahms Waltz in A-Flat Major, Opus 39, #15.

Director and violinist Silvio Ciccone spent 28 years playing musical comedy scores in New York City before joining the trio. Pianist Mary Houseman was active in the local music scene in Altoona. Vocalist Charles Reiner was an early member, but eventually left the group. Cellist John Santone joined the trio in 1938 after leaving his chair in the Johnstown Symphony Orchestra.

The show was a hit and ran until October 1951, when Mary passed away. Her Chickering baby grand piano is still in use today by her granddaughter, Becky, and her great-grandchildren, who inherited her talent and love of music.

Better Off Red

In 1939, the station vastly increased its programming options by joining the National Broadcasting Company's Red Network. WFBG listeners could now tune in to shows featuring NBC stars of the time like Arthur Fields and Fred Hall, singer Ruth Lyon, musical comedians Gene and Glen, bandleader Larry Clinton ("the old Dipsy-Doodler"), actress Betty Lou Gerson, swing vocalist Martha Tilton, and "Professor" Bruce Kaman. WFBG's schedule now included nationally broadcast programs like *Kaltenmeyer's Kindergarten*, *Sunday Drivers*, and *Hilda Hope, M.D.*

Local entertainment fare also continued to be abundant on WFBG. Every Sunday night, *The Amateur Hour* spotlighted local performers demonstrating their talent in the Crystal Studio.

All Courtesy Jeanne Houseman Dalton, Dennis and Becky Beasom

Listeners voted by phone, with a winner chosen each week for twelve weeks. Then, the twelve weekly winners faced off in a grand finale on the stage of the Mishler Theater, broadcast live on WFBG.

Another show, *The College of Fun*, offered cash prizes to callers based on their telephone or social security numbers. Host Willard Fraker asked questions about historical or current events. When the numerical answers lined up with a listener's telephone or social security number, the listener could call in and receive a dollar for each correct answer. Typically, the show received 4500 phone calls each week, and 60 of those were winners.

Other local shows featured music and comedy

performed live in the Crystal Studio by talented regulars such as piano accompanist Alice Mary Connor, musical duo Bob and Gene, the Gospel Trumpeters, and singer/pianist Freddie Glover, who once received 200,000 fan letters at WFBG in one year.

Outlasting All Things Gable

As the Golden Age of Radio rolled on through the 1930s and

40s, WFBG was at the forefront in Altoona. Once again, Gable and Co. had found success bringing an innovative business to the region and using it to meet demand in ways that local people could appreciate.

WFBG was so successful, in fact, that it provided the longest-lasting, furthest-reaching impact of any division of Gable and Co. WFBG-AM led to WFBG-FM, which led to WFBG-TV...which became WTAJ-TV.

And long after the Gable Department Store ended, WTAJ still beams its signal far and wide, reaching millions of viewers—many of whom have probably never heard of Gable's in their lives.

All Courtesy Jeanne Houseman Dalton, Dennis and Becky Beasom

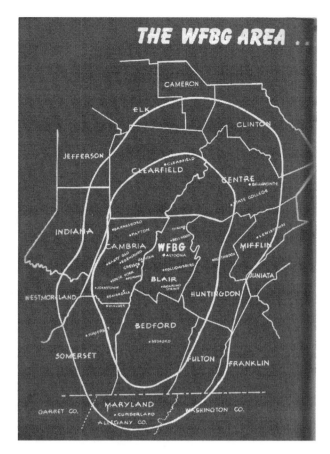

THE WFBG AREA ...

NBC STARS

1. Arthur Fields and Fred Hall (Sunday Drivers)
2. Bruce Kamen, Professor of Kalamazoo Kindergarten
3. Commentor Ruth Lyon
4. Malcolm "Uncle Mal" Claire
5. The Four Showmen of music on NBC

"THIS IS THE NATIONAL RADIO CITY, NEW YORK"

ROADCASTING COMPANY,

All Courtesy Jeanne Houseman Dalton, Dennis and Becky Beasom

60

Chapter Nine

The Brother Who Moved On

1928-1931

The Gable brothers were on a roll.

Robert and George—the official and de facto presidents—had constructed the Arcade Annex on Twelfth Avenue, built the Crystal Studio and launched WFBG radio, and more.

In 1928, they expanded the Arcade significantly, adding two floors, a basement garage, and loads of frontage and square footage. The new garage had room for 50 to 75 cars, with an entrance at the rear of the Twelfth Avenue building. Customers could park for a fee, then walk up a stairway into the store as their vehicles received tire service and a wash from attendants supervised by Sam Constance, formerly operator of the Seventh Street garage.

Courtesy Altoona Mirror

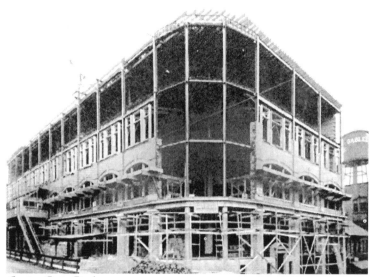

Courtesy George Rowles

The overall size of the Gable and Co. Department Store was now nearly 300 times the size of the original one-room Sprecher and Gable Store on Eleventh Avenue.

And there were more improvements to come. A new addition to the Twelfth Avenue building was constructed by the Gable Real Estate Company in 1930, extending that building 100 feet closer to Thirteenth Street.

The ground floor of the addition was divided into 50 square feet of store space and two storerooms of 25 square feet

apiece. Additional storerooms were installed in the next floor down—two 25' x 60' storerooms, and one sized 25' x 120'. Below that, in the basement, another parking garage was built, providing 100 x 120 feet of space for customers' vehicles.

These expansions brought the Twelfth Avenue structure to the shape and size for which it would be best known, the same general dimensions we see at that location to this day.

In every way that mattered, Gable's was on the rise, with no end in sight. So why did Robert Gable leave the company in 1931? Why, with so many successes under his belt, did he give up the official presidency after only 10 years?

Courtesy Jeffery Holland

We might never know the full story, expressed in his own words—but at least we can look back and see where the road took him as he stepped away from the fabled presidency originated by his legendary father.

Indiana's Calling

It might have seemed like business as usual at Gable and Co. as 1930 melted into 1931. Even in the throes of the Great Depression, sales were good in the expanded Arcade Annex and throughout the store.

A new A&P grocery store had opened in mid-November of 1930 on the Arcade's ground floor, bringing a wide selection of food products to Gable's. Customers loved the convenience of having so much of what they wanted for sale under one roof.

Other plans were in the works, as William F. Gable and Co. approached its 50th Anniversary in 1934. Robert and George would do everything they could to make it an extra-special event for the company and community, one that would help propel them both into the next half-century of prosperity.

Little did Robert know that he wouldn't be at the helm of the company when that anniversary rolled around.

The story broke in the *Altoona Mirror* on Jan. 16, 1931: Robert had been summoned to Indianapolis, Indiana to take charge of a dry goods company there. George had gone with him...and, in the long run, would be the only one coming back.

Indianapolis Getaway

What could make Robert and George leave their precious department store and run to Indianapolis? And what would make Robert not come back?

According to family accounts, a bank was to blame. With business down because of the Depression, Gable's applied for a bank loan. The bank granted it, on the condition that Robert or George resign from the firm. In the bank's opinion, if Gable's was having problems that led it to borrow money, leaving the official and de facto presidents in charge would be a recipe for continued trouble. One of the brothers had to leave to ensure there would be the kind of change in business practices that would make the bank's investment in Gable's a sound one.

It was settled; a brother had to go. But which one, and what would he do next?

After debating the situation at length, the board of directors decided it was Robert who should leave. That just left the matter of where he would go and what he would do after leaving Gable's employ.

Fortunately, a solution soon became evident. A business partner had an opportunity in need of an expert retail executive.

The partner's name was *Pomeroy*.

George Pomeroy, of the Dives, Pomeroy, and Stewart dry goods firm in Reading (the "and Co." of William F. Gable and Co.) had gone in on a deal with the Pettis Drygoods Company in Indianapolis. Pomeroy and a partner, James Swan, had bought out the interest of the president and vice-president of Pettis Dry Goods, H.G. Munro and H.C. Annable, when they resigned from the company. Pettis was having problems, but Pomeroy saw potential with the right people behind the wheel.

To that end, with the holiday season behind them, the Gable brothers left their executive team to mind the store and headed for Indianapolis. Robert would be the store's president and stay in Indianapolis after the initial ramp-up process, while George would eventually go home to Altoona.

They were given control of the floundering Pettis corporation by the board of directors and settled in to work their magic on the Indiana retail enterprise.

But that magic, they learned, did not always work miracles.

Another Store for Robert

Within a year, the Pettis company was in worse shape than ever. By April of 1932, it was bankrupt.

Robert had done his best, giving up his Gable's presidency to serve the same role at Pettis and focus all his attention there. As for George, he'd been mostly focused on the store in Altoona. After Robert's resignation, he'd been elected the new president of William F. Gable and Co. His role was now official, not merely de facto.

But would George's promotion last? When Pettis sank, would Robert try to return to the roost in Altoona?

Determined to turn failure into success, he stayed in Indiana instead. He started a new company, Gable-Truby Co., Inc., and launched a new store in Marion, Indiana, in the building that had housed the defunct Blumenthal & Co. department store.

Robert's partner, W. Stanley Truby, had been an executive at both Pettis and Gable and Co. He came in as vice-president and merchandise manager under President Robert. The two were directors of the company, along with secretary-treasurer and assistant controller James Thomas, also from Pettis via Gable's, and two other former Pettis executives—Herschell Wheeler and L.B. Gable.

The deal came together, and Robert had a fresh start. He embraced the challenge of his third company with excitement and determination, hoping the third time would be the charm.

It wasn't, but Robert found another path to success. He was promoted to managing director of Pomeroy's, Inc., based in Pottsville, Pa. He left Indiana for Pottsville and never looked back.

Meanwhile, the Gable's store in Altoona was left in the care of George. He dedicated his life to the place, presiding over major changes and successes, making the great store everything it could be...loving it as much as his father had, and staying there almost as long.

Courtesy Matthew Germann

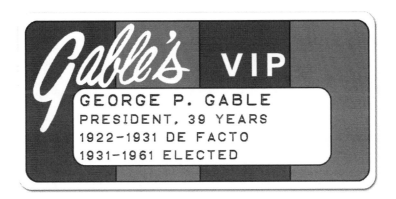

Gable's **VIP**

GEORGE P. GABLE
PRESIDENT, 39 YEARS
1922-1931 DE FACTO
1931-1961 ELECTED

The "A" in "Gable" must have stood for "Type A." William F. Gable certainly had that type of personality, what with starting a successful company while performing copious community service and building top-flight collections of books, autographs, and cattle.

Robert Gable was no slouch either. In addition to working as president of Gable and Co. and several other department stores, he served as a director of multiple civic and business organizations, including the Pennsylvania Retailers Association, the State Chamber of Commerce, First National Bank, Mercy Hospital, the Blair Hotel Co., and the American Automobile Association. He also was a radio pioneer, launching the first station in Altoona and conducting shortwave radio research in his home laboratory in Ant Hills. He and fellow pioneer Charles Leutz introduced the first superheterodyne receiver in the U.S. and co-authored *Short Waves*, a book that explained short-wave radio transmission and reception.

Then there was Robert's brother, George P. Gable. If there had been a contest to see which Gable was the most Type A, he probably would have won it hands down.

The Man Who Said "Yes"

Sometimes, it seemed like George had his fingers in everything. When it came to volunteering, he might have known how to say "no," but he didn't do it very often.

On the business side, George served as the director of the National Retail Dry Goods Association for many years, starting in 1936. He also served as president of the Pennsylvania Retailers' Association from 1943 to 1950. George also was active in the local, state, and national Chambers of Commerce. He directed the Altoona Chamber for years and was named executive chairman of that organization's future planning program.

Courtesy Blair County Historical Society

It was his work with civic and charitable groups, however, that shone the brightest. When it came to those kinds of organizations, he was a powerhouse, lending his time, treasure, name, and tireless energy to every worthwhile cause that came along.

Synonymous With Community Service

"Despite the pressure of his own business in running a big store, he never liked to turn down a request to help in community campaigns, and for years he served continuously in a never-ending series of drives and civic programs," according to a tribute in the *Altoona Mirror*.

"Mr. Gable had a generous heart, and he gave unstintingly of his time and effort, his thought and worry, and his money. For well over a quarter of a century his name was synonymous, not only with the store, but with community service."

George was a director of the Blair County Chapter of the Red Cross and president of the Altoona Community Chest. He served as co-chairman of the Altoona Hospital expansion program from 1947 to 1950, continuing the growth and advancement of that institution. Through his pioneering work with the Altoona Community Council, he helped form the Family Service Agency and Altoona Federation for Community Development. He was a member of the board of the Salvation Army and was recognized for his outstanding service to that organization.

War Footing

During World War II, George really stepped up to the plate, working extensively with the United Service Organization, the USO. He became chairman of the state council of the USO in 1943 and traveled across Pennsylvania enlisting support for the organization.

George also was named chairman of Altoona's Citizen's Service Corps during the war. He served on Pennsylvania's retail war finance committee and as chairman of Altoona's post-war planning commission.

Ever the Type A powerhouse, he did all this while doing his part for a long list of civic and business organizations...and, oh yes, he was running the Gable Company and spending time with his family too.

Talk About Long-Lasting

William F. Gable and Co. underwent plenty of positive changes during George's time as elected president—from 1931 to 1961—and chairman of the board of directors—from 1961 to 1967. The construction of the Arcade parking deck and its later expansion into the four-level Parking Center were hallmarks of George's forward-thinking building program.

Then there was the media empire. WFBG added an FM radio station on his watch, then a TV station. WFBG-TV took to the airwaves in 1953, then was sold and turned into WTAJ-TV, which  is still Altoona's local station today.

Courtesy Georgia Parsons

The Family That Vacations Together

Even with all his other commitments, George still found time for family. His granddaughters, Virginia and Georgia Parsons, visited him often at home and the office.

They also went on vacation with George and Florence, their grandmother. Every summer, they spent blissful weeks in a rented house on Long Beach Island, New York. To this day, they still remember those days as some of the happiest in their lives.

A Friend to All

As a businessman, volunteer, husband, father, and grandfather, George P. Gable worked tirelessly and found constant success...but it was perhaps his friendly attitude that left the biggest impression. Like his father before him, he treated all people with equal kindness and respect.

According to the *Altoona Mirror*, "His tendency to remember people extended to some of the store's earliest customers, and, on the occasion of the store's anniversary, he always would greet throngs of visitors, many of whom, even the most elderly, would make special efforts to go down to greet 'George' and to extend to him best wishes and congratulations.

Courtesy Georgia Parsons

"This never-failing attention to people was one of the elements which made Mr. Gable a great merchant, in the best tradition of merchandising."

The *Mirror* called him "a friend to all" who forged "a heritage of good will, of a

Photo by Gelon V. Smith

readiness to help, to 'get involved,' that has been of untold benefit to the city and the country through every great civic endeavor to which George Gable gave his efforts through the years."

Courtesy Georgia Parsons

Legal Blanks of All Kinds Can Be Purchased at the Altoona Mirror

Altoona Mirror.

Sell, Rent or Buy Through An Ad on The Mirror's Classified Page

SECOND PART ALTOONA, PA., MONDAY EVENING, AUGUST 31, 1921.

Here Are Part of the 506 Employes Whose Service to the Customer Has Been a Gable Ideal For Years

GABLE STORE IN STEP WITH CITY

Big Mercantile Establishment Has Kept Pace With Altoona's Growth for Almost Half Century.

LOYALTY OF EMPLOYES OF FIRM BIG FACTOR

Judicious Use of Advertising Space Credited by Founder as One of Stepping Stones to Success.

GABLE STORE HAS LARGE PERSONNEL

More Than 500 People Comprise Force Giving Service to Public at Great Department Emporium.

GABLE'S FIRST TO MARK BIRTHDAY

Plan Now In World-wide Use Was Originated by Founder of Department Store In 1897.

FIRM WILL CELEBRATE GOLDEN JUBILEE SOON

Completion of Twenty-five Year Period In 1909 Observed In Notable Manner by Entire Community.

SYSTEM OF BUYING ONE OF ADVANTAGE

Products of All Nations Secured for Counters of Gable Store Through Efficient Purchasing Plan.

ONE PRICE IDEA OF GABLE ORIGIN

Founder Originated Many Innovations, Including Money Back If Not Satisfied With Purchase.

ADVERTISING OF GOODS IMPORTANT

William F. Gable Company Consumes Much Newspaper Space 'In Telling Patrons What Is for Sale.

MESSAGE CARRIED DAILY IN THE ALTOONA MIRROR

Name of Local Department Store Created a Household Word Throughout This Section of State.

NOTABLE RECORD OF GROWTH MADE

Expansion Has Been Watchword of Gable's Since Store Was Founded Almost a Half Century Ago.

FOUNDER WAS MAN OF BIG CAPACITY

Born of Hardy Quaker Stock and Reared on Farm Prepared William F. Gable for Larger Field.

STARTED FIRST STORE HERE ON MARCH 1, 1884

Early System of Merchandising Adopted Put Convenience and Comfort for Everybody In Foreground.

A Third Milestone of Gable Progress

(Continued on Page 20)

MEMORY DEPARTMENT

I remember the hat department in the 1940s. My mother, Rhoda Gates, loved hats, and Saturdays would always find us at Gable's. The carpet there was pearl gray and very thick. The hats were displayed on hat stands. My mother would sit at a dressing table with a large, round mirror. The saleswoman would ask what color and style she preferred, then gather a few hats and place each one correctly on the customer's head. It wasn't shopping as we now know it. It was an experience.
Phyllis Gates Deibler

When we lived on the alley above the Cathedral, I spent so many hours downtown after the stores closed and the people were gone, especially in the winter. That area was so peaceful and quiet once the crowds went home. I loved leaving the playhouse after dark to walk home.
Ken Plowman

I always loved the times our Girl Scout troop would sing Christmas carols on those large steps. At least they seemed large to me as a kid.
Debra Hockenbury Whitfield

I can remember going to Gable's to see Santa Claus with my family. My sister and I would be all dressed up for our annual photo with Santa!
Charles Reighard

I won a coloring contest sponsored by the store and got a $25 gift certificate, which I spent in the store. You got a lot for $25 back then! I even bought my brother a chemistry set along with all the things I got for myself. I was probably around 8 or 9 then. I'm 69 now.
Kathy Strasser Humbertson McIntire

Courtesy Ron Keller

I remember at night, my mother and I would walk uptown and look at all the pretty clothes Gable's had in their windows. It was a special outing for my mother and me.
Melinda Rinehart Chamberlain

When I was 9 or 10 years old, my mum and I would take the bus to Gable's. We would go to the shoemaker in the basement to get my shoes fixed. That's what we did back then. They had shoemakers who would fix your shoes, not like today where everyone buys a new pair every month.

Good old Gable's had a toy boat that you could ride for five cents. I just couldn't wait to ride it with its bright lights, which I believe were bright yellow, green, and white. I was so excited to ride that boat at Gable's.

We were poor, of course, and it was a big deal for me to go to Gable's department store. They had everything you needed. They even had hot cashews! Back then, the cashier lady would say, "Would you like to try some hot cashews?" Then she handed me a spoonful.

My mum would be looking for the bargains while I was looking at the toys. The toys were beautiful. Anything you could think of in the way of toys, Gable's had it. And guess what? As poor as we were, my mum would always make sure I got a toy from Gable's during our visit.

Then, we would leave Gable's and catch the bus and head home. Oh, the memories of my childhood store, Gable's.
Al Phelan

Chapter Ten

Half a Century Already?

1934

Hours of His Entire Life." And maybe that was exactly how it was that day in March 1934. Because it's hard to imagine a more special day for George, and Gable's, and the spirit of William F. It's hard to think of a more moving celebration marking a more historic event in Altoona.

Those men and women were there, all 200 of them, to honor the Golden Anniversary of Gable's department store. It was March 7, 1934, and Gable's had turned fifty years old a week earlier.

One colleague after another stepped behind the podium, singing the praises of Gable and Co., its founder, William F. Gable, and its current president. That president, George P. Gable, had tears of joy in his eyes as the room erupted in cheers and applause again and again.

The headline on the front page of the *Altoona Mirror* read, "Son of Store Founder, Surrounded by Business Associates, Spends Happiest

All Courtesy Altoona Mirror

71

"The Greatest Merchandise Event Ever Held"

Preparations for Gable's 50th birthday had been a long time in the making. After all, Gable and Co. was the originator of the department store anniversary celebration, and *this* one, the *fiftieth,* was the *big one.*

The store's buyers, in fact, had been seriously stocking up since early January. Instructions had come down from the top: the buyers had to order enough quality stock at discount prices to make the fiftieth anniversary "...the greatest merchandise event ever held in the history of Altoona."

Spurred on by Sales Manager W. Stanley Truby, returned to Altoona after working with Robert Gable on the failed Indiana stores, the army of buyers was fanned out across the country and getting great bargains to pass along to customers. According to men's furnishings and underwear buyer Raymond Beers, manufacturers were giving Gable's better deals than ever before because of the big anniversary.

Women's high style shoe buyer Walter Simmers came back from the St. Louis shoe markets with orders placed for "wonderful" spring line merchandise. Boys' buyer Henry Wolfgang found great deals in the New York City and Philadelphia markets, while homewares and electrical appliance buyers William Orr and James Long scored awesome prices at the homewares show in Chicago.

Basement buyer Eugene Reinheimer took multiple trips to New York in search of merchandise, even as shoe buyers Myrtle Crawford, Herbert Yost, and Chester Brunner beat the bushes in St. Louis and the Midwestern markets. General Manager J.G. Anspach and china and glassware buyer I.J. Rively attended a china and glass show in Pittsburgh.

And lots more were hitting the road, besides. None of the buyers were sitting around idle in the first months of that year; they were all equally determined to bring in the merchandise that would make the anniversary sale a legend in its own right.

Consider the Stalwart Oak

Even as the company's buyers roamed far and wide, the store's executives and staff planned the details for the anniversary.

The celebration would last a month, they decided, kicking off with the actual birthday on Thursday, March 1, 1934.

On that day, the giant 50th anniversary sale would get underway, including all manner of promotional specials and deals throughout the store. The company's pledge for the sale, signed by George Gable in its newspaper ads: "The policy for Gable's Golden Anniversary is the same as the policy for our FIRST...the country's FIRST Anniversary sale... LOWEST POSSIBLE PRICES."

Gable's would be open from 9 a.m. to 9 p.m., and free souvenirs would be handed out to everyone who attended and registered on the first day.

The store would be cleaned up and decorated to the hilt for that sale, and every department would be fully staffed. All display windows would have the most appealing arrangements of merchandise with a Golden Anniversary theme to draw visitors' attention.

Do You Know...

GABLE'S

Celebrates a Half Century of Friendly Service...the

Golden Anniversary

Beginning

Thursday, March 1st

TRULY THE GREATEST EVENT WE'VE EVER PLANNED

Souvenirs to All Who Register the First Day

The William F. Gable Co.

Courtesy Altoona Mirror

A special logo featuring a "Gable tree" and bearing the slogan "A Half Century of Friendly Service" would be used on commemorative printed items and signage. "We have selected the stalwart oak as the Golden Anniversary symbol," wrote the Gable's team in one of its ads, "because it so truly represents Gable's and Altoona's growth from humble beginnings to their solid, permanent position today. And, also, because William F. Gable, the founder, was a lover of trees and distributed thousands to the children of Blair County."

Even amid the hoopla surrounding the anniversary, the company was keeping the founder, his vision, and his philanthropic works front and center. William F. had been gone for 13 years, but he would still be an important part of the events marking his crowning achievement.

Courtesy Altoona Mirror

50 Years in Black and White

The marketing plan of Gable and Co. had always leaned heavily on print advertising, and the 50th anniversary was no different. Spreading the word was achieved primarily by packing the local newspapers with display ads in the weeks leading up to the big event.

In the first quarter of that year, Gable's advertising department bought what might have been a record amount of space in the *Altoona Mirror* and *Altoona Tribune*. Starting a month before the anniversary, at the beginning of February, Gable's ran ads in every edition, counting down the days until the store turned fifty.

Each ad in the series featured a reference to a historical event and its relation to the date of the anniversary. For example: "13 years before Teddy Roosevelt charged up San Juan Hill, Gable's celebrated their first anniversary."

Each day brought another set of historic touchstones as the big event drew nearer. "Forty-one years before television was invented, Gable's celebrated their first anniversary." "The Apache Indian War was fought the same year Gable's celebrated their first anniversary." "Twenty-seven years before the Titanic struck an iceberg in the Atlantic, Gable's celebrated their first anniversary."

Courtesy Altoona Mirror

Larger ads provided more details of the upcoming event, designed to convince customers just how special it would be and how they couldn't afford to miss it. According to the ads, the celebration would be "Powerful...dramatic...thrilling!" Mail orders would be filled promptly, and free delivery would be offered in the state.

The White Glove Test

Gable's was promising a pretty big shindig, but would the Golden Anniversary live up to its billing? A team of out-of-town inspectors aimed to find out.

The men, from Gable's partner firm, Pomeroy's, Inc., rolled into town during the week before the anniversary. Vice President and Comptroller Thomas H. Hargreaves and General Merchandise Manager J.M. Regan wouldn't leave until they were sure that Gable's anniversary would go off without a hitch.

For several days, Hargreaves and Regan inspected the store from top to bottom, going over every department with a fine-toothed comb in search of imperfections.

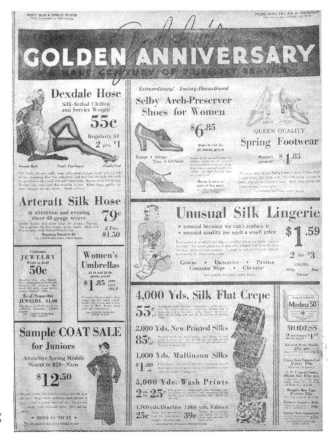

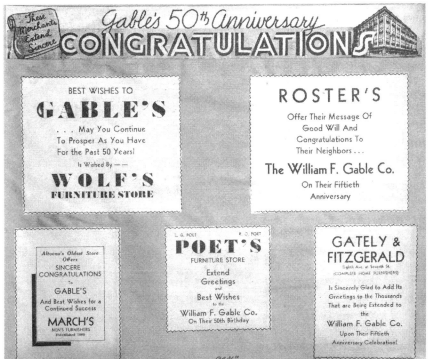

They met with department heads and examined merchandise, making sure everything was ship-shape. They reviewed all preparations for the anniversary, looking for flaws and making suggestions.

When it came time to deliver their report, Gable's executives and staff held their breath. The anniversary was only a day away; if preparations were problematic, they would have to scramble to make last-minute adjustments.

Hargreaves stepped up before them and cleared his throat. Everyone listened closely, preparing for the worst.

All Courtesy Altoona Mirror

And Hargreaves gave them the best instead. He said the condition and appearance of the store were excellent, and the quality and quantity of the sale merchandise also was top-notch. He sang the praises of Gable's management and staff for doing such wonderful work.

Then, he and Regan packed up and left town, returning to the offices of Pomeroy's in Reading. They'd done their part, and the party was about to begin.

The Stage Is Set

On the day before the big blowout, full-page ads touted the highlights. "Gable's Golden Anniversary is a celebration of appreciation for what you have given us... the most precious thing you could have possibly given us...your confidence and your belief in us. Hundreds of enthusiastic workers have been busy for months searching for values worthy of this celebration. Their enthusiasm was contagious. Manufacturers pledged their cooperation. The values that have been secured

exceeded our fondest expectations...and they will exceed yours when you come to Gable's tomorrow.

"Every floor—every department offers new, fashionable merchandise for spring and Easter at Golden Anniversary savings. Hundreds of items are advertised in these nine pages, but there are hundreds more—unadvertised. Visit every department tomorrow, you'll find many Golden treasures worth hunting for. This is truly a Golden opportunity to save on everything you need. The stage is set...everything is ready...the curtain rises at 9 tomorrow morning."

The Curtain Rises

The day before the anniversary, Gable's started a new tradition—closing the store to the public to get ready for the start of the festivities. Employees spent the morning putting finishing touches on everything, preparing for the big sale and related events. That afternoon, they had a half-holiday, enabling them to rest up before the launch.

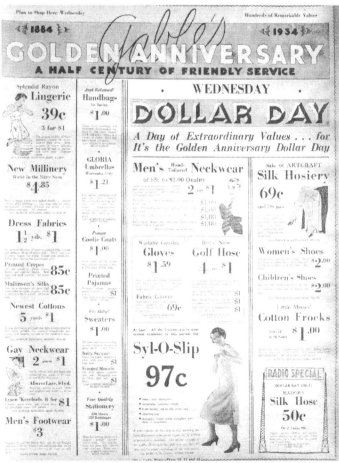

Congratulations GABLE'S 50 years of PROGRESS

Fifty years of continuous service and fifty years
of continued expansion is being celebrated in
Altoona, beginning today, by
The William F. Gable Company

The founder of this great institution embarked into
the mercantile business fifty years ago with perhaps
no idea or no conception that some day this small
store would become the largest department store
between Philadelphia and Pittsburgh.

Fifty years of continued service means fifty years of
continued success. No institution can stand still. It
must either move on to greater things or go backwards and finally to elimination.

The Gable institution stands as a monument to the
confidence that Mr. William F. Gable, the founder, had
in Altoona. It was his ambition to create and to give
Altoona the very best store that could be had for the
citizens of this community. Mr. Gable was the first
in the United States to hold an anniversary sale. This
celebration has been growing and growing until today
it is recognized as the outstanding event not only in
Altoona, but in Central Pennsylvania.

The Mirror Printing Company offers to this great
establishment its sincere congratulations and its best
wishes for future success. It is their hope that those
who are now at the helm of this great establishment
will continue to carry on as the founder did, that in
the days to come it will be not only a great institution
but will become greater as the days go by. We are
proud of this great store.

May it grow and grow and grow.
Sincerely

MIRROR PRINTING COMPANY

Courtesy Altoona Mirror

At 9 a.m. the next morning, Thursday, March 1, 1934, the doors of Gable's opened wide. Finally, after so much preparation, "The 50th Anniversary of the Store That Held the First Anniversary Sale in the Country" was beginning.

People had been crowding the sidewalks outside the Eleventh and Twelfth Avenue buildings, waiting to push inside. As soon as the doors opened, they flooded into the place, a roar of voices and footsteps rushing through the cavernous departments.

As the customers registered and received their commemorative souvenir plates, then fanned out across the floor, George and his staff greeted them and thanked them for joining the anniversary celebration.

Photos by Gelon V. Smith

The decorations were beautiful. The bins and racks and tables were overflowing with merchandise. Everywhere, people were talking and laughing and buying things; many of them had attended their share of past anniversaries. Two women in their 90s had been to more anniversaries than anyone and were thrilled to be there to celebrate the 50th.

Even in the middle of the Great Depression, when so many people had so little reason to be happy, the crowd was able to celebrate a special occasion together. They had helped keep Gable's in business for the first dark years of the Depression; now, Gable's was giving them a day of happiness in return. A *month* of happiness, by the time the whole event ran its course.

Goodwill toward Gable's was so abundant, in fact, that a local supporter, L.P. Patch, wrote a poem titled "Fiftieth Anniversary (W.F. Gable's Store)" that appeared in the *Altoona Mirror* on March 2, 1934. The text of the poem follows:

A commercial venture one day was made,
By a man who believed he was able
To weather the storms of business life,
Which almost everything were rife,
That man, William F. Gable.

March first, eighteen hundred and eighty-four,
He opened in Altoona The People's Store,
A business of small beginnings,
But as oak tree is found in acorn cup,
So his business from embryo, expanded, grew up,
With many rich favorable innings.

First customer was a Mr. Hamilton of Huntingdon, Pa.
The embryo man, a good starter,
And the hundreds and thousands that followed his lead,
Many thousands made Gable's business brisk, successful indeed,
Like a lodge that makes most of its charter.

Let it here be said and emphasized too,
That W.F. Gable was a very hard worker,
And many a night burned the midnight oil,
Lest sly, wily cheats should his business spoil,
An unwelcome task, but it found him no shirker.

What wonder a business so well pioneered
Should grow to its mammoth dimensions,
With George Gable as president and a worthy one too,
Not afraid to branch out in paths that are new,
And all without boastful pretensions.

He is fortunate to have a manager as well trained,
As J.G. Anspach so long at the helm,
With a corps of co-workers tasks ready to do
Who stay on the job and see each on through
Safeguarding interests that nothing o'erwhelm.

On this fiftieth anniversary let Altoonans hail
This store with a patronage able,
And honor a name worthy of great acclaim,
The proud name of William F. Gable.

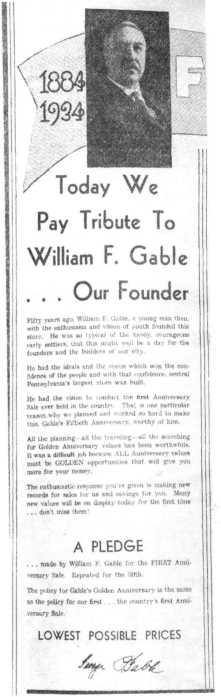

Courtesy Altoona Mirror

Pass the Trimmings

According to the *Altoona Mirror*, some 60,000 people had visited the store on its Golden Anniversary. Gable's scored some of its highest sales figures of all time on that day.

The numbers were great, and the sale would continue... but additional festivities were set for after hours, not open to the public. These events were meant to mark the occasion in a more private way and thank those who'd helped make it a success.

As the business day drew to a close, George Gable hosted a group of local newspaper personnel at a turkey dinner with all the trimmings in the store's main restaurant. As representatives of the executive, editorial, advertising, and circulation departments of the *Altoona Mirror* and *Altoona Tribune* dug in to their meals, George thanked them for everything they'd done to help promote the Golden Anniversary Sale.

"I haven't any doubt but that it was the fine publicity you put out for us in those two splendid editions on Wednesday, which carried such generous greetings from our neighboring business firms and other courteous competitors, that helped this store make this fine day possible," said George.

Courtesy Matthew Germann

After dinner, various guests addressed the crowd, extolling the glories of Gable's and its importance to the local area.

D.N. Slep, president of the Mirror Printing Company, called Gable's the city's greatest retail emporium. Colonel Henry Shoemaker, president of the Tribune Company, said, "Altoona is to be congratulated on having such a store, and the store is to be congratulated on having had such a cultured founder as William F. Gable."

Harold N. Scott, assistant to the vice president of the Pennsylvania Trust Company, talked about Gable's high standing among the financial centers of the eastern United States. "This store nobly stood up to its great and grave responsibilities during the trying era when others which were thought to be as strong as the mighty oak were unable to continue and their business disintegrated," said Scott. "The response one has witnessed here today indicates the wonderful confidence people of this community have in this firm."

Ralph C. Gensel, managing director of the Syndicate Trading Company of New York, said, "I have visited department stores all over the United States, but never have I witnessed a finer response to publicity and to merchandising preparation during any event than that which was demonstrated here today."

George's New Favorite Book

After the media dinner, another event was held in Gable's restaurant, this one focused on the store's management team. Fifty Gable's department managers and various executives of the firm gathered for the occasion, looking back to the past of the company and ahead to what they hoped would be its glorious future.

Various speakers offered remarks, including several who'd addressed the media guests. Weldon D. Smith, president of the Adam Meldrum & Anderson store in Buffalo, N.Y., took to the podium, as did Gable's General Manager J.G. Anspach.

W. Stanley Truby made the biggest impression, though, when he surprised George Gable with a gift. Truby called George to the front of the room and presented him with a gift: a gold-bound book filled with the signatures of everyone who'd assisted in the planning, preparation, and execution of the Golden Anniversary.

Photo by Philip Balko

According to the *Altoona Mirror*, George "was visibly affected, and after voicing his great appreciation for such a thoughtful remembrance paid generous tribute to every member of the large executive staff."

There was plenty of heartfelt emotion to go around that night, but some of the most deeply moving moments would be saved for another event a week later—a tribute luncheon with 200 of George's business colleagues—an event that included, according to the *Altoona Mirror*, the happiest hours of George's entire life.

George's Happiest Hours

At the March 7 luncheon in the Logan Room of the Penn-Alto Hotel, a veritable Who's Who of influential area businessmen spoke in praise of Gable's department store, the company's founder, and its latest president. It was a genuine Gable's lovefest from start to finish, with music by Gable's Golden Trio.

Everyone had good things to say to mark the anniversary celebration. George's brother, Robert, then of Wilkes-Barre, Pa., talked about how great George was, and how he'd always "leaned heavily" on him. Robert had depended on George so much, "Let George do it," had become Robert's motto.

William Francis Gable with the strength and enthusiasm and perhaps the self-confidence of youth—yet with unusual maturity of mind—founded in 1884 on the cornerstones of SERVICE, PERSONALITY, IDEALS and CONFIDENCE, the present enterprising THE WILLIAM F. GABLE COMPANY

The FOUNDER was sensitive, alert, honest, frank, natural and friendly—a MAN of action—one who never turned his back but marched breast forward.

We could wish no greater thing for our Country in this hour of her HISTORY than the appearance of only a few such men as WILLIAM FRANCIS GABLE.

John Lloyd

Another speaker who made a strong impression was Theodore S. Fettinger of Newark, N.J., who'd been the first advertising manager of the Gable store. Fettinger, who'd gone on to head a national advertising agency, said he'd felt compelled to return because he'd once promised William F. Gable that he would be there for the Golden occasion.

Fettinger called William a patron of art and literature and a friend of humanity. He also remembered fellow employees from the old days such as Elbert Hubbard and Alice, who'd gone down with the Lusitania. In addition to speaking off the cuff, Fettinger read excerpts from letters that William had sent him, recounting lofty sentiments and homely philosophies that William had expressed. Hearing these excerpts read aloud—the words of his late, great father—made George feel especially touched.

Courtesy Altoona Mirror

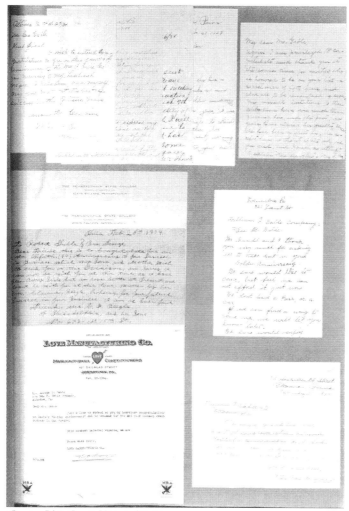

Other speakers included Gable's first customer, Samuel Hamilton; Channing E. Sweitzer, managing director of the National Retail Dry Goods Association; John Jackson of Strawbridge & Clothier, vice president of the Pennsylvania Retailers' Association; and Harry Adamy of Wilkes-Barre, also a vice president of the state Retailers' Association.

These guests and more talked about their appreciation and admiration of William F. Gable and what he'd accomplished. Pittsburgh department store manager Walter Rosenbaum referred to William's original anniversary sale idea, which had been copied by 125 of the biggest stores in the country. Rosenbaum also spoke of Gable's as "a human store" and said, "There is more of the milk of human kindness required in all our business, a more beautiful, helpful and peaceful atmosphere just like Gable's."

On to the Diamond Anniversary

By the time the luncheon was all over, the Gable store and family had been congratulated and praised in just about every way possible. It was hard to imagine a more perfect highlight of the Golden Anniversary.

For George, especially, it had been moving and inspirational. In the driver's seat of the store, he was in charge of leading his father's legacy forward. Now that he'd been reminded of how appreciated Gable's was to shoppers and business partners alike, he was reenergized. He was ready to tackle whatever challenges came next as he guided the company through the next phase of the Great Depression and beyond.

Whatever he did, he was determined to follow his father's example and do those things that would have made his father proud.

Even if William might not have imagined them given what he knew in the times in which he lived.

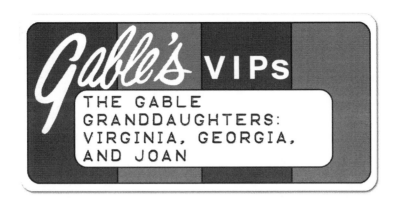

Imagine growing up as one of the grandchildren of George Gable, the great-grandchildren of the legendary William F. Gable himself. Every Sunday, you have dinner at George's house, enjoying delicious meals in a formal dining room. Afterward, George takes you to the Frankstown Hunt Club...or the WFBG radio or TV station atop Wopsononock Mountain...or Gable's department store, where you can roam to your heart's content because it's closed for the day.

Imagine all that, and you'll have some idea of what it was like growing up for Virginia Parsons Brantner, Georgia Parsons, and Joan Parsons Kuraitis.

Sunday Dinner at Grandpa's

As little girls, Virginia, Georgia, and Joan spent many idyllic Sundays with their beloved Grandpa and Grandma Gable. After church, Virginia and Georgia and their parents went to their grandparents' house for dinner.

"It was an old stone house near Baker Mansion," recalls Georgia. "I just adored it. We cherished our time there.

"The home had a lovely rose garden below it where our parents got married. Grandma was always taking care of that garden.

Photo by Philip Balko

83

"Grandpa and Grandma also had a tennis court in the backyard, where I learned to ride my first two-wheeled bicycle," says Georgia.

The big old house was a special place, with lots of room to explore. "When we went in the house, we'd walk upstairs to a foyer," remembers Virginia. "There was a library, a music room, a dining room, a pantry, and a kitchen on the first floor—but no living room, which was kind of different for me as a child.

"The dining room was for special occasions. When it was time to eat, we were called to the dining room, and they would open the big glass doors.

"My favorite place was the kitchen, where Bertha, the cook, worked to prepare meals. My grandmother would help, and I would talk to them both."

Courtesy Georgia Parsons

The library was probably the most remarkable part of the house, though. The fabled book collection of William F. Gable was stored in there, locked inside glass cases. "You needed a key to unlock the cases," says Virginia. "When I got older, I was able to use the key and take out the books. I knew they were very valuable, but they weren't that interesting for me to read as a child."

Hunting for Fun and Frolic

When the family had finished eating Sunday dinner, the girls got to spend the afternoon with their grandfather. Usually, this involved one of three possible destinations: the Hunt Club, the WFBG radio station, or Gable's department store.

"I remember going to the Hunt Club and watching fox hunts," says Georgia. "Everybody had riding outfits with boots on and everything. It was very exciting."

According to Georgia, her grandfather boarded a horse at the club and was a very accomplished rider. "In his house, he had a whole drawer filled with ribbons he'd won for his riding skills. Gingy and I used to play with them."

Georgia and Gingy (Virginia) did some riding at the Hunt Club, too. "My older sister had a horse called Minny," says Georgia. "My younger sister, Joan, and I had a little black Shetland pony named Junior. One of us would get on Junior, and someone would lead us around in a circle. That was about the extent of our riding horses.

Courtesy Georgia Parsons

"But it was fun at the Club, and we could run around and have grand adventures. There was a barn with lots of hay, and we could go in there and climb on the hay bales."

On Top of Old Wopsy

Sometimes, if George had business to attend to at the WFBG-TV station facilities, he would drive the girls up there instead.

"The station transmitter facilities were located up on top of Wopsononock Mountain," recalls Georgia. "We always had a pretty view up there.

"I remember spending time in the station building, talking to the people who were manning the equipment."

"They had all the computers up there," says Virginia. "They were gigantic, as big as a whole room."

But neither the Hunt Club nor WFBG-TV was the girls' *favorite* place to visit with Grandpa George on Sundays.

Run of the Store

What child could resist having a whole department store almost to herself? Not Virginia and Georgia, certainly.

And on certain Sundays, that was exactly what they got. Thanks to the blue laws in Pennsylvania at the time, Gable's was closed on Sunday...but that didn't mean Grandpa George could stay away. As president, he sometimes had work that couldn't wait for Monday, work that could only be done in his office at the store. Which, for Virginia and Georgia, meant it was time to let the good times roll.

"Going into Gable's on a Sunday afternoon was great fun because no one was there," recalls Georgia. "We could just run up and down the halls. It was so exciting."

"Grandpa would take us around and let us do anything we wanted in the store on a Sunday afternoon," remembers Virginia. "We could play with anything. The sales team would probably cringe when they came to work on Monday morning and found everything in disarray."

All Photos Courtesy Georgia Parsons

Not that the girls could ever just help themselves to the merchandise. "I always ran to the toy department, which was my favorite department because I loved the dolls so much," says Georgia. "We were never allowed to have anything, though. We'd pick something up, and Grandpa would tell us to put it back. It wasn't like we got to take anything, but we were allowed to run free through the deserted store, which was great fun for us when we were little."

In addition to playing with toys in the toy department, one of Virginia's favorite things to do in the store was read. She loved the book department, especially *The Happy Hollister* series she found there, which helped improve her reading skills.

Virginia and Georgia also got to see the behind-the-scenes secrets of George's office on the top floor of the Twelfth Avenue building. "I remember going up to his office, which was wood-paneled, had a big desk and a separate bathroom," says Georgia.

"I remember him showing me these gold and silver coins and other valuables he kept in the safe. I thought that was really special."

The Girl in the Chute

The girls' Gable's memories weren't limited to Sunday frolics when the store was closed to customers, however. They also spent their fair share of time in the place when it was open for business.

"I remember going into Gabel's department store with my mother as a child," says Georgia. "When we did that, it was always kind of a special occasion, and you got dressed up and wore dresses and gloves and hats.

"Mother would walk us up to the street car. We took the street car in from Logan Boulevard or we took a bus later on. This was before my mother had a car.

Courtesy Georgia Parsons

"We always felt very special going into the store because all the ladies knew my mother, and she would introduce us as the granddaughters of George Gable. I loved when my grandfather introduced me to people, because he would always say, 'And this is my namesake, Georgia.'"

The girls didn't always toe the line when they visited the busy store, however. They managed to get into some mischief from time to time.

One incident happened during a trip to the ladies' dress department to see Tillie Wolf, the longtime seamstress at Gable's. "Tillie was like a member of the family," recalls Georgia. "She was just an amazing woman and very dear and very special."

When Georgia's mom turned her back for a moment, Georgia went exploring—and found a nearby package chute. Since it looked like a sliding board, Georgia jumped in and took a wild ride straight to the basement.

"Apparently, everyone was looking for me for a long time, and it was a big deal," says Georgia. "They didn't know where I'd gone.

"I was perfectly fine when they found me, but I never got to do it again. I wasn't allowed to go near the package chute after that."

The incident didn't keep her from being a part of other fun—and less dangerous—activities at Gable's, though. For example, Georgia participated in one of the fashion shows at the store.

"When I was about five years old, I was the flower girl in a bridal party at the end of a fashion show," says Georgia. "I got to wear a pretty dress and carry a basket of flowers. The problem was, I wasn't allowed to sit down, because I might wrinkle my dress.

"Poor Tillie, bless her heart, had to walk me around and keep me standing for what seemed like hours. She must have been exhausted by the time I finally got to walk down the aisle in the fashion show."

Gables at the Seashore

Sundays weren't the only magical times the girls got to spend with George. They also shared perfect summer vacations with their grandparents at the New Jersey shore.

According to Georgia, Grandpa Gable rented a house on Long Beach Island every summer. Their family would spend several weeks at the shore with their grandparents, plus a rotating cast of characters.

"Seashore vacations were really magical," says Georgia. "There were always lots of people, and we girls were the only children, so we were the center of attention. We had tons of fun.

"There were several couples who were good friends of my grandparents who were usually there, including Harold and Marge March. Harold always bought kites for us to fly because our house was right on the beach where we could take advantage of the ocean breezes.

All Photos Courtesy Georgia Parsons

"Our Aunt Virginia came down from New York City, where she worked as fashion coordinator at *Life* magazine, and she brought friends with her from the city. One of those friends, in particular, was an actress, and she used to pretend she was a witch at night to scare us. We often called her Dottie Witch, though she was very beautiful and not scary at all."

The area where the family stayed on Long Beach Island was something of an artists' colony, so there were plenty of interesting and eccentric neighbors, as well. One longtime neighbor, Boris Blai, was a world-renowned artist and sculptor who founded the Long Beach Island Foundation of the Arts and Sciences and counted the famous architect Frank Lloyd Wright as a friend. Blai and the Gables were such good friends, he sculpted a bust of George and presented it to him in Altoona in 1953.

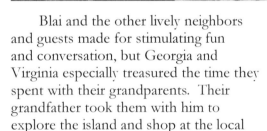

Blai and the other lively neighbors and guests made for stimulating fun and conversation, but Georgia and Virginia especially treasured the time they spent with their grandparents. Their grandfather took them with him to explore the island and shop at the local fish market to stock up for meals. "I remember my grandmother making big lobster dinners with corn on the cob and blueberry pie," says Georgia. "I don't know how she cooked for all those people, but somehow she did, and it was wonderful."

Florence even had a way of making rainy days special for the girls, providing a box of toys for them to play with when they couldn't go to the beach. "That toy box was special for us and very much fun. My grandmother was always so thoughtful," says Georgia.

Looking Back with Love

Many years after those idyllic vacations and Sundays with their grandparents, Virginia and Georgia cherish those times as some of the best of their lives.

They fondly remember the little things their grandmother did to show her love—like making their favorite foods when they weren't feeling well. "I particularly liked the egg custard she used to make," says Georgia. "If I had a stomach ache or wasn't feeling well, grandma would arrive at our house with an entire tray of little cups of egg custard that were especially for me. For Gingy, she made blueberry pies."

Courtesy Georgia Parsons

Holidays were always magical in those days too. "We had our Christmas at home, and then we'd go to our grandparents' house and have an even bigger Christmas. That was where we got bicycles and larger gifts."

But George taught the girls to give as well as receive… to make a difference by helping those around them. In fact, generosity is one of the things that Virginia admired most about George. "Whenever he went through the store and saw someone in need, he'd help that person. I remember the kindness he had for others."

Courtesy Georgia Parsons

Golden Gable Girls

These days, Virginia and Georgia live in St. Petersburg, Florida, and their younger sister, Joan, lives in Whitefish Bay, Wisconsin. They sometimes reminisce about their lives as George's granddaughters.

Their grandmother Gable passed away in 1958, and George remarried, but they still adore the memory of the grandparents who brought so much love and affection to their lives.

"I loved the Cubby Bear stories Grandpa used to tell me," says Virginia. "I think he made them up on the spot, and they were wonderful.

"He had a mustache that tickled when he kissed me. He smoked a pipe, and I would smell the tobacco smoke around him.

"Our grandparents were a huge, huge part of our lives when we were growing up," says Georgia. "We are so lucky to have such fabulous memories of them and their lovely home and the store and the wonderful people in it.

"I wouldn't trade those memories for anything."

Photo by Philip Balko

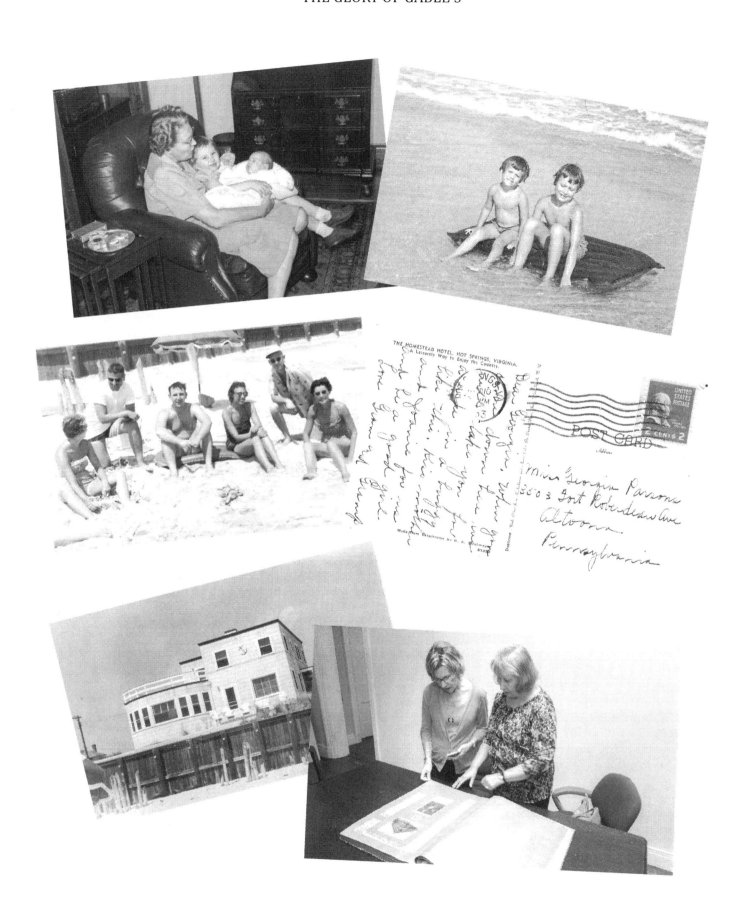

Chapter Eleven

What Depression?

1935-1940

You might think the Great Depression would slow Gable's down. You might think it would at least make the company more conservative when it came to making expensive moves.

And you would be wrong, if that's what you thought.

If anything, George Gable and his team loosened the purse strings to update the store. They understood that when money is tight, retailers have to work harder than ever to keep consumer dollars flowing. They understood that customers are most generous when they get a little entertainment with their low-priced quality merchandise.

That's why, riding high on the momentum from the Golden Anniversary in 1934, they cooked up plans to make the Greatest Show in Altoona more captivating than ever for local shoppers.

Meet the New Gable's

Starting after the 51st anniversary in 1935, Gable and Co. initiated a series of major improvements to the store properties. By the time the work was done in time for the 52nd anniversary in 1936, the changes were so extensive that the place looked entirely different.

As the *Altoona Mirror* put it, "A patron who, if there has been any, who has not been in the store since the fifty-first anniversary in 1935, would scarcely know the interior of the Gable buildings."

Every department was updated in one way or another. It must have cost a small fortune to complete all the work, and that in the heart of the Great Depression. But George and his team thought it was important. The additions and improvements were made with one thought in mind, as noted in the *Mirror:* "the best service to and convenience of the patrons of the Gable's stores."

"Confidence on the part of customers is created by clean paint, well-balanced color scheme, and a logical arrangement of accessories and furnishings which enhances the appearance of the merchandise by giving full expression to its value," according to the *Mirror*.

Courtesy Frank Barry

Putting on the Ritz

On the main floor of the Eleventh Avenue building, the book and stationery departments were moved to a new location. New fittings were installed, and a brand new greeting card section was added.

The toiletries department was doubled in size and refurbished extensively, making it "one of the beauty spots of the Gable's stores," according to the *Mirror*. A new perfume counter was added to this department—first of its kind in Gable's.

Also on the first floor, the shoe departments were completely remodeled. The three main departments were compressed into two—a style shoe department and an orthopedic one. Between the two, a brand new "Peacock Parlor" was set up to handle nothing but Peacock shoes. A big Peacock emblem was mounted in the middle of the area, centered in a chrome circle with a pleated silk and gold background.

Another first floor change involved the candy department, which was moved from under the stairs to a "choice location" between the main doors on the Eleventh Avenue side. Modern new display cases were brought in, and new lines of sweets were ordered, as management aimed to create the biggest candy department in any store in the state.

The glove and leather goods department moved, too, occupying the space left empty when books and stationery changed location.

Other first floor changes included replacing or repainting all the fixtures. The ceiling was painted white, and the columns were all made square and painted ivory. "The effect is one of great beauty and very pleasing and soft to the eye," the *Mirror* said.

From Furs to Lingerie

The columns also were squared on the second floor, with painting and new fixtures to match the first. The ready-to-wear, millinery, and fur departments were extensively remodeled, with a new sweater booth in ready-to-wear and new racks to go around.

In the yard goods department on the same floor, new silk booths and a monogramming counter were added. A new department for maids' and nurses' uniforms also was set up, with all new fixtures.

One of the biggest changes was found on the third floor, where all the children's departments were relocated and consolidated from elsewhere in the store. Everything for kids was now located on three, with clothes for everyone from infants to high schoolers. It was a policy that was "greatly appreciated by patrons," according to the *Mirror*.

Also on the third floor, the lingerie department got a major facelift, spruced up with new furnishings and fixtures. A new picture framing department opened on the fourth floor, adjacent to the photo studio.

What About the Twelfth Avenue Store?

Meanwhile, plenty of work was done to renovate the Twelfth Avenue building as well. In the basement, for example, the new Thrifty Home Store took over space formerly used for storage. The Thrifty Store also was given more than 8,000 square feet on the first floor, running from 1114 to 1116 Fourteenth St. In years gone by, that space had been occupied by the Liszman barber shop, the Smull shoe repair shop, and an indoor miniature golf course.

Managed by A. Galfond, formerly of Glosser Bros. in Johnstown, the Thrifty Store carried carpets, rugs, linoleum, draperies, furniture, china, and all manner of home furnishings. The color scheme—ivory and green—matched that of the rest of Gable's department store.

On the first floor, the grocery department underwent significant upgrades, including the installation of new counters, scales, and cash registers. A new "epicure's department" was added at the foot of the stairs, featuring gourmet delicatessen merchandise.

The second floor house furnishing and paint departments were both updated too. On the third floor, a new suite of offices was installed for the personnel manager and staff. In addition, the model home show rooms were redecorated and refinished.

Who Are You Calling a Dummy?

Along with the many improvements throughout the store in 1936, Gable's invested in upgrading another vital part of its business: the display mannequins.

A set of new high-end mannequins was purchased for use in the Eleventh Avenue windows. Sculpted by renowned New York City artist Cora Scovil, the mannequins were modeled on famous movie stars, including Marlene Dietrich and Ann Southern.

According to Gable's display manager, H.L. Greene, Scovil's mannequins were "the finest and most natural that it is possible to obtain." In addition to the appeal of their movie star-based faces and forms, the new mannequins had flexible arms and legs and natural, silky hair done up in the latest styles.

The Changes of '39

As extensive as the improvements of 1935-1936 were, more changes took effect by the 55th anniversary in 1939.

In the Eleventh Avenue building, a round of general overhauling, remodeling, and regrouping of merchandise affected most departments—some more than others. Eight new fitting rooms were installed in the ready-to-wear department, for example. New sections also were added to the rayon underwear department, which was enlarged and remodeled.

A new electric ice cream freezer, ice cream hardeners, an exhaust fan, and new lights were added to the restaurant. The three shoe departments then in existence were merged under one management, plus completely remodeled.

The nut and orange dispensing booth, previously operated by an outside vendor, was taken over by Gable's, remodeled, and expanded.

A new pipe club was set up in the Esquire Room

Courtesy Altoona Mirror

restaurant, with pipes, tobacco, and a dark oak pipe rack all supplied free of charge by Gable's. Members had 131 pipes and high grade tobacco like Prince Albert and Sir Walter Raleigh at their disposal, for use in the Esquire Room. The only requirement was that the members be regular patrons of the Esquire Room restaurant.

Like the first floor, the second floor was renovated and redecorated. The beauty shop was remodeled on the third floor, with the old sign replaced by a neon one and a gas hot water heater with a 50-gallon copper boiler installed to improve efficiency. Also on the third floor, new fitting rooms were added to the junior department, the corset department was remodeled and redecorated, and a new women's bathroom was installed.

During the past year among the many important changes made in the William F. Gable company's stores was the remodeling, refurnishing, redecorating of the "Gift shop." This shop has always been a fascinating one to lovers of the beautiful in art, in fine china, and decorating merchandise, but this has been greatly enhanced in the new "Gift shop" as there has been such a wonderful advance in the opportunity to display the many fine articles sold in this department, as is disclosed in the photograph shown herewith.

Courtesy Altoona Mirror

As for the Twelfth Avenue building, all the floors were sanded, a project that took weeks to complete. Among other improvements to the second floor, a wallpaper inspection room was added there. On the third floor, partitions were erected to separate the furniture floor-display from adjoining stock rooms.

Everything in the store was spiffed up, expanded, and updated, proving Gable's good health and commitment to keeping its store on the cutting edge...again, while the Great Depression was still underway. And George and his team weren't done yet.

By the next anniversary, the company had undergone even more improvements.

The Greatest Event in History?

Was Gable's 56th anniversary in 1940 the greatest event in the company's history? The front page story in the *Altoona Mirror* said so.

Thousands of guests were expected to visit the store during the month-long celebration. According to George Gable, more than $1,000,000 worth of "highest quality and up-to-the-minute merchandise" had been brought in for shoppers to explore. The merchandise would be on sale "at such prices as to afford sensational values along the entire gamut of the more than 100 departments which constitute this great store, now embracing almost an entire city block."

Visitors would receive free souvenirs, and special gifts would be handed out to patrons who had shopped at Gable and Co. during its first year in business. There would even be an exhibit of merchandise that was purchased in the original Gable's store during its first year in business.

Courtesy Matthew Germann

The very act of getting to the store would be a gift, as Gable's had arranged for its customers to get free transportation on all Altoona and Logan Valley street cars and buses between the hours of 8:30 and 9:30 a.m. on the first day of the anniversary sale, March 1st. Shoppers also could ride free from outlying areas that morning on Blue & White Bus Lines buses. Guests who traveled by car would have free parking in all Tenth Avenue parking lots until 6 p.m.

Eager to kick off a new decade, George and his staff were pulling out all the stops. "Our anniversary sale is more important in our history than the Christmas season in that we begin another fiscal year in our business," said George on the eve of the big event. "Tomorrow our sales force will total 850 capable and courteous persons. This includes our regular sales force, coupled with several hundred extra salespeople."

After years of anniversary celebrations, the Gable's team had gotten in the habit of trying to make each one bigger than the last, using them to generate excitement about the store and showcase the latest improvements.

This time around, those improvements included new fitting rooms and a "surgical department" in the ladies' foundation department, an enlarged shoe repair department, new equipment in the restaurant, a new produce department in the basement under the management of Jack Lambert, a new dairy department, and extensive painting and redecorating throughout the store.

Once again, Gable's reached another anniversary bigger and better than ever, unbowed by the economic storm of the Great Depression. But how would it stand up to the world war racing its way, and the changes it would bring to the Altoona area and the country as a whole?

Courtesy Altoona Mirror

Gable's 56th ANNIVERSARY

Tomorrow--Exciting Anniversary Savings for

Founder's Day

A Short Biography of the Founder

William F. Gable, Founder of The William F. Gable Company, was born on a farm in Chester County, February 12, 1856. In early manhood he went to Reading, Pennsylvania, and attended the Reading Commercial College. Graduating from there, for five years he became bookkeeper for a firm of lumber dealers by the name of Boas & Roudenbush of Reading; from there he took a similar position with Dives, Pomeroy & Stewart, well known as the leading Dry Goods Company of Reading, and they still are.

On March 1, 1884, his first connection with the business interests of Altoona was formed and he became a partner in the firm of Sprecher & Gable in the formation of the "Daylight Store." A few months later, Mr. Sprecher's interest was purchased by his former employers, Dives, Pomeroy & Stewart, and the firm then became William F. Gable & Company. Under this caption the business continued and constantly expanded as additional success and prosperity rewarded adherence to the strict and upright principles of dealing. In 1919 the business was incorporated as The William F. Gable Company. Its growth has been vigorous and natural and today occupies the position as the largest department store of Pennsylvania, outside of Pittsburgh and Philadelphia. It is remarkable when you think that this great business institution started with a capital of only $800.00.

William F. Gable was always ready to embrace new and progressive ideas, at the same time he hung tenaciously to his principles which were; First, one price to all; Second, good quality merchandise; Third, your money refunded cheerfully without argument. His early slogan was "Lowest prices East or West of the Alleghenies" and that slogan has been held ever since. There is a strong family spirit, a spirit of hearty cooperation, in the Gable store, William F. Gable's attitude was a constant aid and sympathy with his organization. A quotation taken from one of his letters, and later engraved on a silver loving

cup presented to him by his employees, fully explains his viewpoint, William F. Gable said, "There is no line drawn in my mind or heart between employee and employer." The welfare and happiness of his assistants in the operation of his business were among his greatest concerns.

William F. Gable was an untiring worker as he rarely slept over five hours a night and worked practically the entire time between. You could find him at his desk from the time the store closed until the early hours of the morning. In the quiet hours of the night he had an opportunity to think out his business problems.

William F. Gable was one of the outstanding book and autograph collectors of his time. It is a well known fact that he had one of the finest collections ever made in the State of Pennsylvania.

William F. Gable was very much interested in agriculture and had the farm in Chester County, of over 1,000 acres, where he was born. On this farm there was a great herd of approximately 100 head of registered Guernseys and in 1912 this herd produced the world's finest milk, winning the Panama Pacific Exposition prize.

William F. Gable was a many sided man but his first interest was The William F. Gable Company and the people of Altoona. Today the store is operated on the principles of the founder and his ideas are emulated to some of the smallest details. Proof of this you will find in the values offered for Founder's Day. We believe them to be the "Lowest prices East or West of the Alleghenies" for merchandise of similar quality. We know they are excellent values and if you are not satisfied we will cheerfully refund your money. This is "Your Store," the store of the people of this community. For 56 years we have faithfully followed the principles of the Founder.

It Was Values Like These for Tomorrow That Helped Make the Founder Famous!

Doveskin Lingerie
Full cut and neatly tailored Vests, Band Panties, Bloomers, Stepins and Briefs. Regular and extra sizes. Former value 59c.
39c
Gable's Lingerie—Main Floor—11th Avenue

Beacon Blankets each
Second selection of 3.98 and 4.50 Blankets. Solid colors, jacquard patterns in light and dark colors. Slight imperfections will not hurt wearing qualities.
2.98
Gable's Domestics—Main Floor—11th Avenue

Stamped Cases 2 pairs
Stamped Pepperell Pillow Cases, hemstitched for crocheting. New and attractive stamping patterns. Work several pairs in your spare time.
1.00
Gable's Art Needlework—Third Floor—11th Avenue

Doeskin Gloves
Regular 1.98 value washable doeskin Gloves in slip-on and gauntlet styles. Four button length in white, pink, blue, green, navy and red.
1.29
Gable's Gloves—Main Floor—11th Avenue

Cannon Bath Mats
Dropped patterns of Cannon first quality Bath Mats. Not all colors in each style but a good selection. Values 1.19 to 2.50 each.
88c
Gable's Linens—Main Floor—11th Avenue

Cannon Bath Towels
39c value, first quality colorful block pattern Bath Towels. Soft yarns. 23x46 size. Blue, green, gold and peach.
29c
Gable's Linens—Main Floor—11th Avenue

Girls' Pajamas
Stock up your little Girls' lingerie wardrobe now . . . Crepe Pajamas in pink, blue and peach colors. Sizes 8 to 16.
83c
Gable's Youth Centre—Third Floor—11th Avenue

Men's Shirts, Shorts
"Fruit of the Loom" Shirts and Shorts. Shirts made of fine combed cotton sizes 34 to 46. Shorts made of broadcloth, sizes 30 to 44. $1 for 1.00
29c
Gable's Men's Shop—Main Floor—11th Avenue

Women's Neckwear
Something frothy and feminine at your neck and the rest of the dress takes on a lovely look. Pique, lace, organdie Neckwear.
50c
Gable's Accessories—Main Floor—11th Avenue

New Cotton Fabrics
Lovely designs and colors to choose from: Stripes, checks, plaids, sports designs and novelty patterns. Values to 39c yard.
27c
Gable's Fabrics—Second Floor—11th Avenue

Infants' Dresses 2 for
Hand-made Dresses for Infants' sizes 6 months to 2 years. Hemmed and scalloped bottoms, some with collars. In White only.
1.00
Gable's Youth Centre—Third Floor—11th Avenue

Girls' Wool Sweaters
Slip-on, short-sleeve Sweaters and long-sleeve, coat style Sweaters in sizes 3 to 6x and 8 to 16. Pretty styles and pastel colors. 1.59 value.
1.19
Gable's Youth Centre—Third Floor—11th Avenue

4-Pc. Canister Sets
A grand housewares value! 4-piece decorated Canister Sets in red, black, and green. Containers for flour, sugar, coffee, tea. Regularly 69c.
44c
Gable's Housewares—Second Floor—12th Avenue

Men's Sweaters 2 for
Grand for sports, work and many other uses. Men's sleeveless Sweaters in sizes small to large. Regular 1.00 to 1.95 values. 59c each.
1.00
Gable's Men's Shop—Main Floor—11th Avenue

Boys' Wool Sweaters
Grand for school, and dress-up occasions. Plain shades in these slip-over style Boys' wool Sweaters. Full zipper jacquard patterns. Sizes 30 to 38.
1.56
Gable's Youth Centre—Third Floor—11th Avenue

Wallpapers Single Roll
Spring Wallpapers in a complete assortment of colorings. 10c and 15c values. Blues, greens, pinks, tans, white and others. Sold only with border.
7½c
Gable's Wallpaper—First Floor—12th Avenue

See Following Pages for More Founder's Day Specials Tomorrow!

Courtesy Altoona Mirror

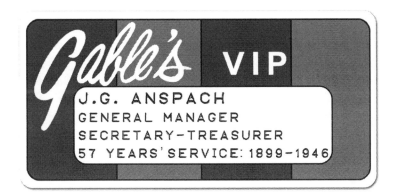

J.G. ANSPACH
GENERAL MANAGER
SECRETARY-TREASURER
57 YEARS' SERVICE: 1899-1946

There was an important business meeting at 7 p.m. at the Penn-Alto Hotel. That's what George Gable told J.G. Anspach as he hurried him out the door. Anspach, the treasurer and general manager of Gable's department store, didn't even raise an eyebrow. Big deal last-minute meetings came with the territory. They had, in one way or another, since J.G. had first started working at Gable's 54 years ago.

Why should tonight be any different?

Courtesy Altoona Mirror

Keeping the Spirit Alive

Born in Mifflinburg, Pa. in 1875, J.G. had come to Altoona in October 1889 at the age of 14. He got a job at Gable and Co. shortly thereafter...and never left. Moving up through the ranks, he learned retailing from William F. Gable himself, and carried those lessons forward as a Gable's executive after William died in 1921.

In the years that followed, J.G. continued to play an influential role in the hierarchy at Gable's. For most of his career—which eventually lasted 57 years—he worked as general manager and treasurer of the store.

During that time, he served as an important link to the days of William F. Gable, keeping his wisdom and vision of the company alive for later generations of store management. George Gable, for example, learned extensively from J.G. during his own time rising through the ranks of the various departments.

When George became president, J.G. remained one of his most reliable executives and advisors...not to mention one of his best friends. The two were good enough friends, in fact, that George didn't hesitate to rush him out the door on a Wednesday night for a 7 o'clock meeting, a meeting for which J.G. hadn't even properly prepared. George knew he understood and accepted the inconvenience. J.G. knew he was appreciated, which went a long way with him.

And, when he walked in the Penn-Alto dining room, he was *surprised*.

A Night to Remember

"Happy Birthday, Mr. Anspach!" That's what the 96 guests in the Penn-Alto dining room sang when J.G. walked in with George Gable. Gable's Golden Trio themselves backed the singers with their violin-cello-piano arrangement.

Did J.G. have tears in his eyes as the guests launched into "For He's a Jolly Good Fellow"? It seems like a pretty safe bet.

After all the anniversary celebrations he'd mounted for Gable's over the years, it was J.G.'s turn to blow out the candles. His closest family, friends, and co-workers had turned out to honor him on his 68th birthday, hammering home a point that J.G. already knew quite well in his heart.

He had led a good life, and people loved him.

Now, they were coming through for him. It wasn't a typical milestone birthday, marking a new decade—70 or 80—or three-quarters of a century—75—but here they were anyway, for his 68th. Was it because he'd been having some issues? Some medical problems? Did they want to throw him a big party while he could still enjoy it?

All that matters is, it was a night to remember.

So Many Tributes

There was a turkey dinner, courtesy of George, of course. Then George talked at length about all the wonderful things J.G. had done to make the company a success.

Then, one coworker after another got up and said the same kind of things. Elvia Wagner, a member of Gable's Quarter Century Club, talked about their lifelong friendship and how it was still going strong. Merchandise specialist Fred Starrett talked about J.G.'s fine sense of timing, which was so important in keeping up with variations in the merchandise market. Sales and promotion manager Stanley Truby talked about J.G.'s efficient style in carrying on the store's operations.

And there were more: stylist H.O. Jones; George's assistant, S.A.

Courtesy Altoona Mirror

Hamilton, who had been the store's first customer; and David Little, who had helped set up the event. J.G.'s best pal and fishing buddy, John E. Sheep, got up and told stories about the trips they'd taken and the fish they'd caught…just before handing him his birthday gift, a solid gold shrine jewel.

A Perfect Moment

What a night!

Can there be any doubt that it made J.G.'s week…his month…his year? Maybe his lifetime? That he thought back on it often in the years to come, even as illness took its toll? Even as he felt himself slipping, little by little, though he never *ever* stopped going to work at Gable's every morning?

Can there be any doubt that when his body gave way three years later, on May 20, 1946, and the lights started winking out in his mind, one by one, cluster by cluster, one of the last to go was the memory of that night in '43, when the Golden Trio played "The Gang's All Here," and 96 people sang along, all smiles, all eyes beaming right at him? Can there be any doubt that that single perfect moment flashed through his mind one last time?

Just before he heard a certain voice for the first time since 1921, and he looked back over his shoulder…and everything was different. Yet the same. The same as he remembered.

And he said the name that went with that voice. Said it like a question, though he knew without a doubt whose voice it was. He knew without a doubt, but he said it anyway.

William?

MEMORY DEPARTMENT

My Aunt Helen Haller was the secretary-treasurer at Gable's for many years. She started in the accounting department and worked her way up. She retired when the store closed.

Gable's was like my home away from home. I worked there, too, in the credit office, and I did part-time work in a variety of departments. My first job was on Saturdays during the Christmas season, at the cash desk in the accounting office, counting the daily sales from the previous day. After that, I did gift-wrapping for the holiday and inventory in January.

Terra George

I remember when my mother worked for Gable's. I would ride the bus there and go to the fourth floor, where the offices were located. I spent some time at a young age helping "Squeak." She worked the switchboard. My mother worked in the printing office.

Christina M. Lascoli-Clancy

My next-door neighbor was the basement store manager, Lester McCracken. He and his wife, Dottie, were the nicest people. She would ride the bus every day to Gable's, just to have lunch with him. She would either bring it packed, or they would eat at the basement restaurant.

Mary Bowers

I often rode the bus from Ashville to downtown, and Gable's was my favorite! Mr. Lato, who had the shoe shop on the bottom floor, was from Ashville too. He was always so nice to me! I remember buying lots of costume jewelry—rings, mostly, which I wore on every finger! I would also purchase very nice clothing through a layaway upstairs.

Catherine Klepser

Courtesy Anne Dixon

99

Mr. Little was the floorwalker, and he was not little. He was a tall, distinguished man who walked through the store departments, making sure everything ran smoothly. He was always gracious when greeting the customers.
Phyllis Gates Deibler

I remember when I was in the Cherub Choir at First Lutheran Church. Miss Little would take us over to sing Christmas carols at Gable's. Then, we were invited to have hot chocolate.
Pamela Kelley

I remember going downtown on a city bus, usually on a Saturday afternoon, with my grandfather. My favorite time for going to Gable's, however, was Christmastime.
Cheryl Deihl

My mother graduated from Bellwood High School in May of 1945. After graduating, she went on to Altoona School of Commerce, working at Gable's the whole time. She stayed on at Gable's after graduating from the School of Commerce, working as a personal shopper. She continued to work there till I was born in August of 1952.

Mom said that every morning, rain or shine, a man would come to the office carrying an umbrella and proclaim what a beautiful day it was. I wish I could remember what his name was.
Constance M Holland Cullison

My grandmother and I could spend hours shopping at Gable's. On Saturday afternoons, we would go to Gable's, sometimes having lunch in the restaurant in the basement. I remember that the women's lingerie department where my great aunt worked also was in the basement.

Gable's had many departments, even a candy department. I had coats, shoes, and toys from Gable's. My grandmother had a Gable's charge, and we still have the little metal credit card for her account.
Christine Glunt

When I was young, there were no malls. Everything was what we called "uptown." Some people called it downtown, overtown…and we called it uptown. Everything was there. Sears, Penney's Gable's, shoe stores, everything you needed was in the uptown area. We used to go there all the time. Sometimes we rode the bus, and sometimes we walked. It wasn't too far away, so mostly we walked.

Photo by Gelon V. Smith

At Christmas time they always went crazy with the displays. They had different groups singing Christmas carols on the steps. At night, we would go over and listen to the Christmas music. We used to walk over the one bridge, the Fourth Street Bridge, and go up through town, then back down and over the Twelfth Street Bridge because the railroad shops would decorate the trees in the big yards of the shops. So we would walk and see the trees, and there was a bakery on the other side of the bridge where we would stop and get cookies for Christmas.
Frank Barry

Chapter Twelve

Life During Wartime

1941-1945

It felt like the whole world was on fire. Battles raged every day around the globe—on the ground, in the air, in the sea. Scores of lives were lost in Europe, Asia, Africa...the Atlantic, the Pacific...and countless islands in between. Every newspaper, radio, and newsreel blared the latest reports on Axis atrocities, Allied advances, and all the innocent lives extinguished as a consequence. All-out war and its effects were felt everywhere, a monstrous storm that threatened to consume all human civilization.

Gable's department store was no exception. On the surface, it seemed that business as usual continued daily, providing a haven of normalcy on the homefront...but the effects of the war were plain for all to see.

Rationing in Action

For one thing, the availability of certain goods stocked in the store changed dramatically. Sugar, butter, coffee, lard, cheese, tea, milk, meat, and other foods were needed for the war effort, so suppliers were unable to provide enough to keep up with customer demand. Rationing was implemented to ensure that such products, stocked in limited amounts on store shelves, were distributed fairly, and did not become unaffordable.

The same went for products manufactured with nylon, silk, rubber, or oil. Gasoline was rationed, as well, which affected the cost and timing of delivery.

As a result, the way that Gable's did business changed dramatically during the war. The company had to adjust its processes across the board to fit the new reality, changing the way it ordered, stocked, priced, and sold merchandise. Accounting systems had to be adjusted, as the ways in which earnings and expenses occurred were altered. Even time-tested marketing techniques and advertising formulas had to be revised.

It wasn't always easy. Just dealing with rationing requirements could be a complicated task for merchandisers and consumers alike. For example, the War Price and Rationing Board offered the following guidance in the *Altoona Mirror* on March 2, 1944:

On Sunday, Feb. 27, the new ration token program went into effect and consumers are expected to receive many benefits from it.

Since red and blue stamps in book No. 4 are now worth ten points each, housewives will be enabled to more efficiently budget their purchases as the length of validity of the first group of stamps will be three months. It should be borne in mind that all red and blue "A-8" stamps will be worth ten points each.

One of the important factors of this new plan is a great saving in time that will result. Housewives, upon making purchases, will no longer be compelled to compute the amounts appearing on the face of the stamps, as in the instance of brown stamps in book No. 3 which are marked "8," "5," "2," and "1." When a purchase is made in a multiple less than ten, the consumer will extract a ten-point stamp and receive the difference in "change," or red or blue tokens as the case may be, red stamps being used for meats, fats, butter, cheese, etc., and blue stamps for processed foods.

Not so simple, was it? The cornerstone of the retail industry—the transaction between retailer and customer—had fundamentally changed, and both sides of that transaction had to make the best of it.

Gable's, ever a nimble organization, did just that, and continued to succeed. Even in the heat of wartime, George Gable and his team kept the merchandise flowing and the cash registers ringing…even as the composition of that team was itself changed by wartime demands.

Undermanned Anniversary

By Gable's 60th Anniversary in March 1944, 85 of its employees had left the store for the armed services. Those 85 men and women enlisted or were drafted into the U.S. Army, Navy, Marine Corps, and Coast Guard, joining the forces fighting the war at home and abroad—leaving gaps in Gable's staff that were difficult to fill.

According to the *Altoona Mirror*, "Those left behind must fill their places to the best of their ability, but all will be exceedingly glad when the war is over and everyone is welcomed back to their old positions, and they will be better employees on account of the benefit that their experience in the service has been to them."

Courtesy Frank Barry

Courtesy Frank Barry

Courtesy Frank Barry

The staff shortage didn't seem to make the 60th Anniversary any less festive, though. When the doors opened at 9 a.m. on March 1, customers poured in, rushing to receive their free souvenir—a cake-plate with a gothic letter "G" in the center, a follow-up to the free plate handed out at the Golden Anniversary in 1934. Even in a time of shortages and rationing, the crowds found plenty of merchandise and great bargains throughout the store. It was a testimony to the hard work of Gable's 63 buyers and executives, who traveled more than 180,000 miles (over seven times the distance around the world) annually to purchase merchandise.

Special displays also were set up to mark the anniversary. For example, the history of the Pennsylvania Railroad was portrayed via artifacts and photos in the store windows along Eleventh Avenue. Visitors could explore the story of the railroad from its earliest days to its role in the modern war effort.

There were many reminders of the war throughout the store, of course. After all, it was the defining event of the times. But there were plenty of distractions to take customers' minds off it, at least for a little while. Walking the floors of Gable's, they could almost forget that the world beyond was still in flames.

Gable's Backs America

Gable's put its best foot forward for the Diamond Anniversary, putting on its usual great show and spectacular sale. But the company made a powerful impression in its support of the war effort too.

For example, when the U.S. Treasury Department appealed to department stores to help sell war bonds and stamps, the Gable's team went all-out. In recognition, the Treasury Department awarded the staff the Gold Star citation for extraordinary results in the sale of war bonds. The entire staff was honored at a dinner on January 26, 1944, at the Penn-Alto Hotel, where G. Ruhland Rebman of the Treasury Department presented the award to George Gable.

Photo by Gelon V. Smith

Booking a Legacy

The store and its staff also played a vital role in the National Victory Book Campaign, which was dedicated to collecting books and sending them to servicemen. By early 1943, Blair County had collected more than 12,456 books, becoming the third of Pennsylvania's 67 counties to surpass the assigned quota. Gable's staff and shoppers helped the book drive succeed, and further support came directly from George Gable, who served on the executive board of the county Victory Book Campaign and was chairman of the storage and destination committee. When the Victory Book Campaign organization and the National Retailers Association asked Gable's department store to serve as a warehouse for Blair County's incoming books, George accepted.

"One more
Notch to go..
You're Next Hirohito!"

The William F. Gable Co.

From that point on, hundreds of cartons of books were shipped to Gable's under the direction of Distribution Committee Chairman W.H. Mann and E.W. Snavely of the Miller School. Once the books were sorted and packed, they went directly from Gable's to the camps that were most in need of them. It was only fitting that book lover William F. Gable's store helped get books in the hands of American servicemen.

Telling Time Without a Watch

In addition to guiding the store in selling war bonds and stamps and collecting books for servicemen, George Gable volunteered for the USO. He became chairman of the USO's state council in 1943 and did what he could to help the group support and entertain service members and their families during the war. He also was named chairman of Altoona's Citizen's Service Corps.

But maybe the most important work he did was keeping Gable's running during difficult times, keeping it as ship-shape as it had been before the war. People needed distractions and a place that still felt normal, a place that was as much a social hub and support network as a business...and George and his team provided it.

The familiar ebb and flow of Gable's schedule continued without interruption. Every January, there was a New Year's sale. Every March 1st, there was an anniversary sale. There were Easter sales, summer sales, back-to-school sales, Christmas sales...and then, it started all over again.

It felt like peacetime. It felt like life. It helped people get through the shortages, the sacrifices, the drills, the blackouts...the loss of loved ones. It helped people remember what would be waiting for them when the world stopped burning.

And there came a day when that very thing happened. Victory in Europe (VE) Day arrived in May 1945. Victory over Japan (VJ) Day came in September of that same year. People returned home from the war. Some of them went back to work at Gable's.

And the store ticked along like clockwork, as it always had. Customers came and spent their money, and employees restocked the shelves. Painters applied a fresh coat of paint to every square foot of the store, as they did every year. Diners ate in the restaurants in the Downstairs Store and Twelfth Avenue Arcade—more than 40,000 of them every month. Phone calls flooded the switchboard at a rate of 2,400 a day, all handled by a staff of three operators. The lights were switched on in the morning and off after closing time at night, burning 85,000 kilowatt hours per month.

And George Gable, like his father before him, looked around at all the activity, *felt* the pulse of the store around him, and nodded. He knew the numbers by heart. There was no need to check the watch in his pocket.

The store told him what time it was just fine.

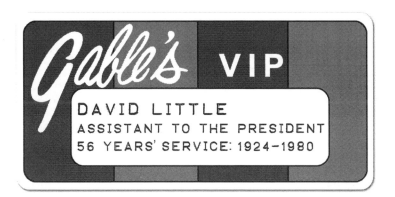

Courtesy Jim Shannon

"Mr. Service." That was what they called David A. Little, but it could just as easily have been "Mr. Personality" or "Mr. Entertainment." Or "Mr. Big," even. After all, he was a giant in many ways.

Or "Mr. Gable's," because that's what he was to so many people over so many years. As much as any president of the company—more, perhaps—he was the face of the store. The voice of it, too.

And what a *face* it was, with that ski slope nose and airplane hangar door grin and those enormous dark-rimmed glasses. And what a *voice* it was, booming over crowds of shoppers on the sales floor like the trumpeting of an elephant over herds of antelope on the veldt.

And what a *guy* he was. The word "charisma" comes to mind. The word "hilarious," too.

Do they even *make* them like David Little anymore?

Nothing Little About Him

They gave him his own day, did you know that? The next time Aug. 21st rolls around, pay tribute to "Mr. Gable's," why don't you? Greet your friends and neighbors with hearty handshakes, big laughs, and slaps on the back.

Make sure folks understand how happy you are to see them. Do what you can to help out in any way possible. Leave the world a little brighter than you found it.

In other words, do things Dave Little style.

Starting in 1924, he brought his unique *joie de vivre* to Gable's department store. He was a force to be reckoned with—in a *good* way—and brought his special *oomph* to every job he did, whether it was truck driver, credit manager, floor manager, service superintendent, or assistant to the president.

But he especially kicked it up a notch for those last three. Those are the jobs where he shone the brightest, the ones for which he's best-known.

They all sound a little vague, don't they? "Floor manager." "Service superintendent." "Assistant to the president." Like there's room for interpretation. Room for improvisation. Also room for the wrong kind of person to take advantage.

Or for a beloved guy with a larger-than-life personality to make thousands of people feel good about spending money at Gable's. Good enough to spend more than they'd planned.

Good enough to make them want to come back again and again.

Hazel Bilka, for example, remembers shopping at Gable's as a little girl with her grandmother. "Mr. Little would rush across the store when he saw my grandmother. He always greeted her as Mary McCartney (her maiden name). Then, he would turn to me and tell me my grandmother was the most beautiful girl in all of Altoona, and when they were in school together, she could dance like an angel. Needless to say, we both enjoyed shopping at Gable's and talking to Mr. Little."

George Sheedy remembers him well too. "He walked around and greeted people. He talked to all the ladies, and you'd hear him clear across the store. 'Oh, Mrs. So-and-So!' And everybody turned their heads. Everybody knew that voice.

"If somebody had a complaint or anything else, they'd run to Mr. Little, and he would put his arm around them and soften things up. He was a company man, but he made you feel as though he was on your side," said George.

Never Too Little, Too Late

"Host." "Greeter." "Problem Solver." These job titles all fit Dave to a "T." He was at his best when walking the main floor, welcoming folks to the store, asking about their families, smoothing over any rough spots that happened to arise.

No person was too insignificant, no problem too big or small, to get the Little treatment. The *Altoona Mirror* said it best: "If a customer has a problem, it becomes Dave's problem— and, in the true Gable

PERSONIFICATION OF GABLE'S — Officials of the William F. Gable Co. met at luncheon to discuss plans for David A. Little day to be observed at the store tomorrow. Being presented with a certificate of esteem (left to right) by Robert S. Powers, Gable's president, is Mr. Little, who is assistant to the president, with Miss Helen Haller, secretary-treasurer, and Mrs. Eleanore Geesey, personnel director, while standing are: Charles L. Vagnier, controller; Carl Haller, merchandise manager; Jack Mitchell, vice president, merchandising; Atty. Marion Patterson, vice president, legal, and Fred Deichert, advertising director.

Courtesy Altoona Mirror

tradition, he makes sure it is solved to the complete satisfaction of the customer."

Have you ever had that kind of person in your life? In the store where you shop? Then you know why President Bob Powers gave him his own day on Aug. 21, 1971.

"This day of recognition is long overdue," said Powers. "This is our invitation to Dave's thousands of friends to come in Saturday and greet him, just as he has been doing to everyone, and will continue to do in the exciting years ahead."

Dave's friends took him up on the invitation. They poured into the store to shake his hand, slap him on

ALTOONA MIRROR, ALTOONA, PA., FRIDAY, MARCH 3, 1978

GABLE'S QUARTER CENTURY CLUB held its 67th annual meeting Tuesday, Feb. 28, at the store's restaurant. In attendance were (from left): Seated—Mrs. Margaret Eichelberger, Myrtle Crawford and Mrs. Eleanor Geesey; standing—David A. Little Jr., store president Robert S. Powers, Merrill M. Doran, Eugene V. Hildebrand, Raymond G. Crouss and Alfred Jenner.

the back, wish him well…but Dave, being Dave, usually did all that first, and best.

As for "the exciting years ahead," they turned out to be exactly nine…nine years until Dave, and most everyone else at Gable's, got the boot. Nine years until the store closed its doors for good.

The Little Equation

After 56 years of service, Dave's roar was banished from the store…but what a 56 years they had been.

In all that time, had there ever been a day when he hadn't wanted to go to work? Had there ever been a moment when he'd been at a loss for words? Had there ever been a customer he hadn't liked or had gotten into it with?

Considering these questions from a statistical point of view, the odds tell us one story. They tell us to be realistic.

But considering these questions from the point of view of Dave Little, we know the true story to be quite different. We know for a fact what Dave would tell us.

And we know, if he were standing right here in front of us, selling his take with all the cranked-up-to-11 personality at his command, that the percentage of doubt in our minds would be exactly the same as the percentage of people who met Dave and didn't like him.

You do the math.

All Courtesy Altoona Mirror

108

Chapter Thirteen

Changing of the Guard

1946

J.G. Anspach saw the end of the war, and there was something to be said for that. He lived to see VE Day and VJ Day, to know the Allies had won, and all the sacrifices had not been for nothing. As General Manager and Secretary Treasurer, he got to welcome back returning servicemen and servicewomen to Gable's. He got to shake their hands and hug them, to see the tears glistening in their eyes…to dab the tears away from his own eyes too.

He got a glimpse of the future, as well—an inkling of the plans George Gable had in mind for the store. In the process, he saw a vision of things that William F. Gable would never have imagined, at least not exactly, though the great man would certainly have approved if he'd known. William F. would have signed off on that vision in a heartbeat, and so would the man he'd hired all the way back in 1899—J.G. Anspach.

Good old J.G. Anspach, who'd carried the torch for the old man since his death in 1921. Good old J.G. Anspach, who'd been a kind of Jedi Master to William's boy, an Obi-Wan Kenobi to George Gable's Luke Skywalker.

Good old J.G. Anspach, who on May 20, 1946, set out to drive to Altoona Hospital with his wife. They were going to see their daughter, Evelyn, who was a patient there at the time.

But along the way, something went wrong with J.G. He lost control of the car, and his wife had to steer it off the road. A nearby postal employee raced him to the hospital.

As they worked on him in the emergency room, did J.G. still think he might get to go to the office later that day, as he'd intended? Did he still hope he might get to see Gable's big plans for the future come to fruition? Did he think he might get to give George Gable a bit more sage advice handed down from the William F. era?

We'll never know, but we do know those things did not come to pass. We know the beloved General Manager was not revived that day.

As the medical staff stepped back from the table where he lay, did J.G. open his eyes to another world? A familiar world where horse-drawn carriages rolled through the muddy streets, and a tall, dignified man waved from the door of a quaint little department store on Eleventh Avenue, calling his name? Maybe whistling and waving for him to join him? Maybe telling him it was time to get back to work?

We'll never know that either.

J.G. RIP

J.G.'s death sent shock waves through Gable's and the local community. He'd been such a beloved and influential figure that his passing made an extraordinary impact.

A tribute appeared on the editorial page of the next morning's *Altoona Mirror*. "All who knew Mr. Anspach will testify to the fact that there was a great deal more to him than his knowledge of affairs and business competence, great as these were. He possessed that valuable quality which can best be summed up in the word character; this quality was evident not only in his own life but it left its mark, as it inevitably would, upon the great business house whose policies he had a hand in directing for so many years.

"A man of tremendous energy, he knew how to overcome obstacles, while at the same time he was always genial, friendly and companionable and without a doubt, he contributed in large measure to the extraordinary intimate relations that have always existed between the William F. Gable company store and its patrons and friends.

"All who knew Mr. Anspach will remember him with affection as a man of charm and dignity. The Gable company store will miss his leadership and guidance and the entire community will mourn the loss of one who always stood for progress and progressive policies. From first to last he was the good citizen, level-headed, well informed, generous of his time and energy."

Crowded to Overflowing

The store closed early on Thursday, May 23, as a tribute to J.G., and to enable Gable's staff to attend his funeral service in the Stevens Memorial Chapel on Eighth Avenue in Altoona. They did just that; according to the *Mirror*, "The chapel was crowded to overflowing with friends, Gable company executives and business acquaintances of Mr. Anspach's long career."

Pallbearers included George Gable, David Little, and John Sheep (J.G.'s longtime fishing buddy). Earnest Richardson, a retired bishop of the Philadelphia Methodist Conference and lifelong friend of J.G., conducted the service

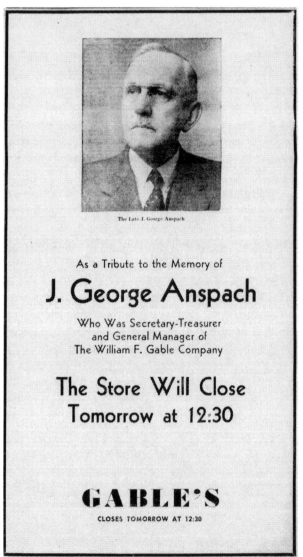

The Late J. George Anspach

As a Tribute to the Memory of

J. George Anspach

Who Was Secretary-Treasurer and General Manager of The William F. Gable Company

The Store Will Close
Tomorrow at 12:30

GABLE'S

CLOSES TOMORROW AT 12:30

Courtesy Altoona Mirror

alongside Rev. J. Resler Shultz of the First Methodist Church, which J.G. attended. "No one of unworthy or ignoble character could have achieved this," Richardson said of J.G.'s 57 years of service to Gable and Company.

They interred J.G.'s remains in the mausoleum at Fairview Cemetery, and everyone drifted away. Did some retire to local taverns to remember their departed friend and console each other? Did others go home alone to sit in shadows and contemplate the void he'd left in their lives? We don't know.

But what we do know is that Gable's reopened for business the next morning, and life moved on. And soon after that, the executives did what they had to, as difficult as it might have been.

They replaced him…though it took multiple people to fill his shoes.

Musical Chairs

With J.G. gone, George Gable assumed the title of general manager of the store—though certain responsibilities that had formerly come with that title were divided up among other staffers.

For example, David Little was promoted from first floor manager to service superintendent, taking charge of a newly created Customer Service and Customer Relations Division. The new division, and Little, would handle many tasks that had previously fallen under J.G.'s purview. As Little moved up, Emery Horton moved into his spot as first floor manager.

GEORGE P. GABLE

DAVID A. LITTLE

Meanwhile, several other personnel took up titles and duties that had belonged to J.G. E.C. Callaway was given the position of secretary and treasurer of the corporation. Bertha Hennessy, who had been George Gable's secretary, became assistant secretary of the corporation. W. Stanley Truby stepped into the job of general merchandise manager and assistant general manager.

Other job changes also were announced as part of the realignment. Fred Stoltenberg took full charge of building maintenance and servicing. Advertising Manager Samuel Patton added Director of Publicity to his list of titles.

And so, the store and company moved on, sustained by the depth of their talented, close-knit staff. One of Gable's stars was gone, no question, but William, Robert, and George had built the place to last. In years to come, the lineup would continue to change, and the team would be all the stronger because of it.

That would be especially important as Gable's raced toward its next big innovation, the one that would end up being its most lasting legacy. Personnel with mastery over a whole new range of disciplines would be needed to make it work.

The department store that had brought radio to Blair County was about to bring television there too.

W. STANLEY TRUBY

111

All Courtesy Altoona Mirror

Courtesy Altoona Mirror

TILLIE WOLF
SEAMSTRESS
44½ YEARS' SERVICE: 1935–1980

Courtesy Altoona Mirror

Tillie Wolf sewed and sewed. Her sewing machine never stopped running, filling her department with the sound she knew and loved so well.

Chickita chickita chickita chickita

Every day, for more than 44 years, Tillie sewed whatever was laid before her…repaired it, altered it, unstained it, monogrammed it. She took in and let out the legs of trousers, the sleeves of shirts, the hems of dresses and gowns and skirts. She fixed buttons and collars and pockets and flies, zippers and cuffs and inseams and waists and straps. There was nothing, repeat, *nothing*, that Tillie couldn't sew.

And for a very long time, even after she stopped, her handiwork was *everywhere* in Altoona and plenty of places beyond.

A Common Thread

When Tillie was young, she went to business school, preparing for work as a secretary, but it was sewing that got her the job at Gable's department store. She learned to work a needle and thread at home, to run a sewing machine like a concert pianist playing a Steinway…and lo and behold, there was a place for someone like that at the People's Store. George Gable liked the cut of her cloth, and he put her in the alterations department, and that was where she stayed.

Chickita chickita chickita chickita

"I felt like one of the family," she said, but she was wrong. She was part of *many* families through the years, too many to count.

She was close to the Gable's family, sure…worked on the kids' clothes through the years, did the alterations on all the Gable girls' wedding gowns. But then there were all those *other* families, too, all over Altoona—all over Blair County, and deep into Bedford and Centre and Cambria counties and beyond, too. Everywhere you looked, there were alterations by Tillie, done with the same care and precision as those done for the Gables themselves.

Chickita chickita chickita chickita

How many times did she see her handiwork on someone walking toward her at the store, or on the street, or in church? How many times did someone stop and thank her for fixing a dress *just so*, for bringing new life to a blouse or hat or slacks that they'd thought were ruined for good?

How many people can say they sewed up an entire town? That their work ran through it as a common thread, like a single long thread stitching everyone together, with one person at the root?

She could. Tillie could.

In Stitches

People loved Tillie, and they do to this day. Her name is one of those that still come up when you ask around about Gable's back in the day. She is still *synonymous* with it.

They loved her for the quality of her work, and the kind of person she was. A sweetheart, through and through.

And Tillie loved them back.

Chickita chickita chickita chickita

"It wasn't just hello and goodbye," she said of Gable's, and the way the customers and employees interacted. "There was a feeling in this store, a feeling like it was home."

Tillie never wanted to leave. She often worked through vacations, and never retired. Gable's bosses didn't argue with her about that.

"Tillie, you can't retire. We need you." That was what the store's last president, Robert Powers, told her once. "Yes, we can replace you, but we cannot replace what you do."

That was what the last president of Gable's said to the woman who turned out to be its last seamstress. For she had sewn herself into the fabric of the place so well that she remained a part of it right up to the end.

Chickita chickita chickita chickita

And beyond that, *far* beyond that. Never mind that it's been over 35 years since Gable's closed; there are still people around who have towels she monogrammed, or still have dresses or blouses or trousers or bathrobes or jackets she repaired. Who still have wedding photos in which her handiwork is on display, or photos of themselves with Santa in the outfit she sewed together for him from scratch.

Or still have memories of her stitched into their own memories, their own hearts, their own lives. Memories of her work, her smile, her laugh, her way of altering the drabbest of days in the most magnificent of ways.

And the way she worked that sewing machine like a concert pianist playing a Steinway.

Chickita chickita chickita chickita
Chickita chickita chickita chickita

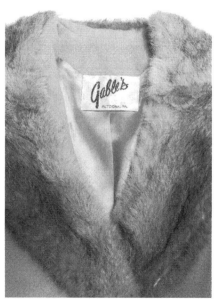

Courtesy Blair County Historical Society

Courtesy Matthew Germann

Memory Department

I have so many wonderful memories of "my" Gables from 65 years ago. For example, I remember that when we entered the store from the uphill side, we walked into the Arcade. On the right was a lunch room. My mother and I always had lunch there or walked west two blocks where the YMCA had a cafeteria.

I also remember modeling at the store. Gwen Holton and I were picked to be models in the fashion show in the second floor dress department.

I remember there was a wonderful area where sewing machines were displayed in a long row. Mother bought a White model in 1939.

My uncle, John Davis, who was in the Navy in 1942, came home and opened a fish department in the basement alongside the butcher shop.

Going to Gables was always such a treat.

Joan Hunter Miller

My great uncle, Colin Blake, managed the shoe department at Gable's for many years, after decades of having his own shoe store in downtown Altoona. He was such a proper and gentlemanly man who knew so much about good fit and shoe quality. The luggage department was just across from the shoes. My cousin and I often practiced our ballet in those aisles because they were stacked so high that we would rarely be seen.

My other great uncle, Charles Blake, was the bus driver on the line to Gable's. He always sent us off with the happiest wishes as we arrived at Gable's front door with the lovely display windows around it.

Debbie Conley Foreman

My Mom and I would take the Second Avenue bus across town. We always went to Gable's and got Spanish peanuts to eat on the way home. After all these years, I still have two Gable's plates.

Alice Jane O'Donald

We went there every Saturday and always ate in the restaurant. I sure do miss it.

Wanda Albright Cummins

In 1954, when I was 7 years old, one of my Christmas gifts was the first two editions of "Tom Swift," on sale at Gable's as a set for $1. From then until high school, I would walk about two miles to the store after school every month or so and check for new editions. I loved their book department!

Wayne Campbell

The biggest factor behind Gable's success was its general manager, David Little. Everyone knew and liked David. He might as well have been known as "Mr. Gable."

Al Confer

I remember my mom taking me to Gable's on my sixth birthday. I had 16 dollars, and all I wanted was a Rifleman gun, which they had. Then, I went to the basement and watched them shine shoes.

David Tarry

I remember at Christmastime in the 1950s, there was a mechanical Santa in the window, and he read all the letters sent to him from us kids. There was a mailbox outside in front of this window where letters to Santa could be deposited.

I remember the electric train display on the second floor. While walking up the wooden staircase, I could hear the faint sounds of the trains progressively get louder as I got closer to the second floor, and suddenly, there they were! WOW! What a sight to see, all those really neat trains! In those days, electric trains were the most popular and most technically advanced toy on the market. Those were the days!

I also remember how sad it was to climb those same stairs and hear no sounds of trains running, because Christmas had passed, and the train display was taken down till next year!

Ron Keller

Courtesy Altoona Mirror

Chapter Fourteen

The Department Store Will Be Televised

1947-1956

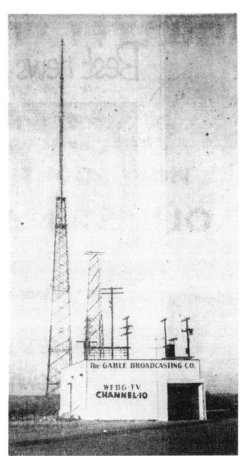

Courtesy Altoona Mirror

Lightning blazed down out of the sky at 8:15 on Saturday morning, Feb. 28, 1953. The blindingly bright bolt crashed into the new 163-foot antenna on top of Wopsononock Mountain, sizzling through metal struts and wiring.

Just like that, Altoona's new TV station was fried. Would WFBG-TV, launched by the Gable Broadcasting Company, make its on-air debut, which was scheduled to happen the next day?

No one could say for sure.

It Was Almost Channel 9

Maybe George Gable had jinxed it. After all, in an interview in the *Altoona Mirror,* he had said, "It was a long, and sometimes discouraging, project to get started. But it looks like everything is going to work out fine now."

It was true that the station had taken a long time to get off the ground.

George had been dreaming of it since the first experimental telecasts in 1943; he'd been convinced that becoming a TV pioneer was the right move for Gable's since 1947.

That was why, in August 1948, George had applied to the Federal Communications Commission, the FCC, to have Channel 9 allocated to the new station, WFBG-TV. So why did it take until February 1953 for WFBG-TV to get around to scheduling its first broadcast?

Do the words "red tape" ring a bell? Two months after George's original application, the FCC announced a 90-day freeze that ended up lasting two years. It was starting to feel like WFBG-TV would *never* get a license for Channel 9.

So why not try for another channel? George finally decided he had nothing to lose by giving it a shot. In early 1950, he enlisted the aid of the Blair County Association of Radio Service Engineers to mount a new application. The Association circulated petitions and worked with the Gable Broadcasting Company to prepare a new application. Petitions in hand, George and his newfound supporters went to the FCC with a new request: to grant WFBG-TV a license to broadcast on Channel 10 in the very high frequency (VHF) band instead of Channel 9.

The new application worked...eventually. It took *more than two more years*, but the approvals finally came through for George and his team. The Gable Broadcasting Company was granted a construction permit on Dec. 31, 1952 to build a television station to operate on 316,000 watts.

On January 2 of the following year, the FCC gave final approval to the Gable application. By then, George had laid the groundwork for the project, ordering equipment for the station from the General Electric Company of Syracuse, N.Y. Some, he kept in storage in warehouses in Altoona, while other items—like the giant antenna—were too big to store and would have to be delivered later.

Not that later was that far off anymore. Channel 10 would soon be a reality, broadcasting to Altoona and the surrounding area...and yes, it would someday become *that* Channel 10, the same one we still watch today, though the call letters would eventually change from WFBG to something very different.

A Station Grows on Wopsy

With the construction permit in place, a small army of technicians, mechanics, and builders hired by Gable's went to work at the TV station's site atop Wopsononock Mountain—known locally as "Wopsy." It was the perfect location, situated 2,580 feet above sea level. The antenna would reach 2,727 feet above sea level, making the transmitter one of the highest in the industry at the time.

It also helped that the site was already owned by Gable's. A broadcasting facility was already in place, used for FM transmission by WFBG radio. Once the FM gear was pulled out, the building would be the perfect structure to house the new TV studio, control room, transmitter, and other necessary components of the operation.

Having an existing facility to build on would help reduce construction time...and that was good, since the timetable for completion would be tight. Naturally, George chose the upcoming anniversary week to debut the new station, the time of year when Gable's was most celebrated. So from January to the first week of March was all the time the work crews had to get the whole project up and running.

After so many years of waiting for the license to go through, they would have to hurry up and finish the extensive technical arrangements in a limited amount of time.

Built to Broadcast

When the workmen removed the WFBG-FM gear, it was donated to the engineering department of what was then the Pennsylvania State College. With space opened up in the building, the next order of business was to bring in the TV equipment that would replace it.

Gable's workers retrieved the gear that had been stored in Altoona warehouses during the application process. Meanwhile, George requested additional equipment, including the giant antenna, from General Electric.

As equipment was ordered and taken out of storage, carpenters Dave and Roy Fluke worked overtime to frame and finish new rooms in the WFBG

building. Space was blocked off for the studio, projection room, darkroom, announcer's booth, preview room, and control room.

As the interior layout took shape, the technicians worked on installing power supplies and wiring the place for the demands of television. Workmen from W. Floyd

Bush of Martinsburg put up three big power transformers on top of Wopsy, ensuring a steady flow of electricity to the new station. The transformers were mounted on poles outside the building, and the leads were inserted through metal shielding into the transmitter inside the rear of the place. Electricians rigged sets of 200 amp switches inside the building to control the power input from the transformers to the transmitter.

When construction and installation were complete, programming would be funneled through the master control panel in the control room, then sent to the transmitter. From there, the video/audio signal would be beamed out into the surrounding region via the towering new antenna.

Though shipping and erecting that particular piece of equipment was a spectacle in itself.

All Courtesy Altoona Mirror

Raise It!

WFBG's 86-foot, $47,000 antenna was so big and bulky, a special truck had to deliver it from General Electric in Syracuse. The trip took ten hours along a specially-planned route, since the big truck couldn't navigate certain sections of Route 220. A special permit from the Pennsylvania Department of Highways was necessary, since the antenna was longer than the state motor code allowed.

On the afternoon of Tuesday, Feb. 17, 1953, workmen unloaded the antenna and put it in place. Using steel winch cables attached to a wooden spire, they hoisted the antenna high above an 89-foot steel base, or cradle, that they had constructed to hold it…then lowered it into the base.

"There's nothing to it," said George Hayes, the Penelec communications engineer who was supervising the installation. "That is, if you have good weather and everything goes right."

Fortunately, it was a clear, still day, and the process went smoothly. Workers welded the antenna to the base, creating an assembly with a combined height of 163 feet.

The new 12-bay antenna had 48 transmitting elements—24 for video and 24 for audio transmissions. It contained an automatic de-icing system that kicked in at 27 degrees and shut down at 35. Once the wiring from the transmitter was connected, WFBG had the high tech firepower it needed to beam its signal throughout the region. All over Blair County and beyond, household television receivers would pick up that signal and convert it into images and sound for the enjoyment of the viewing audience.

TV Guide 101

What exactly would all those folks be watching? In some cases, network programming, beamed in from distant locations. Network signals would be received by a microwave facility atop Laurel Mountain near Johnstown, then transmitted from there to WFBG atop Wopsy. The Laurel Mountain transmitter, owned by the American Telephone and Telegraph Company, would make it possible for all manner of nationally produced news, sports, and entertainment programs to reach people in WFBG's viewing area. This programming would be drawn from all networks, though WFBG-TV was affiliated primarily with NBC. The first shows scheduled for broadcast on the station included *Cisco Kid, Boston Blackie, Unexpected, I Married Joan,* and *Roy Rogers*.

Other programming would originate in-house from the Wopsy facility.

This microwave transmitter located on Laurel mountain near Johnstown will transmit all network television signals to a similar installation at the WFBG-TV station atop Wopsononock mountain. The microwave transmitter at Laurel mountain is owned and operated by the American Telegraph and Telephone company which takes care of transmitting all network television programs.

Live shows would be staged in the studio there, shot with state-of-the-art cameras from General Precision Laboratory. The plan was to move the studio off Wopsy eventually, to the fourth floor of Gable's department store. Films and slides could be displayed in the projection room, then converted into electronic signals for broadcast.

News film shot in the field could be developed in the darkroom, then played in the projection room and put on the air during newscasts. A newsreader could describe it on a set in the studio.

Commercials could be performed live in the studio or projected from film. They also might consist of text and images on slides, described by someone in the announcer's booth.

Whatever the programming, it would be seen in the preview room, next door to the projection room. Video and audio would be checked by an operator on special monitors in that soundproof room; since the walls would be glass all around, the video also could be previewed by personnel in the projection and control rooms.

And so, a mix of live and filmed programming would fill the schedule of WFBG-TV, providing plenty of content for viewers to watch. Starting it all off would be a special show about Gable's department store, with an appearance by George himself.

If, that is, the station could recover from that blazing bolt of lightning that fried it the day before its scheduled debut.

A True "Gable's Charge"

The lightning bolt had been a strong one. According to a woman in Wehnwood, its electrical charge had been so strong that it had caused her doorbell to ring spontaneously.

The effects of the bolt crippled WFBG for hours, as the Gable Broadcasting Company team leaped into action. After waiting so long to be ready to go on the air, George and his crew were determined to make the next-day deadline for the station's first broadcast.

At first, it looked like they might not make it. Then, it looked like they might. The technicians and workmen finished repairing the lightning damage by mid-afternoon. All equipment was back up and running.

But the cheering was short-lived. Test transmissions were plagued with "ghost images" that blurred the video signal. Again, the crew dug in, working to find the cause of the blur and repair it in time for the big show.

121

Eventually, they figured it out. A radio frequency was bleeding into a projector cable from the outer wall of the projection room, which wasn't insulated. Chief Engineer George Burgoon and master control operator Kenneth Brubaker concluded that insulating the interior of the projection room wall might solve the problem.

And they were right. Insulating that wall blocked the outside interference and made the WBFG signal crystal clear. Finally, the station was ready for its official debut. The Gable Company's biggest and most cutting-edge venture of the 1950s was about to premiere, and the world of local broadcasting would never be the same.

Let the Gablevision Begin

How many viewers watched the first program shown on WFBG-TV on March 1, 1953? It's hard to say; we don't have the ratings for that particular telecast. But what we do know is this: It was the beginning of a TV tradition that continues to this day. George Gable brought Channel 10 to life that day, and it still beams news, sports, and entertainment throughout Blair County and beyond all these years later.

During that first live broadcast, George himself spoke to viewers about the station's historic launch and the department store's 69th anniversary celebration. Managing Director Jack Snyder spoke too, and announcers Ted Reinhart and Charlie Nelson introduced various features and performances.

WILL HANDLE KEY JOBS AT GABLE TV STATION

Now! Congratulations To TV Station WFBG From Penn Furniture

Better See... **Motorola TV**

**WELCOME
WFBG-TV**
and
**CONGRATULATIONS
GEORGE P. GABLE**

HOTELS
William Penn and Colonial

Seventeen prizes were given away in a 69th anniversary drawing—$1500 worth of prizes, including Magnavox and Philco TV sets.

That first show ran from 8 to 10:30 p.m. and was followed by a movie. After that, at midnight, WFBG-TV concluded its broadcasting day. The station went dark for the night, but it would be back on the air the next day. And the day after that. And many more days after that.

Its first day on the air had indeed been a momentous occasion, though not for the exact reasons that George was aware of back then. How could he have known that WFBG-TV would be the longest-lasting part of the Gable empire, outlasting even the department store? How could he have known that decades after the store ended, people would still be watching Channel 10?

Even though it would not belong to the Gable Broadcasting Company for very long at all.

SHOP BY TV
with
THE GIRL FROM GABLE'S
EVERY TUESDAY
and FRIDAY
At 4:00 P. M.
on
WFBG-TV
Channel 10

Triangle's Buyout

WFBG-TV got off to a strong start and quickly became part of local viewers' daily habits. Each week's programming included network shows as well as local shows like *The Girl from Gable's*, an early ancestor of infomercials that featured a female host displaying and talking about products on sale at Gable's.

The operation on Wopsy ran smoothly, with plans in place to move the studio downtown. George Gable, in fact, had reserved space on his department store's fourth floor, adjacent to the TV station's business offices, to house the studio.

So why did he sell it? Why, on Jan. 10, 1956, did the FCC approve the transfer of ownership of WFBG-TV—and WFBG-AM radio in the bargain—to Triangle Publications Inc. of Philadelphia? Why, on Feb. 20, 1956, did George sign the final settlement papers, consummating the deal?

The **GABLE BROADCASTING CO.**

**Proposed
WFBG-TV**

All Courtesy Altoona Mirror

Courtesy Altoona Mirror

He had dreamed of owning a TV station for years. He had patiently struggled to make his dream a reality, persevering in the face of extreme delays by the FCC, assembling a team with the specialized knowledge it took to build, equip, and operate a station in the early days of the TV era. A department store tycoon, he had put his mind to the problem of breaking into TV broadcasting...and he had succeeded.

Why, then, was WFBG-TV sold to Triangle Publications just three years later? Especially because, according to George himself in the *Altoona Mirror*, "Prior to the negotiations which resulted in today's sale, I had always contended that WFBG and WFBG-TV were not for sale at this time."

The official explanation from George, in the *Mirror*, went like this: "When I learned that Walter Annenberg as president of Triangle and Roger Clipp as head of its radio and television division had expressed some interest in these properties, quite frankly I felt that were we to sell to any one, as some day inevitably we would, it would not be possible to place our community trust in better hands."

That's what George said...though it seems a little vague, doesn't it? Somehow, it seems like there must have been more to it, doesn't there? Had he gotten in over his head with the TV project? Was the station losing money? Was the department store side of the company in need of a cash infusion?

If there *was* more to it, we might never know. Maybe all that really matters is that George Gable let go of his passion project after a brief three years and handed it over to the next in a series of owners who would carry it forward into the future.

All the Angles

When WFBG-TV and WFBG-AM were acquired by Triangle Publications Inc., they joined a media empire on the rise. Triangle already owned WFIL-AM-FM-TV in Philadelphia, WNBF-AM-TV in Binghamton, N.Y., and a 50-percent stake in WHBG in Harrisburg, PA. On the publishing side, the company owned TV Guide, Seventeen magazine, the Philadelphia Inquirer, and other national publications. Now, Triangle had a foothold in Altoona as well.

Though, to hear company owner Walter Annenberg tell it, Triangle's takeover would only have a positive impact on the stations and the region. "We intend to operate the Altoona stations in accordance with our basic belief that to merit public confidence, we must render outstanding service to the community. It is our intention to do everything we can to serve constructively every worthwhile community interest."

Triangle's radio-television division general manager, Roger Clipp, expressed similar sentiments. "We are most conscious of broadcasting's responsibilities to the communities served. The additions we have planned for the stations' service and others which we may develop will be based on sound experience and in the belief that our responsibility is constantly to strive to improve upon the best that the industry can provide."

According to Clipp, there would be "no sweeping changes in policy or personnel" at WFBG-TV or WFBG-AM. Jack Snyder would continue to serve as managing director, and George Burgoon would stay on as chief engineer.

There would be changes in programming, though, some arising from a partnership with Penn State University. "By terms of a proposed arrangement between Pennsylvania State University and the Triangle ownership, the Altoona stations will originate on a regularly scheduled basis educational programs direct from the campus of the university," said Clipp. "We view this as a far reaching step in the development of educational television, and we are gratified by the enthusiastic cooperation of Dr. Milton Eisenhower and his staff at Pennsylvania State University."

New programs arising from this agreement included *Home and Farm* and *University Chapel Service.* Another new show, *University of the Air,* was an adult education series featuring faculty members from more than 25 colleges and universities. In addition, Triangle planned expanded local news service with a strong focus on coverage of community events.

Station to Station

And so, the die was cast for the new era of WFBG-TV—one without the ownership or involvement of the Gable Broadcasting Company. It was a change that didn't seem to bother George Gable, who said, "I am deeply grateful that Triangle saw fit to conclude these negotiations for I now know that our fondest hopes for continuing outstanding broadcast leadership in this community will be fully realized."

But you have to wonder, don't you, what he thought when he watched Channel 10 in years to come. Was he proud to have had a hand in bringing that TV station to life? Did he regret selling it? Did he have any idea that it would outlive him, his store, and his company? That it would, in effect, become his greatest achievement...though he no longer owned a stake in it?

Because that is exactly what happened, as WFBG-TV became WTAJ-TV (Television for Altoona and Johnstown) in 1972...became the home of local personalities like Big John Riley and Tom Casey...aired decades of local and national news, sports, weather, and entertainment... converted from analog to digital...and continued its march into the high tech future with no end in sight.

Just as William F. Gable was responsible for the planting of trees throughout Altoona, his son, George, planted a seed in the media marketplace—one that grew and changed the landscape in decades to come, long after George was gone.

As long as somebody somewhere is watching Channel 10, whatever its form—virtual reality, perhaps, or some kind of braincast or dreamwave we can only imagine—George's legacy will live on, and the spirit of Gable's will never die.

Photos by Philip Balko

Gable's VIP

NADINE SHADE
"FLYING SQUAD" MEMBER
33 YEARS' SERVICE: 1947–1980

There was a woman at Gable's who could do everything...except for one little thing. But she didn't find out about that until 33 years down the line.

The Flying Nadine

You name it, Nadine Shade could do it—except that one little thing. Otherwise, they wouldn't have put her on the Flying Squad when they hired her out of high school in 1947.

Photo by Philip Balko

Members of the Flying Squad were real Jacks or Janes of all trades, expected to fill in anywhere in the store at the drop of a hat. They were real go-anywhere, do-anything types, fast learners who were dependable and didn't mind a challenge.

Nadine fit right in. She went where the Squad sent her with maximum positive attitude, and mastered each new set of duties with minimal training. She went from the jewelry department to the handbag department to the silverware department to the grocery department. She sold women's clothes, men's clothes, children's clothes, and all manner of shoes. She worked upstairs, downstairs, all around the house, and coworkers in both buildings of the store got to know her.

They respected her too, and that meant a lot. They knew, when they saw her coming, that she wouldn't let them down. This was a girl who could do everything. *Almost* everything.

And she went where they sent her, even if it meant leaving the Flying Squad. Even if it meant spending all her time on the job running an elevator.

The Rises and Falls of Nadine

As an elevator operator, Nadine didn't stay in one place any more than she had on the Flying Squad. She rode the car up, then down, then up, then down, remaining in constant motion.

Always, there were the passengers, riding along from one floor to the next—first to second, third to fourth, fourth to basement. "It was always busy," recalls Nadine. "People were always standing in line to get the elevators, especially during sales...and Gable's had *lots* of sales."

Nadine got to know many of those people, learned their names and the names of their spouses and kids and what jobs they had and what made them tick. She got to know the store bosses too, from taking them up to the offices or down to the sales floors. Then there were the radio stars, whom she ferried to and from the studios of WFBG. Always, there was someone interesting in her car, and something new to be learned or considered.

And sometimes, the very act of operating the elevator was a thrill. "We had three elevators, but only one of them was automatic, where you pushed a button, and the car took you to the floor you wanted," says Nadine. "The other two, you had to run manually.

"One, we called the hotbox. It didn't have a gate, but it had doors that you had to pull open. To go to another floor, you had to turn a handle. You called out whether the car was going up or down, and you turned the handle again when you reached the floor you wanted. Then, you called out the floor number and made sure everyone watched their step getting in or out of the car.

"The third elevator was similar to that one, but it had a gate instead of a door. You had to run it manually and call out the floors. It was located in the arcade."

But one day, the ups and downs ended for Nadine. She found out she was pregnant, and the head nurse at the store—who also was a personal shopper, by the way—persuaded her to take some time off to have the baby.

It turned out Nadine was good at that, too...good at being a mom. There was really only one thing she wasn't good at, though she was years away from finding out about that.

Nadine's Finger

Two months after giving birth to her son, Nadine asked to return to work at Gable's. This time, instead of the Flying Squad or elevators, she was assigned to the store's receiving room.

The receiving room was located on the alley between the Eleventh and Twelfth Avenue buildings, where trucks delivered merchandise for sale in the store. Packages were unloaded from the trucks and placed on a conveyor belt that carried them into the receiving room. There, team members put the boxed merchandise on long tables, where Nadine and her coworkers attached price tags to each item.

"I had about eleven different departments to take care of, including jewelry and handbags," remembers Nadine. "My job was to count everything for those departments and check to make sure it was all there. I also had to determine if there were any damages. Then came the price tagging."

In the beginning, Nadine used price tickets with pins on them, which she attached manually. Eventually, though, the company brought in Monarch marking machines, which automated parts of the work.

"We loaded the machines with rolls of pins and rolls of tickets," explains Nadine. "Then, there was a dial that we could use to change the department number and price. We just ran the machine and put tags on the items, then folded them and sent them on to the departments.

"We had a technique for each type of item. With men's shirts, for example, we always put the tag on the back. With women's blouses, we put the tag on the neck."

Not that using the machine was free of danger. Once, Nadine brought it down hard on top of her hand, sending waves of pain shooting through her.

"I remember my coworkers thought one of those pins had gone through my finger," says Nadine. "They called in the electrician, who helped get the machine unjammed. Thank God, I hadn't gotten a pin through my finger or had it severed or anything like that.

"After I got my finger out, one of the shipping clerks rushed me over to the doctor. At that point, I had tears on my face, because I'd been crying. But things worked out okay. I had a mark from the machine, but it hadn't done too much damage."

The One Thing She Couldn't Do

The occasional mishap aside, Nadine never got tired of working at Gable's. She never met a job she didn't like or couldn't handle in the store either. As competent as she was, there wasn't a thing she couldn't do with a little training and practice.

Except one. Even after 33 years working under the great George Gable and Robert Powers, becoming a seasoned hand at everything from ringing up groceries to running elevators to price-tagging merchandise, getting to know just about everyone in the store, Nadine still couldn't *save it.*

When the end came for Gable's in 1980, there wasn't a thing she could do to help keep it afloat. She wasn't an executive; she didn't have the expertise or power to stop the collapse.

But she *did* have the ability to keep it alive in a different way—in her *memories.* And over thirty years later, those memories are still going strong. The world of Gable's is still going strong.

Memories and Souvenirs

Nadine remembers Christmastime at Gable's, when the store was always busy and decorated and filled with music. "The day before Christmas, we always had a singalong. All the employees would go to the first floor on Eleventh Avenue, and Dave Little's sister would conduct us in singing Christmas carols."

Nadine remembers the display windows too, and how beautiful they were. Jim Pennypacker, the head of display advertising, often gave her artificial greenery from the displays when it got damaged. "In one of the windows, they had a parrot cage, and Jim gave that to me too when they were done with it. I still have it hanging out here in my yard after all these years."

But Nadine has more than a parrot cage left over from her days at Gable's. She has a drawer full of costume jewelry, plus lots of clothes and shoes that she purchased with her 30 percent employee discount. "I have a black leather coat trimmed with fake fur too, and a storm coat with a furry lining, both from Gable's."

She also has two greeting card display racks from the store, given to her by building superintendent Red Hildebrand when they were replaced with new models. "I had a carpenter add some shelves to the tops of the units. I still have them in the corner of my living room."

In addition, Nadine has program booklets from the annual dinner meetings of the Quarter Century Club, and a pin that President Robert Powers gave her when she joined the group. "I was invited to join the club in January 1975. I went up to Mr. Powers' office, and he gave me that pin, with a little diamond on the inside. He gave me a hundred dollars too. He was such a nice man."

Nobody's Perfect

Looking back from her home in Riggles Gap, Nadine thinks of the store often. "I really miss that store," she says. "It was just a good place. You never had any trouble.

"I always said we were like a family. I always looked forward to going to work. I've never found another place that good."

So there's one other thing Nadine couldn't do, when you come down to it. She couldn't help stop the store from closing...and she could never find another place quite like it. She could never find another Gable's.

And maybe she shouldn't feel bad about that, because she isn't alone there. Neither could anyone else.

Photo by Philip Balko

Courtesy David Seidel

1950 Staff Courtesy Helen Hildebrand

Chapter Fifteen

Put Up A Parking Lot

1956-1966

George Gable knew an opportunity when it came calling.

It was 1956, and Bell Telephone was expanding its local operations. Bell had a bit of a problem though; the company needed to rent more space in downtown Altoona.

Fortunately, George had the solution to that problem—8,800 square feet of space ready to lease. It would be more than enough room to house Bell's new business office when it moved out of the existing Bell building.

That just left one more problem. Bell was going to hire 150 new employees to staff its expanded facilities. Where would they all park when they went to work?

George had the solution to that problem too.

Laying the Groundwork

Bell Telephone's expansion would be a big one, part of a $2,524,000 program to establish Altoona as a main toll switching center for west central Pennsylvania. The program, announced to the public on Feb. 16, 1956, would use cutting edge centralized automatic message accounting (CAMA) equipment to charge for long distance calls. It was a stepping stone in the effort to develop long-distance calling services with reliable billing capabilities for providers and true ease of use for callers.

But the CAMA equipment would take up a ton of space in the Bell building at 1119 Sixteenth Street in downtown Altoona. Even with moving the test center, district traffic headquarters, and employment office to rented space next door at 1109 Sixteenth St. and overflowing beyond that into 7,500 square feet in the Acme building on Seventeenth Street, there wouldn't be enough open square footage for all that CAMA gear.

And that was where George Gable came in.

He had 8,800 square feet available in a building adjacent to the Gable Arcade building on Twelfth Ave. He would be glad to put it to use, especially for such a big project that would have such a positive impact on the downtown central business district.

So Bell's space problem was solved. George's building at 1309-11 Twelfth Avenue was big enough to house the business office. With the business office gone, the Bell building would be big enough to

contain the CAMA equipment. As for the new employees who would operate it, George had an idea about where they could park. It would involve the biggest building project that Gable's had undertaken since 1928.

George was going to build a parking garage.

This picture reveals the streamlined attractiveness of the new Bell Telephone company business office at 1331 Twelfth avenue. The office opened to the public at 9 o'clock this morning following a formal dedication ceremony.

Here Mayor Robert W. Anthony snips a satin ribbon to symbolize the opening of the new business office of Bell Telephone. Robert L. Hite, (left), president of the Altoona Chamber of Commerce, holds one end of the ribbon while Bell Office Manager Richard C. Becker hold the other. Vice Mayor Charlie Adams stands behind Mayor Anthony. Girls at rear are telephone company employees.

What Went Down

The garage would go up in stages, starting with the ground floor. According to George, further levels would be added based on the demand from parking patrons. Those patrons would include Gable's shoppers as well as Bell employees and other downtown shoppers and workers.

"This parking garage will give Altoona additional facilities right in the heart of the downtown business section," said George. "Shoppers will be able to visit all the major stores."

With so many people in need of downtown parking, could there be any doubt that the garage would grow beyond the first stage? George certainly sounded optimistic about the facility's potential: "The Gable management shows its faith in Altoona's future by its present planned expansion and joins with the Bell Telephone company in the confidence that Altoona's central city business area gives every promise of continued growth and progress."

Before anything could go up, however, there were things that had to come down. In the weeks that followed the garage announcement, workmen demolished a row of buildings along Twelfth Avenue. Businesses had to vacate the whole strip from 1301 to 1311 Twelfth Ave., including Thrifty Cleaners, the Wilbert Kuhn Antique Shop, the American Cancer Society, Beck's Beauty Supply, and Toole's Art Shop.

With those properties flattened, construction was finally ready to begin.

Ribbon-Cutting Before Breakfast

General contractors J.C. Orr and Son took the reins, directing the small army of subcontractors who would erect the Twelfth Avenue garage.

As months passed, the steel framework of the huge structure took shape—and it was bigger than expected. Though George had originally said that the initial stage would only include the ground floor, the first version of the garage would consist of *three* levels.

Meanwhile, Bell's new business office up the street also was coming together. J.C. Orr worked on that job too, remodeling the leased space to the tune of $187,000.

At 9 a.m. on Monday, October 15, 1956, Altoona Mayor Robert W. Anthony cut the ribbon and officially opened the place for business. City patrolman Christ Hauser, an officer on beat 3, then marched in and became the first customer to pay a phone bill in the new office. The VIPs then adjourned to the Pennsylvania Room of the Penn-Alto Hotel for breakfast.

On the way, they all got a good look at the garage underway on the corner. They couldn't miss it. The latest manifestation of Gable's progressive attitude and determination was rising amid clouds of dust and the rumble of machinery. It was only a matter of time until it opened to the public.

Triple-Decker Parking

Pouring concrete to cover the decks of the new parking garage wasn't easy. The employees of the New Enterprise Stone and Lime Company had a heck of a time transporting the stuff from the street and pouring it in the right place, especially as they got further from the outer edges. They ended up filling buckets on handcarts and wheeling them to the alley side of the building, where the buckets were picked up by a crane. The crane swung each bucket out over the deck, then lowered it to the point where workers could dump its contents.

It was difficult, time-consuming work, and it wasn't done until Wednesday, Nov. 21, 1956. At that point, all three decks were fully surfaced and drying in the sun.

They would stay that way for over a month, as the concrete took that long to "cure." Even then, they wouldn't all open at once.

The two lower decks opened on Saturday, Feb. 2, 1957. Drivers now had access to 50 parking spaces on the middle deck and 22 spaces on the bottom deck—a total of 72 spaces. They could enter the middle deck from Thirteenth Street and the bottom deck from the alley off Eleventh Avenue.

133

Stairs provided access from the bottom to the middle level. From there, patrons could walk through a covered passage into the home furnishings department of the store.

It didn't take long for that passage and its protection from the elements to become popular. According to George Gable, "This feature of the parking facility has already proved attractive to all parking patrons, but especially to women shoppers."

When the 100 x 120 square foot top deck was finally opened, 60 more spaces were added, bringing the grand total to 132. The top deck also featured stairway access to the middle level and the covered passage into the store.

Once again, George's vision had brought something grand into being. Sprawling from the Twelfth Avenue store building to Thirteenth Street, the Arcade Parking Center looked imposing, another monument to the continued dominance of "the Gable block" by the department store company.

And it wasn't even done yet. It wouldn't be finished for years to come.

Dealing Another Deck

You can never have too much parking. That much became clear after the opening of the top deck of the Arcade Parking Center. Even with 132 spaces available, the public wanted more. The new garage was always full, leaving drivers to trawl the local lots and streets for somewhere to park, wasting time that could have been better spent shopping at Gable's.

The writing was on the wall. It didn't take long for George Gable to initiate an Arcade Parking Center expansion.

Construction was in high gear by mid-1959.

The project, again managed by J.C. Orr & Son, added a new top deck to the facility, increasing the total parking area by 24,000 square feet. The resulting 84 new parking spaces were accessible from Twelfth Avenue via a two-way ramp. A

Courtesy Altoona Mirror

protected pedestrian walkway also led to and from the new deck, and a new entrance connected directly to the second floor of the Gable Arcade building on Twelfth Avenue.

Opened on Sept. 1, 1959, in plenty of time for the holiday shopping season, the Parking Center expansion was a grand slam hit. People loved the convenience of being able to walk right into the store while being under roof for much of the time. Downtown workers like the Bell Telephone people loved the ease of parking near their workplace and the store with its shopping and restaurants.

The expanded parking center became a real showpiece for William F. Gable and Co. "One of the things of which we're proudest is the enlargement of the parking garage on Twelfth Avenue at Thirteenth Street," said George Gable on the company's 76th anniversary in March 1960. "By completing the second floor deck over a half of a city block, we have parking space for our customers and covered approaches to the store at every level."

After the expansion, Gable's offered hourly parking space for 204 cars. There were also 22 spaces that could be leased on a monthly basis, bringing the grand total to 226.

But was it *enough*? Could the vehicles of the store's growing clientele be contained in those 226 spaces? If so, for how long?

The answer turned out to be seven more years.

Pave It Again, Sam

Yet again, as time passed, it became clear to the bigwigs at Gable's that demand had exceeded capacity at the Arcade Parking Center. The only way to keep up, as always, was to expand the Center.

A new parking deck was added to the facility, boosting the available parking space by 25 percent. A new rate was put into effect, dropping to ten cents for the first hour and 10 cents for each additional half-hour. Direct entrances into Gable's Arcade were installed on every level of the updated garage.

The expanded Parking Center opened to the public on Nov. 4, 1966. Once again, patrons rushed to fill it...but Gable's didn't rush to expand it.

Should've Invited Joni Mitchell

The Arcade Parking Center was such a hit, it even attracted hitmakers from the music business. Concerts were scheduled for the top deck of the Center in August 1967 featuring some very well-known pop music performers.

The "WVAM End of Summer Yacht Party" would feature two shows with top talent of the times—the Turtles, the Vogues, and the Spencer Davis Group on Wednesday, Aug. 23, and Sonny and Cher on Thursday, Aug. 24. The timing was perfect when it came to popularity: Sonny and Cher had one of their biggest hits that year with "The Beat Goes On," and the Turtles were riding high with the success of "Happy Together." Bringing such top talent to Altoona was a real coup for the event promoters.

Unfortunately, only one of the shows went off as planned at the Parking Center. The Turtles-Vogues-Spencer Davis Group concert was a hit, but Sonny and Cher were rained out. Tickets for the event said it would happen "Rain or Shine" at 9 p.m., but the weather was just too foul that day, and organizers had a change of heart. They moved Sonny and Cher to the Altoona Skating Rink, which was historic in its own right, though the Gable's connection had been lost.

Still, as the original venue for the event, the Parking Center had its profile raised significantly. William F. Gable and Co. had shown a willingness to try new things and embrace change...a willingness that would become even clearer in the very near future.

Other changes were in the wind, starting with a major changing of the guard just three months later. The top man, George Gable, was on his way out, and the company would be sold a year after that.

Very soon, all bets would be off. The age of stability was drawing to a close.

Gable's

Get Your Tickets to the WVAM-Gable Yacht Party, Aug. 23 and 24

Sonny & Cher
The Turtles
Spencer Davis
The Vogues

| Either Show 3.75 tax incl. |
| Both Shows 5.25 tax incl. |

All Courtesy Altoona Mirror

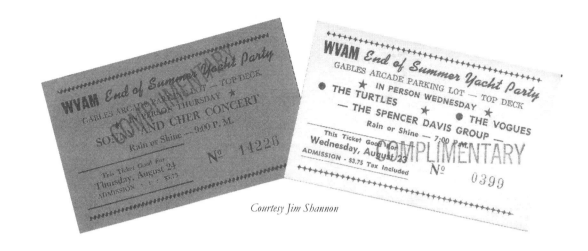

Courtesy Jim Shannon

Photos by Gelon V. Smith

Photos by Gelon V. Smith

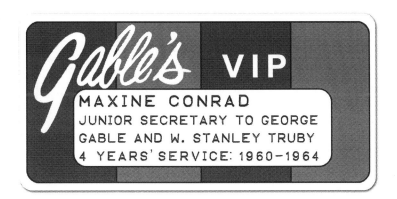

Gable's VIP

MAXINE CONRAD
JUNIOR SECRETARY TO GEORGE
GABLE AND W. STANLEY TRUBY
4 YEARS' SERVICE: 1960-1964

Courtesy Maxine Conrad

Every day, the hobos would sit outside George Gable's office, beside Maxine Conrad's desk. And every day, when George came out of his office, he would do something for them...the same thing every day.

Back then, Maxine was working as a junior secretary to George and his vice president, Stanley Truby. Every afternoon around 2 o'clock, three or four hobos showed up and waited for George.

"To get to the top floor, where the offices were, they had to ride the elevator from the mezzanine," says Maxine. "They would get off on the fourth floor and walk right into the executive offices like they belonged there."

There were different men every day, according to Maxine, but they had one thing in common. They all smelled bad.

"The smell was horrible," recalls Maxine. "They lived on something called canned heat that smelled awful. It really lingered too. I had to spray with disinfectant after they left."

When George emerged from his office, he always did the same thing: He pulled out his wallet and gave each man a dollar bill. Then, they would get up and leave.

And three or four other men would show up the next day at the same time.

"These men looked like they rode the rails," says Maxine. "I guess word got around out there among the hobos that Mr. Gable was handing out money.

"This happened every day that I worked there, like clockwork. I never knew how it started or why, but it never stopped the whole time I was there.

"As far as I was concerned, it just showed how generous Mr. Gable was, and what a wonderful place Gable's was to work," says Maxine.

May I Have The Entire Building, Please?

Fresh out of high school in 1960, Maxine landed the junior secretary job after an interview with the personnel director and a meeting with George Gable. She was hired on the spot and started the following Monday.

The job was a perfect fit. Maxine had loved Gable's department store for as long as she could remember. "I shopped at Gable's a lot growing up. Mom and Dad would take me there on Monday and Thursday nights, because the store would be open till nine then."

Maxine loved the place, from the mesmerizing window displays to the characteristic smells. "Entering the first floor of the Eleventh Avenue building, you walked right into the cosmetics department. The perfume and cologne smelled so good—and then there was the candy department off to the side. You don't find those kinds of smells in department stores anymore."

When she went to work there, the magic of the place never wore off...especially when it came to her fellow employees.

Maxine always felt like she was part of one big happy family. "Everybody knew everybody," she says. "You couldn't walk through the store without someone saying hi and calling you by name."

The hospitality started at the top, with the company's president. "Mr. Gable made it a point, almost every day, to walk through the store and talk to the customers. He talked to the personnel too, and knew them all by their first names. He knew their families and asked about them. He always took time for the staff.

"George Gable was a very caring person," remembers Maxine.

Case in point, when Maxine got engaged, George told her to take a walk through the store. He said he wanted her to pick out a wedding present.

"'I don't care what it is,' he told me. 'I don't care how big or expensive it is. I want you to pick anything you want out of the whole store.'"

So what did Maxine pick? A kitchen or laundry appliance? A piece of furniture? An expensive piece of china or jewelry?

None of the above. Since she was raised not to abuse a privilege, she settled for a coffee pot. "But God love him for giving me that opportunity," she says. "It just made me feel so special, that Mr. Gable treated me like I was one of his family.

"But he was that way with everybody, and everybody liked him because of it. As for me, I loved him to pieces. He was so good to me," says Maxine.

Rockin' Around With Brenda Lee

As a junior secretary in the executive offices, Maxine handled the overflow work from the president and vice-president's personal secretaries. "Mr. Gable's secretary's name was Roberta. He was very fond of her and called her Bert. Mr. Truby's secretary was Helen Overdorf.

"Bert and Helen's offices were beside their bosses' offices. My desk was out front in the reception area."

Maxine's duties included typing, bookkeeping, managing the stock ticker, and answering the phones. All incoming calls went to her phone first, and she directed them to Bert, Helen, George, or Stanley as needed.

Her favorite part of the job was collecting the money for each day's sales from all the departments. "On Monday and Thursday nights, I would work until nine, when the store closed. Then, I would go down to the mezzanine, which was where all the departments brought their proceeds for the day. Being young, I thought that was a big deal, collecting all that money."

Once in a while, though, Maxine got to feel like even more of a big deal—like the time she got up close and personal with a famous singing star. "WFBG sponsored Brenda Lee to come to Altoona and do a show at the Jaffa Mosque," remembers Maxine. "Mr. Gable asked me to chaperone her while she was in Altoona, which was terribly exciting.

"There I was, just out of high school, and I was taking care of a big name performer. I rode along in the limousine that picked her up at the airport and made sure she got to her show on time. The next day, I had breakfast with her before she left. It was a wonderful experience."

Malts in the Basement

Having breakfast with Brenda Lee may have been an exciting experience, but having a malt or bobwhite in Gable's basement was pretty great too.

Maxine loved going to the ice cream counter in the basement and ordering a malt, which was "to die for." According to her, "Anyone who worked at Gable's at that time, that's the first thing they would tell you about: the malts they had in the basement." The bobwhites, made with root beer and ice cream, were delicious too, she says.

Her favorite restaurant for lunch, though, was the one on the mezzanine. "It had a glass enclosure, so you could look out into the store," says Maxine.

The view was always entertaining. She remembers there were always crowds moving through the store, going from department to department. In those days, it was the center of Altoona, the place to go for just about anything.

"They had the candy department, hosiery department, jewelry department, beauty shop, photo studio, you name it," remembers Maxine.

Courtesy Altoona Mirror

"There were other stores in town, but people went to Gable's because of the friendliness, selection, and prices."

Courtesy Altoona Mirror

Maxine continued to shop there long after she got pregnant and quit her secretarial job in the executive suite. She missed Gable's when she and her husband moved to Michigan, then resumed shopping there when they moved back during the Detroit riots.

She still misses it to this day, long after the store's closing in 1980. She says she's not the type of person who lives in the past, but she still thinks about the memories and happy times she had at Gable's.

Courtesy Maxine Conrad

"It was just such a wonderful, wonderful place to work and shop. I know that sounds corny, but it was.

"I loved the place, the customers, and the people I worked with—especially George Gable. I'll never forget how he used to invite us into his office when there were parades on Twelfth Avenue, so we could watch them from his office windows. Later, when I got engaged, he made a gift of my engagement photos. When I quit to have my baby, he gave me a baby gift.

"He was such a gracious, caring man, and the store reflected that," says Maxine.

ITEM	BLDG	FLOOR	ITEM	BLDG	FLOOR
CCESSORIES	11 TH AVE	1 ST	MATERNITY SHOP	11 TH AVE	3 RD
ADJUSTMENT OFFICE	12 TH AVE	2 ND	MEN'S CLOTHING	1 T AVE	1 ST
ADVERTISING OFFICE	12 TH AVE	4 TH	MEN'S FURNISHINGS	1 TH AVE	1 ST
ART NEEDLEWORK	12 TH AVE	1 S.	MEN'S WORK CLOTHES	1 TH AVE	BASEMEN.
ARTIST MATERIALS	11 TH AVE	4 TH	MILLINERY	1 TH AVE	2 ND
BATH SHOP	11 TH AVE	4 TH	MIRRORS & PICTURES	12 TH AVE	2 ND
BEAUTY SALON	11 TH AVE	3 RD	MODEL ROOMS	12 TH AVE	3 RD
BEDS & MATTRESSES	12 TH AVE	2 ND	NOTIONS	11 TH AVE	1 ST
BLANKETS & SHEETS	11 TH AVE	4 TH	PAINTS & WALLPAPER	1 TH AVE	4 TH
BOOKS	11 TH AVE	BALCONY	PARCEL CHECKING	11 TH AVE	4 TH
BOYS' CLOTHING	11 TH AVE	3 RD	PERSONAL SHOPPING	11 TH AVE	4 TH
BRIDALS & FORMALS	11 TH AVE	2 ND	PORTRAIT STUDIO	11 TH AVE	4 TH
			PICTURE FRAMING	11 TH AVE	4 TH
CANDY	12 TH AVE	1 ST	RADIOS	12 TH AVE	2 ND
			RANGES, GAS & ELECTRIC	12 TH AVE	2 ND
CHILDREN'S WEAR	11 TH AVE	3 RD			
CHINA & GLASSWARE	12 TH AVE	1 S.	REFRIGERATORS	12 TH AVE	2 ND
CLOCKS	12 TH AVE	1 ST	RESTAURANT	12 TH AVE	BASEME
COATS & SUITS, WOMEN'S	11 TH AVE	2 ND	REST ROOM, MEN	11 TH AVE	BASEMEN.
			REST ROOM, MEN	12 TH AVE	2 ND
COSMETICS	11 TH AVE	1 ST	REST ROOM, WOMEN	12 TH AVE	1 ST
CREDIT OFFICE	12 TH AVE	2 ND	REST ROOM, WOMEN	11 TH AVE	BASEMEN
CURTAINS	11 TH AVE	4 TH	ROBES & LOUNGEWEAR	11 TH AVE	3 RD
DRAPERIES	11 TH AVE	4 TH	RUGS, FLOOR COVERINGS	12 TH AVE	2 ND
DRESSES, WOMEN'S	11 TH AVE	2 ND	SERVICE ON APPLIANCES	12 TH AVE	2 N.
ELECTRICAL APPLIANCES	12 TH AVE	1 ST	SHEETS & BLANKETS	11 TH AVE	4 TH
EMPLOYMENT OFFICE	12 TH AVE	4 TH	SHOES, CHILDREN'S	11 TH AVE	2 ND
EXECUTIVE OFFICES	12 TH AVE	4 TH	SHOES, MEN'S	11 TH AVE	1 ST
			SHOES, WOMEN'S	11 TH AVE	2 ND
FOUNDATIONS	11 TH AVE	3 RD	SHOE REPAIR	11 TH AVE	BASEMENT
FURNITURE	12 TH AVE	3 RD	SILVERWARE	12 TH AVE	1 ST
			SPORTSWEAR & BLOUSES	11 TH AVE	1 ST
GIFT SHOP	12 TH AVE	1 ST	SPORTSWEAR, BETTER	11 TH AVE	2 ND
GIFT WRAPPING	1. TH AVE	4 TH	STATIONERY	11 TH AVE	1 ST
			TABLE CLOTHS	11 TH AVE	4 TH
GIRLS' WEAR	11 TH AV	3 RD	TELEVISIONS	12 TH AVE	2 ND
GLOVES	11 TH AVE	1 ST	TH IFTY HOME STORE	12 TH AVE	14 TH ST
			TOYS	12 TH AVE	1 ST
HANDBAGS	11 TH AVE	1 ST	UMBRELLAS	11 TH AVE	1 ST
HANDKERCHIEFS	11 TH AVE	1 ST	UNIFORMS	12 TH AVE	3 RD
HOSIERY	11 TH AVE	1 ST	VACUUM CLEANERS	12 TH AVE	2 ND
HOUSECOATS & ROBES	11 TH AVE	3 RD	WASHERS & DRYERS	12 TH AVE	2 ND
HOUSEWARES	12 TH AVE	1 ST	WATCHES & REPAIR	11 TH A.E	1 ST
INFANTS' FURNITURE	11 TH AVE	3 RD	WIG BOUTIQUE	11 TH AVE	ND
INFANTS' WEAR	11 TH AVE	3 RD	WINDOW SHADES	11 TH AVE	4 TH
INTERIOR DECORATORS	12 TH AVE	3 R.			
JEWELRY	11 TH AVE	1 ST			
	12 TH AVE	1 ST			
LINENS	11 TH AV.	4 TH			
LINGERIE	11 TH AVE	3 RD			
LUGGAGE	12 TH AVE	1 ST			

Courtesy Frank Barry

Memory Department

Gable's would send keys in the mail. The keys were a chance to unlock a golden treasure chest.
Chuck Markel

I grew up in Catfish and remember going to downtown Altoona, which meant going to Gable's. We shopped there a lot. I remember what a big deal the parking garage was.

I still have my mother's plastic credit card from there, as well as a little key ring full of treasure chest keys that I kept. Also, I remember they had an electric foot measuring device in the shoes department.
Sheri Loose

My father used to sell our Shelties at Gable's when I was growing up. My father's name is Richard Shannon. My classmate's mom, Virginia Mock, used to work where they sold candy.
Linda Shannon Foust

I dearly remember Gable's. I was a student at BGHS High School, Sixth Avenue building at the time, and I remember walking over the bridge to Gable's before getting the bus to go home from there. We would visit the candy counter and the restaurant in the basement. I remember buying milkshakes at that restaurant, and they were called bobwhites. As young kids, we always visited Santa at Gable's, and each child received a wrapped gift. I also took our children to visit Santa, too.

My Royal Cameo China was purchased at Gable's before our wedding in 1970, and I still use it for special occasions to this day. During our high school days, we always bought/wore Sebago Roamers (loafers) at Gable's. I think the shoe department was in the basement. My older sister worked for WFBG (maybe in the 60's), and they were located on one of the floors at the store. I think we all miss the wonderment that was Gable's and shopping along the avenue.
Kathy Bleicher

Courtesy Matthew Germann

141

We used to come from First Lutheran Church to sing Christmas carols on the steps inside Gable's. Good memories...
Leigh Martino

I worked for Gables after graduating from high school in 1963. I worked in a little office in the basement, and my boss was Mr. McCracken. I was there for my birthday and remember Mr. Gable coming down and wishing me a happy birthday. I was told he did that for everyone. It was a great place to work.
Mary Bettwy

I loved inventory time when I worked at Gable's. The store was closed, and we counted merchandise all day. A big, long table of food was set up for all the hungry workers.
Florine Markley

I remember in the late 50s and early 60s going on special trips to Gable's with my

Courtesy Anne Dixon

grandmother, Margaret Iuzzolino. We dressed up in our Sunday best with hats and white gloves, and hand-in-hand rode the bus downtown. We would visit all departments of the store, and she would tell me about what to look for in shirts for PapPap and scarves for the aunts, among other things. I loved when Nana would show me the china and silverware; it was always so elegant.

We always had lunch, a little more shopping, and a quick stop for a piece of chocolate! That was our secret! My Mother and I shopped at Gable's a lot, but those dates with Nana will always remain special.
Nancy Iuzzolino Pepe

Courtesy Frank Barry

Courtesy Jeffery Holland

Chapter Sixteen

Order of Succession

1959-1967

George Gable watched as the hands went up around the boardroom table. As his life, and the life of the store, changed completely in that one quiet moment on Tuesday, March 21, 1961.

The results of the vote had never been in doubt. The board, including George, had agreed on the outcome earlier. But seeing it played out before him now, irrefutably, irreversibly, was harder to take. It was more definite, more permanent, more real.

Afterward, many things wouldn't be much different. George would still have a voice in decisions. He would preside over special events and serve as a company spokesman. He wasn't about to leave the store and company that he'd done so much to build through the years.

But the hands in the air told a tale he couldn't deny. Part of his life was over.

Not that change was something new to him. After all, he had just remarried on Feb. 10, 1961, to a woman named Betty Barr Harpster. His first wife, Florence, had died Sept. 24, 1958, after 36 years of marriage.

He wasn't living in the same place either. He had moved from the elegant family home near Baker Mansion to a place in Riggles Gap. So things had been changing quite a bit in his world.

But *this*...this went *deep*. The man at the far end of the table—his brother-in-law, W. Stanley Truby—had taken his place. George would still be chairman of the board; the hands were in favor of that.

GEORGE P. GABLE
Chairman of Board

W. STANLEY TRUBY
President

Courtesy Altoona Mirror

143

But he wasn't president of William F. Gable and Co. anymore. For the first time in history, the company president didn't have the last name Gable.

A Company in Crisis?

What was the reason for the change at the top of Gable's? It's safe to say it didn't happen because of a lack of improvements to the store. By 1961, Gable's was looking better than ever thanks to the initiatives of George and his team.

A major modernization program had begun in 1955 and continued for years after that, breathing new life into all the Gable's properties. "The $800,000 program reflects Gable's decision to stay a central city store and add its strength and prestige to the current revitalization of the downtown core area of Altoona," George said in February 1961, leading up to the company's 77th anniversary.

Courtesy Jeffery Holland

A key part of the modernization program was the refinishing of the front of the Eleventh Avenue building—the first major change to the exterior of the place since 1913. Planned by architects Hunter, Campbell & Rea and executed by J.C. Orr and Son, the Eleventh Avenue project included rebuilding the display window area with stainless steel frames and new show window interiors; replacing old revolving door entrances with swinging doors and heated vestibules; and installing a drip-free canopy along the front of the building, complete with a catch-basin into which all runoff was drained.

Workmen also put in granite trim around the doors and under the windows, with aluminum panels finished with porcelain enamel above the windows.

In addition to the Eleventh Avenue storefront work, the modernization project included the development of Bell Telephone's business offices on Twelfth Avenue and the various phases of the Arcade Parking Center construction, which started in 1956. By September 1960, the Parking Center featured 204 standard spaces, plus 22 monthly rentals.

On top of all this, there were many updates to the interiors of both store buildings during the modernization…and

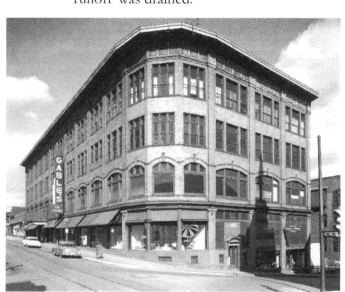

Photo by Gelon V. Smith

the company wasn't done yet. "Gable's has other improvements in mind for the coming years to continue this program," said E.C. Callaway, the firm's secretary-treasurer.

Gable's didn't sound like a company in crisis, did it? It didn't look like a company in need of a shakeup at the top.

The Gables Building has been the heart of downtown Altoona for the past century.

So why did the hands go up around the boardroom table on March 21, 1961? At the age of 63, was George ready to cut back or retire? Was he showing signs of the illness that would drag him down just a few years later? Or was more going on behind the scenes than we will ever know?

Were there as many secrets in the air as upraised hands on that day when the board voted out the son of William F. Gable?

Anniversary as Usual

The 77th Anniversary Celebration was George's last as president of Gable's—not that it seemed, on the face of it, any different than any other Gable's anniversary. If George knew he was on his way out of the presidency in a mere three weeks, he didn't let on.

"Gable's may be 77 years old, but its face and heart are young," he said. "We're going to prove once again we've got the best store in Central Pennsylvania during our great 77th anniversary sale. And we'll prove it during all the rest of 1961."

There were seven days of celebration, starting with Anniversary Day on Wednesday, March 1. Each day after that had its own theme: Leadership Day on Thursday, Old-Fashioned Day on Friday (with all the clerks dressed up in 1884-era costumes), Founder's Day on Saturday, Homecoming Day on Monday, and Basement Day on Tuesday. Then, on Wednesday, March 8, the whole thing drew to a close.

"Through it all, Gable's will have the best quality at the lowest possible prices," said George. "That's been the slogan for Gable's since my father began business with John R. Sprecher 77 years ago."

As usual, Gable's provided free bus transportation for patrons to the store. As always, older customers were given complimentary automobile rides to Gable's. It was just another anniversary. George Gable was in charge, as he had been for decades, and all was right with the world.

Until it wasn't.

Consciously Un-Gabled

Imagine what it must have felt like to see it all happen in '61. For most of your life—maybe *all* of it—George was president of Gable's. He, as much as his store, was an institution in Blair County.

Then, the evening edition of the *Altoona Mirror* lands on your doorstep. The headline on the front page reads, "Truby Succeeds Founder's Son As Gable's Head."

All Courtesy Altoona Mirror

Reading on, you realize it probably won't make much difference in your daily life. George will serve as chairman of the board of directors, so he'll still be around. "I will stay active in the store and in the community," he tells the *Mirror*.

And Truby was a vice president since 1952 and assistant general manager before that, so it's likely he'll maintain the status quo, for the most part. He's old school Gable's, on staff since Oct. 15, 1922. He started as a cash boy making $2.50 per week and worked his way to the top, so he obviously has a love for the place and an interest in keeping it running smoothly.

The new vice president and general counsel, Marion Patterson Jr., also has longstanding ties to the firm. His father, Justice Marion Patterson Sr., served as counsel and director of Gable's for many years.

Still, just knowing George won't be president anymore must leave you with a funny feeling. Who knows what's coming next? Is nothing sacred? When will the changes end?

Will Gable's go on being the place you've come to love and rely on for so many years?

Farewell to a Giant

Maybe illness *was* to blame for the shakeup, after all. It looked that way during the next two years, as George gradually ran out of steam. By early 1963, his health was failing so badly, he was forced to withdraw completely from work and all his many community activities. He just couldn't keep up his Type-A lifestyle anymore, as much as he loved living that way.

Gone were the days when he would walk the floor of the store, greeting customers and asking employees about their families. He didn't go to the store much at all anymore; he *couldn't*.

He went on that way for four more years, always declining. By the time of Gable's 82nd anniversary in March, 1966, he was well out of the limelight. His photo adorned the usual front-page coverage of the event, right under the photo of his father, William, but it was Stanley Truby on the front lines, actively promoting the celebration. It was Truby who was talking about the event's theme—"Go and Grow with Gable's"—and the latest improvements to the store, like the new restaurant with Colonial décor, the new cash registers, and the new lighting fixtures in the Twelfth Avenue building. George was still Chairman of the Board, but he wasn't really in the mix much anymore.

Then, one day in 1967—Feb. 13—it happened. It was a little over a month before his 69th birthday on March 18...but there wouldn't be a celebration to mark that event.

Because George Gable was gone.

He died in bed at his home in Riggles Gap, and his body was found at 8:30 in the morning. The man who had carried on the legacy of William F. Gable for so long had gone to join that very man, his father, wherever he was.

A Missed Man

Was George really gone? The echoes of his life were so strong that it seemed like he was just as present after death as before.

Everyone, it seemed, wanted to hold onto him. As president, chairman of the board, businessman, community activist, or just a guy who appreciated those around him and treated everyone fairly and with kindness, he had made the kind of impression that doesn't fade fast. He had endeared himself to the people in his orbit.

A tribute in the *Altoona Mirror* put it like this: "It is quite possible that there have been few men indeed in the history of Altoona whom as many persons called 'friend' as George P. Gable."

It didn't stop there. "He had a prestige with few precedents in the community. It was not just the prestige of a well-known and influential name. It came from the man himself, his unfailing courtesy and consideration, his smiling readiness to help in every civic endeavor.

"Those who knew him well knew also that his thoughtfulness of others extended to the little details, always a letter of thanks for a bit of help in some of his many civic efforts; always a kind word for friends and strangers, as well as visitors to the store.

"Mr. Gable had a generous heart, and he gave unstintingly of his time, and effort, his thought and worry, and his money."

The *Mirror* tribute went on to talk about how people gravitated toward him, responding to his friendly personality. "His tendency to remember people extended to some of the store's earliest customers and, on the occasion of the store's anniversary, he always would greet throngs of visitors, many of whom, even the most elderly, would make special efforts to go down to greet 'George' and to extend to him best wishes and congratulations.

"There are many indeed who will miss his helping hand and his sympathetic ear. With the passing of George P. Gable, the community has lost a man who was, in truth, a friend to all, but behind him, he has left his heritage of good will, of a readiness to help, to 'get involved,' that has been of untold benefit to the city and the county through every great civic endeavor to which George Gable gave his efforts through the years."

Low-Key to the Last

We can only imagine the vast crowds who would have turned out to honor George at the end—the throngs of well-wishers who might have mobbed his funeral to pay homage to the man who'd meant so much to them. We can only imagine because those crowds weren't invited...to the funeral, at least.

There was a viewing from 7 to 9 p.m. on Tuesday, Feb. 14—Valentine's Day—at the Stevens Memorial Chapel in Altoona. The place was packed with people who'd come to see off their beloved George, because they knew they wouldn't have another chance. The funeral service was held in the same place the next day at 2 p.m....and it was private.

George Gable was buried at Alto Reste Burial Park without the crowds or bells and whistles. Despite his achievements and standing in the community, he had stayed a humble man right up to the end. In planning his funeral and burial arrangements, he had known that what mattered most was the way he had lived, not died.

And he had pulled out all the stops in that life of his, for sure. He had held nothing back.

But that, in a way, could be a curse to the company he left behind. Gable's without George was like the Walt Disney Company without Walt Disney. With his visionary influence gone forever, how would Gable's find its way forward? Especially with certain storm clouds on the horizon, like the rise of a potentially troublesome competitor in the suburban Eldorado area.

The Logan Valley Mall, which had existed as an open-air shopping center since November 1965, was expanded and enclosed in 1967. The new and improved mall had its grand opening on

June 8, just four months after George's death. The place was still in the formative stages, but local business people could clearly see its potential as a challenger for Gable's crown as top retailer in Altoona.

Were Stanley Truby and the rest ready to face this and other challenges? Would they guide the company to a brighter tomorrow, or one that was somewhat...less bright?

Gable's, and Altoona, would not have to wait long to find out.

All Photos by Philip Balko

Rejoice Christ is Born

THE WILLIAM F. GABLE COMPANY
ALTOONA, PENNSYLVANIA

GEORGE P. GABLE, PRESIDENT

December 23, 1954

Dear Don:

All of us at Gable's want to thank you for
the fine window that you designed for the Christmas
Season.

The idea of Cathedral windows, and then the
beautiful way it is worked out, is surely a credit
to you. You are a very talented young man.

With thanks again, I am

Sincerely yours,

George Gable

Mr. Donald Kuny
933 First Avenue
Altoona
Pennsylvania

Mr. Donald Kuny
933 First Avenue
Altoona, Pennsylvania

THE WILLIAM F. GABLE COMPANY
ALTOONA, PENNSYLVANIA

LARRY BOOKHAMER
THRIFTY HOME, FURNITURE, SUPPLY
& SEWING MACHINE REPAIR DEPTS.
7 YEARS' SERVICE: 1961–1968

Larry Bookhamer took some wild rides down the delivery chute at Gable's back in the day.

The chute, which went all the way from the fourth floor to the delivery room, sometimes got blocked by a package. That was Larry's cue to go for a ride.

"I'd go up to the top floor and crawl into the chute," he remembers. "It was really polished and slick from all the packages that had gone down it, so once I

Photo by Philip Balko

started, I couldn't stop till the end. I'd zip right down that chute and blast whatever was blocking it out of the way.

"I'd come out on a table in the delivery department with a couple of guys looking at me, laughing. It was a real hoot," says Larry.

Those rides were a lot like his whole career at Gable's, which also was pretty wild. How many other employees could say they wore the clothes off a mannequin's back, stocked an entire house with *just about everything*, and was fired twice and quit once (make that *thrice*)?

Extreme Makeover: Gable's Edition

Larry started working at the store as Christmas help in the Thrifty Home department in 1961. He mostly did stock work and cleanup, though his boss, Henry Young, also taught him how to cut rugs and perform other tasks in the department.

In the summer of 1962, Larry was promoted to the furniture department, where he assembled and repaired furniture with a crew of five to six other employees. It was a job that kept him on the road a lot, as he and his coworkers traveled to customers' homes to repair furniture they'd bought from Gable's...a free service, in those days.

"We drove to homes all over Altoona and surrounding communities," explains Larry. "We went to towns that were farther away too, like Bellwood, Cresson, and Tyrone.

"We fixed nicks and scratches on Gable's furniture, which didn't take long. Sometimes, it took longer to get to the place than to do the job.

"But sometimes, the work was more involved, like a broken leg on a table or chair or damaged upholstery or whatever."

Larry's biggest job as part of the furniture crew came when a family ordered everything they needed to fill their new home in Duluth, West Virginia. "The husband was transferred to Duluth because of his job, and he bought a whole house worth of furniture. He and his wife ordered everything from a sofa and chairs to beds, plus the linens that went with them. They didn't just order furniture; they ordered furnishings and housewares too.

"It took us two weeks to deliver and set all that up. A driver and I made trips to Duluth, leaving Altoona around five in the morning, then getting back around eight or nine at night.

"We delivered the items and put them where the couple wanted them. They were very nice and always gave us a meal, so we didn't mind a bit," says Larry.

Musical Chairs the Hard Way

Not all customers were equally informed and supportive, however. According to Larry, one customer actually tried to return a rocker/recliner that hadn't been *purchased* at Gable's. And he got away with it!

"The rocker/recliner was broken, and the customer called Gable's about it. Dave Little wanted to keep this person happy, so he arranged to have the chair picked up and gave the customer credit for it.

"But it turned out the rocker/recliner was from *Wolf's*, not Gable's," recalls Larry. "Can you believe that? But it all worked out. We contacted Wolf Furniture, and they came and picked it up, then gave Gable's credit for what they'd given the customer. Everybody was happy in the end, and it gave us a funny story to tell later."

Having a good sense of humor was definitely an asset on the job. Larry and the crew liked to kid around and play practical jokes on each other to get through the day.

But one of those jokes led to disaster when it involved a Gable's customer. According to Larry, a customer ordered a phonograph needle, and one of the guys decided to have a little fun with it.

"He had a weird sense of humor," says Larry. "He put that tiny needle in a big refrigerator box filled with paper, then sealed the box and delivered it to the customer as a gag.

"She was not amused. She found his employee number on the label, which identified him, and she called the store and complained. The guy was gone within two hours."

The Mannequin Stripper

Larry ended up being fired too, over a different situation. "I was helping deliver a dryer, and I dropped my end of it, and it got all scratched up. Gable's fired me over that."

When he couldn't find work elsewhere, however, Gable's relented. Larry returned to the fold, and things were fine and dandy…for a few months. After another screw-up, he got fired a second time.

And came back again when the job market showed no love for him. Gable's rehired him, but this would be his last chance. "If I blew it again, it would be strike three," he says.

Larry worked as a stock boy and cleaner, then got the opportunity to move into the supply department. Managed by Red Hildebrand, the supply department provided bags, pins, boxes, ribbons, wrapping paper, and other supplies to sales clerks. Supply department personnel also served as fill-ins for other employees throughout the store.

The new job was a good fit, and Larry enjoyed it. He especially liked being down the hall from the alterations department, where Tillie Wolf, the head seamstress, worked. "I got to be friendly with Tillie, and she'd give me the clothes off the mannequins," says Larry. "If they were my size, she would pass them along when they were taken off the mannequins. No one seemed to mind, because those clothes would just be thrown out anyway."

Free clothes and a decent job with a nice boss. Who could ever leave such a sweet setup?

Larry could, actually. This time, when he walked out the door, he quit instead of being fired. His boss, Red, told him about a job with higher pay elsewhere in town; he even offered to give him a recommendation. So Larry left Gable's—voluntarily this time—and tried the new job on for size.

But it didn't fit. "I was supposed to cut boxes with a hydraulic machine," he remembers. "I asked what happened to the last guy who did that job, and they told me he left because he lost some fingers. He lost three or four of them, they said.

"That was all I needed to hear. I worked the new job for six hours or so, and then I got on the phone to Red and asked if I could come back to Gable's. He said they hadn't filled my job yet, so I could come back the next day."

UnforgettaGable

By the time Larry returned to Red and the supply department, he had been fired twice and quit once. But that wasn't the end of his comings and goings.

He quit working full-time at Gable's once more, in November 1966, to take a job as a custodian in the Altoona School District. Gable's still had a strong hold on him though. He went back in the middle of 1967 to work as a part-time employee repairing sewing machines.

Finally, in late 1968, he left for the last time. "My youngest son was born in July of '68. Working part-time at Gable's, on top of my full-time schedule in the school district, was just too much. It was keeping me away from my family too much," says Larry.

Decades later, he still thinks back fondly on his time at the store…and the old days in Altoona. "I remember when the traffic downtown was bumper to bumper," says Larry. "And the crowds were shoulder to shoulder.

"It was always like that in Gable's. When I worked in the supply department, I had to push carts through the store to deliver supplies and pick up packages. There were lots of times when it was so crowded, I couldn't move.

"It was exciting," recalls Larry. "Everything was happening at Gable's, and I was in the middle of it all. I was *part* of it all."

Photo by Philip Balko

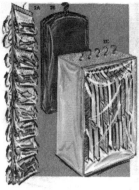

SPRING NOTIONS

Gable's

PROTEX CLOSET & TRAVEL NEEDS

2A—Shoe file stores 18 prs. Rugged quilted gold vinyl; clear pockets. . .3.00
2A1—Matching handbag file with 8 sections. . .3.00 Pak-lite travel bags in light but sturdy coated nylon—water, stain, dust resistant. Side zipper and snap lock for packing ease. Navy or taupe.

2B—Dress bag holds 4 to 5 garments, 54" long. 6.00
2B1—4 suit bag; 40" long. 5.00
2C—Family storage bag of sturdy vinyl. Clear front, zip-open door, quilted top. 2 para pockets. Holds 30 garments. Aqua, gold, pink or green. 25" wide x 20" deep x 54" long. . .5.00

3A—Triangle's "Replace-a-covers" for Danish style furniture cushions. Leather grained fabric backed vinyl —easy care; zip off. Seat 23x23x3½; back 16x23x 3½". In black, orange, avocado, turq. Back & seat. . . . . Set 5.00
3B—Matching stack or bench pillow cover. Zips. 17½ x 17½ x 3". Colors above. 2.00

3C—Skier Glamour Garde protects hair-do. Shower, sleep, shop in it. Velcro tabs hold it firmly in place. With jumbo shower cap of vinyl lined nylon lace. 3.00
3D—Equality car umbrella clips to car visor. Comes in handy sheath. . . . 2.00
3E—Equality foot vibrator with 2 D cell batteries. Plastic case. 5.00

Dandee notions for you.
5A—Golden finish snap-on hanger aids fit closet rod; for 120 garments. 20/3.00
5B—Auto safety flasher. Chrome body; revolving red light, extra heavy suction cup. Uses 3 D cell batteries. (not incl.). . . 4.00
5C—Automatic shoe shiner; 2 brushes, buffer. 4 D cell batt. not inc. 4.00

Daniels' handy travel aids.
5D—Dryer kit includes line, sewing kit, laundry bag, suds, hangers. . .2.00
5E—Auto litter bin fits over car hump. 2.00
5F—Travel iron operates on AC/DC. Cord incl. 3.00
5G—Ironing board to fit in your suitcase! Silicone cover on foam pad. 23½x 9". Truly portable! . .3.00

Barrys' "Wrap saks"—for beach, bath or lounging. One size fits 8 to 16.
6A—Coachman-type cotton terry wrap, lace trimmed, double breasted. Patch pockets. In pink, white, turquoise. 7.00
6B—Poppy print cardigan of cotton terry has side slits. Jumbo pocket. Blue, orange, pink. 6.00

6C—Ben Hur's "Darling" sunglasses go square! Black, white or tortoise frames. One of a large asst. 3.00
6D—Wing's permanent press bra, treated to stay fresh for dozens of washings. Kodel polyester contoured padded cup. 32-36A; 32-38B. White. 1.59
6D1—Unpadded, 32-36A; 32-38B; 34-40C. . 1.59

BARRY'S ANGEL TREADS— SO COMFY

The softest things on two feet! Washable; colorfast; cushion bubble soles; fully lined. Sizes S 4-5½, M 6-7½, L 8-9½.
7A—Sweetheart roses on crisp glazed chintz. Has elasticized instep. Black, blue, pink, red. . .2.00 pr.
7B—Floral sling back scuff—so comfortable! Orange, turquoise. 2.00 pr.

7C—Ballerina of plushy Velva cotton terry. Blue, pink or white. . .3.00 pr.
7D—Scuff of cotton terry. Cerise, pink, turquoise, white; yellow. . . .2.00 pr.
7E—King Barry scuffs for him. Of luxurious Velva cotton terry with bubble sole. Blue, brown, white. Sizes S 7-8½, M 9-10½, L 11-12½. . . . . 3.00 pr.

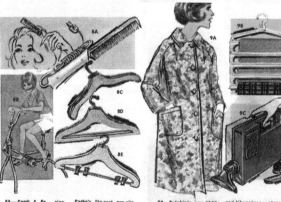

8A—Comb & Go...electric comb to style, straighten, tease and dry hair, even if tinted. 6' cord. 110-120V. AC. 6.00
8B—Slimtrim helps work off inches, improve muscle tone. Full movement handlebar is activated by pedaling. Chrome with gold-tone baked enamel. Supports 400 lbs. 30.00

Garbe's Sta-neet non-slip hangers of styrofoam reinforced with steel. Serrated edges hold garments firmly —no crease, stretch, wrinkle! Safe for sheers—won't tear, mark clothing. White, green, blue, yellow.
8C—3 dress hangers. 1.19
8D—3 all purpose. . .1.29
8E—2 suit hangers with plastic tip clips. . . .1.29

9A—Dolphin's new "100 Proof*" raincoat—bonded fabric and vinyl that's colorful and appealing, yet water, spot and stain proof*! Has raglan sleeves, patch pockets. A vivid floral in pink/blue/gold or pink/aqua. 8-18. . . . . . .9.00
9B—Pandora Rack-A-Slack. 5 slacks or skirts hang securely in space of 1. Rug-

ged fiberglass—strong, light, won't rust, stain, crease or break. Clear and asst. pastels. 2.89, 2/5.00
9C—Kembric's handy hand vacuum is excellent for small jobs. Works on 4 D cell batteries (not incl.). Attachments include utility pick up nozzle, crevice nozzle, rug and upholstery brush. 6.00

GLOBETROTTING WITH KLEINERTS

10A—Oriental Savawave—a striking new bathing cap. White, black, teal blue, hot pink, sand, red. 5.00
10B—Little boy style Savawave of rubberized terry. Bathing cap in red, blue, orange, yellow. 5.00
10C—Travel case of gold streaked plastic. Pouch, 4 fittings. Pk., yel. . . .3.00

10D—Hopsacking makes these Espadrilles something special. Black, champagne, gold, pink, turquoise. S (5½-6½); M (7-7½); ML (8-8½); L (9-9½). . . . . .3.00 a pair
10E—Andiamo tote in chic Oriental print. New wet look vinyl; waterproof lining. Hot pk., grn. . . .5.00

Courtesy Matthew Germann

Memory Department

When I graduated from high school in 1961, I followed in Mom's footsteps and went to work in the credit office at Gable's. Marg Gordon was still there and was my supervisor. The boss was Bill Fink, and Bob Powers from accounting sometimes substituted. Lina Reese was in the accounting office upstairs, and I worked up there a couple times when they needed an extra hand.

Janice Knee ran the billing machine, Nora Misitano made charge plates (they were metal back then), and Edna Heller was one of the tellers where people paid their bills. There were a number of others in the office at the time whose names I have forgotten.

The furniture department was right outside the credit office. The Twelfth Avenue building was called the Arcade and had a revolving door. On the first floor of the Arcade was a neat little restaurant. Also, when I was a child, there was an African-American lady, a podiatrist or something, at the Arcade; Mom would take me to her to massage my feet and help fit me with shoes.

Down on the first floor of the main building, there was a mezzanine with a door that opened onto Fourteenth Street. They sold books up there. Below the mezzanine was the notions department, where you could find sewing stuff, ribbons, etc. There was an elevator next to notions, and in front of the elevator was the jewelry department. That's where my husband and I bought our wedding rings in 1963. More to the front of the store was the candy counter.

Men's and ladies' clothing was down there too. I remember one time I had just bought an outfit in the ladies' department. We're talking slacks, jacket, vest, and blouse. Big bucks! Then, I went to another department for something. As I was paying, I laid my bag with my outfit on the counter. While I was distracted talking to the clerk, a woman came up to the counter and laid her package on top of mine, which I didn't notice, then walked away with it all. When I discovered what she did, she was long gone. It was a hard lesson learned that I carry with me to this day.

There also was a lunch counter in the basement. One day, an older woman was there, kind of leaning on the counter, looking like she was drunk. No one would serve her. Some of the other employees and patrons eating there were concerned about her. One went to her and determined that she was a diabetic, then called to a waitress and demanded a glass of orange juice. It helped bring her around a bit.

It seemed like just seconds till Mr. Dave Little, Mr. George Gable, and some other big wheels were there. They were livid that she had been ignored! The waitresses were reamed out in front of everyone. The lady was taken away to be cared for.

Also in the basement, in addition to the usual bargains, was the shoe repair shop. That shop sold shoe strings, polish, and anything else shoe-related.
Linda Garman

In 1963, I graduated from St. Francis College and needed a suitcase to use on job interviews. I bought a Pullman hard case three suiter at Gables. I saw this suitcase, and it was a good deal for the price. I paid with a check. About two months later, I received a call from Gable's and was told the item I purchased was priced incorrectly, and they wanted me to pay the difference. The only way they knew who purchased the item was that I had paid with a check. I was married with three children at the time, and money was tight. Needless to say, they might still be waiting for the difference.
Virginia Parsons Brantner

I still have the gold cable-knit Bobby Brooks sweater that my aunt, Margaret Detwiler, bought for me in Gable's in 1964. All the girls in my high school had mohair sweaters, and thanks to my aunt and Gable's, I was able to have one too.
Paula Fogarty

I was in high school in 1964. My friends and I decided to skip school, take the bus to Gable's from Roaring Spring, and have a fun day. My parents were not aware I did this.

We were having a blast in Gable's basement when I turned around...and ran right into my aunt! Needless to say, I was in trouble!

But I still loved that store. Christmas shopping at Gable's was a highlight of the season, and dinner at Crist's restaurant after. What we would give for one more day at Gable's with our parents and family.
Karen Sell

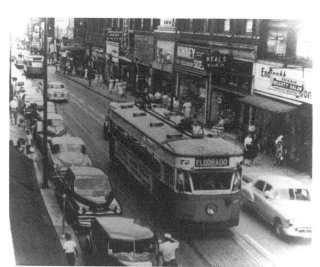
Courtesy David Seidel

I remember in the mid-60s traveling by bus downtown from Eldorado with my good friend, Nancy Vetakis, on Saturday mornings. Her dad, Frank Vetakis, worked in Gable's in the sewing machine department. We would have lunch in the basement, which was considered trés chic at the time. I can still remember the delicious vegetable soup they made. Then, we would go from floor to floor, checking out all the interesting merchandise.

Another fond memory I have is working in the lingerie department under the tutelage of my friend's mother, Mrs. Evelyn Hanelly. She was the most patient, sweet, kindhearted person ever, as was everyone who worked in that department. I only worked there from Thanksgiving to Christmas, or if they were having a big sale. I learned a lot from that experience and loved every minute. Gable's also had a talented "window dresser" during that time period. I don't remember her name, but she was a young gal with lots of new trendy fashion ideas and really kept the windows looking top notch!
Rebecca Dumm DiMino

Chapter Seventeen

The Goods, the Bad, and the Anniversary

1968

It was like moving Christmas Day to late March.

Gable's biggest event every year was the Anniversary Sale, and it was sacred. It had been held on the anniversary of the store's founding—March 1—since the first such event was launched by William F. Gable back in 1894. It had always been one of Gable's greatest claims to fame, as just about every other retail outfit in the country, and around the world, for that matter, had launched their own anniversary sales in the years that followed. Gable's anniversary sale had been the *first*.

Changing the date of the sale—so well-known to Gable's customers—was unimaginable. Throwing away all that event recognition and customer habit—which had taken so many decades to establish—was sheer madness.

And yet, in 1968, that was exactly what Gable's did. For the first time in history, Gable's Anniversary Sale would not be held on its anniversary.

It would be held three months later, in June, instead. That way, winter weather could not interfere with it.

"Three out of five times in recent years, we've had a March blizzard—or at least a heavy snowstorm—on opening day," explained Gable's President W. Stanley Truby.

Courtesy Altoona Mirror

155

"We've decided, for the benefit of our customers, and our own benefit, to give up March as an anniversary date."

It seemed like sacrilege. There would still be a "birthday sale" on the anniversary date in March, but the full-blown anniversary sale would have to wait until June.

Just like that, a long-held tradition went out the window. On the date of the store's 84th anniversary in 1968, a two-day birthday sale kicked off. The store was open Friday, March 1, from 9 a.m. to 6 p.m. and Saturday, March 2, from 11 a.m. to 5 p.m....and that was all. For the first time, the big weeklong anniversary sale would happen three months after the actual anniversary date.

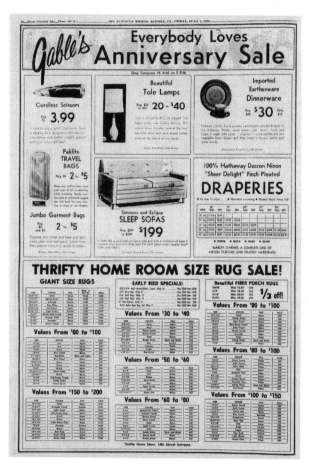

The sole buyers came from Wheeling, W.Va. They were brothers with the last name Good—though whether that name foretold the kind of men they were and the effect they would have on Gable's remained to be seen.

Sidney Good Jr., 41, and Laurance, 35, were department store people. Their outfit back in Wheeling, L.S. Good & Co., was something of a success story, and they were looking to expand.

Gable's, it turned out, was looking to sell. George Gable, retail giant that he was, had been dead for more than a year, and things just weren't the same without him.

It felt like Gable's had crossed a line somehow. Like the store had forgotten its heritage and gone off track. Was it then that Gable's started on the long, dark road that would eventually lead to its downfall?

And was it any wonder, with the anniversary sale rescheduled, that even bigger changes were on the way in the immediate future?

A "Good" Deal

They moved the anniversary sale to June, but there was actually a much bigger Gable's sale in March that year. *Everything* was sold, as a matter of fact, though the sale wasn't even open to the public.

WILLIAM F. GABLE CO. OFFICIALS — Flanked by President W. Stanley Truby (left) and Vice President Marion D. Patterson (right) are the two new owners of the William F. Gable Co., Sidney S. Good Jr. and Laurance F. Good, both of Wheeling, W.Va., where they are owners of the L. S. Good & Co. department store. In Altoona, they are chairman and vice chairman, respectively, of the Gable board. The Goods were attending an 84th anniversary sale luncheon given by the Gable firm.

For certain key stakeholders, the thrill was gone…especially with the threat of the Logan Valley Mall looming over the horizon. Some thought it was only a matter of time until the mall overtook the downtown business district—with Gable's as its centerpiece—and became the area's preeminent retail destination.

Some of those who owned shares of the company were ready to cash them in and move on with their lives. Owning and directing the store didn't hold the same allure it once had for a faction of the Gable family who controlled large blocks of stock.

So the Goods, when they entered the picture, were not seen in a bad light. They were able to make a deal with the ownership of Gable's to acquire the store, and all interested parties seemed to be happy with how it came together.

On March 31, 1968, just a month after Gable's birthday, Altoona's renowned retail institution changed hands. For the first time, the William F. Gable Co. was owned in full by out-of-towners with no connection to the Gable family.

And people started to talk. Word spread as folks wondered if the Goods would live up to their name or prove to be the opposite. But it was still too soon to tell.

The Goods, for their part, seemed inclined to let their actions do the talking. In the months after the sale, they commuted back and forth from Wheeling, making plans and setting things in motion, preparing for the new reality they intended to shape within the walls of those sacred buildings on Eleventh and Twelfth Avenues.

Good Will Hunting

Gable's annual press luncheon was special that year. For one thing, it was held later than usual, on May 31, in conjunction with the anniversary sale. Also, it was held in the Oneida Room of the Penn Alto Hotel instead of the usual Pennsylvania Room.

But the most special part of the occasion was the guest list—in particular, the two new faces at the head table. For the first time, Sidney and Laurance Good were attending the longstanding luncheon, being introduced to the local media as Gable's new owners. It was the Goods' official coming-out party.

Photo Courtesy Altoona Mirror

The two men grinned and nodded as President W. Stanley Truby talked about their achievements and hopes for the future. "They have brought their store up from $1.5 million to more than $5 million gross income in the past six years," said Truby. "They are very interested in stores of our type, with excellent merchandise."

When Gable's new chairman, Sidney Good, got to say his piece, he emphasized staying true to tradition and community. "We want to do everything we can to further associate with Gable's and with the Gable family," he said. "I hope you all can be as proud of us as I know we'll be of Altoona." Vice Chairman Laurance agreed.

The Goods' comments went over well with the media folks. There was applause all around. They liked the implication that the new owners would honor the store's traditions—like making huge ad buys in local newspaper, radio, and TV outlets. When Truby and the Goods confirmed buys of 24 pages in the *Mirror*, tied in with plentiful radio and television spots, you better believe the applause was long and loud.

Though, clearly, not all traditions would be preserved. After all, the anniversary sale and press luncheon had been rescheduled. And then there was the matter of the giveaways.

For decades, Gable's had given away souvenirs to customers during the anniversary sales. There had been plates, ashtrays, vases, coins, and other commemorative gifts…but no longer. Starting with the 84th anniversary in 1968, the public would no longer receive complimentary souvenir prizes to mark the occasion. According to President Truby, it was Gable's belief that the public was tiring of gimmicks and trading stamps.

Was it true? That year's sale was called the "Everybody Loves Gable's Anniversary Sale"…but would everyone still love Gable's after being denied the free gifts they'd come to expect?

Or would the lovefest that played out at the press luncheon carry over into the general population? Would everyday folks show the same goodwill to the Goods that the media people had?

Making Good on the Deal

One thing became certain as the year went on: the sale to the Goods was a done deal. On October 29, Altoona City Council authorized Councilman William Stouffer to execute the deeds required to complete the transfer of the store properties to the new owners. So there was no going back.

Gable's, and the Goods, could only move forward—and 1969 lay ahead. Would it be as tumultuous for the local department store trade as it would be on the nationwide cultural and sociopolitical landscape?

Let's just say, *major* changes were in the air. So yes, 1969 would be a transformative year for Gable's as well as America.

Courtesy Altoona Mirror

MEMORY DEPARTMENT

When I was growing up in Hollidaysburg in the 1960s, Gable's was the place to go for great clothes. Service from the sales staff was always friendly, knowledgeable, and helpful. It was a time when, if you were visiting the city of Altoona, it was a good idea to look your best. After all, you just might run into someone you might know! Thanks to Gable's, most people on the street during those days were properly dressed.

During the early and mid-60s, I was a high school student in Hollidaysburg. One place where high school students went on Saturday night was the YMCA. It was an important spot to meet friends and dance to pop tunes on the basketball court. Living at 803 Penn Street, I always looked forward to the 15-minute walk to the 'Y' located at that time on the corner of Penn and Walnut. And, of course, I wanted to dress to impress!

Several days earlier, my dad and I visited Gable's to purchase a pair of pants. I was able to find a perfect pair, but they needed to be hemmed. The Gable's folks said they would be ready Saturday. On Friday, I asked my dad if he could drive me to Gable's to pick up my new pants so I'd have them for Saturday night. He said no! I tried and tried to get him to take me, but for some reason that I can't now remember, he simply would not take me! I had no idea what to do. I was frustrated, to say the least. The dance was the next day, and I really needed those pants. No new pants to wear to the dance when they were in a store waiting for me? Impossible situation!

I woke up Saturday morning to a dreary day with drizzle and a little sleet. It was probably around 37 degrees or so. I asked Dad again, begging him to take me to Gable's to pick up my pants. And once again, he said no. What was I to do? I didn't know anyone who had a car who could take me. Besides, because of the weather, it was not a great day to be driving.

I had only one option. I located the receipt, placed a waterproof poncho over my winter coat, and walked to Gable's! So in late morning, I started. I walked to Dysart Park, then through the woods to Lakemont, then on the road all the way to Gable's.

My poncho and boots were dripping wet when I walked into the store. It was amazing that anyone let me in. I went to the second floor shedding water with each step. I handed over the soggy receipt to an astonished-looking saleswoman. She located the pants, and I made sure she wrapped them twice in plastic. Without saying much, I left Gable's and walked home. I guess the round trip was about 13 miles.

Unfortunately, I do not remember if the pants were a hit with anyone at the 'Y' dance that Saturday night, but Gable's helped me to feel great while motivating me to realize at a young age that if you want something badly enough, you can get it.

Frank T. Koe

Photo by Gelon V. Smith

I bought my wedding gown at Gable's in May 1967. I had been watching and dreaming about a certain gown on a floor model. When I went shopping for a senior prom gown, the wedding gown was no longer on the model. When I asked the sales lady, she said that it was on the sale rack. I found it and bought it with the $25 that I had saved for a prom gown. I later went back and bought a prom gown. I wore the wedding gown on Sept. 20, 1967, when I married my "Soldier Boy." This September, it was 50 years since our wedding.

Annetta L. McAlarney Simington

Gable's had a billboard with a two-piece Jansen bathing suit that I just had to have. I got it after two months on layaway.

Gable's was a cut above when it came to fashion. My sister and I bought these outrageous (for our town, anyway) outfits like Cher wore, with paisley print and flared bell-bottom pants. I wish I still had them!

Catherine Klepser

We used to go to Gable's for our Boy Scout supplies. They had the most to offer in terms of uniforms, camping gear, books, etc. And the salespeople were always friendly. They also had great toys and old coin and stamp collections.

Bob Summers

During my college winter breaks, I was lucky to get a job in Gable's Christmas Trim-a-Tree Department. Fifty years later, the ornaments I bought there are still some of my favorites.

We were lucky to be in the path of Mr. Gable's daily walks through the store. He was so friendly and invariably had something pleasant to say about his employees.

Olivia Anslinger Carniglia

Gable's Book Department was a curved balcony over the top/back of the first floor. You entered it from the side street. The manager there knew how to help a mom with a daughter who loved poetry and art. Her choices were usually spot-on, except for my first copy of Walt Whitman's Leaves of Grass. I was a bit young for it at ten, but grew to love it over the next few years. She chose art books that I would get lost in from every country. It was always great to linger there.

My aunt and I often explored Gable's after she took me to my class at Ruth Barnes' School of Dance, just a few blocks away. Buying a new petticoat or a classic novel were my great joys with one so beloved, as was the treat of a hot fudge sundae.

I remember two things in particular about the Bargain Basement. My aunt took me there when I was about 12. I had saved enough money to actually buy my mother a dress. It seemed like such a big deal, but as I remember, it was a simple cotton house dress with pink flowers. Also, when I was a teenager, a girlfriend of mine taught me how to be a good, discerning shopper in that basement. It was a good and caring lesson.

Courtesy Frank Barry

I remember that the girls who were seniors would lend their names and pictures as part of the marketing in the young girls' clothing departments. They were role models to younger girls, and it made buying there seem nicely advised.

Debbie Conley Foreman

My husband, Dave Jenner, worked in Gable's men's furnishings department at Christmas while he was in college. His dad, Al, managed the paint department, and his mother, Kay, managed the book department at Gable's.

Marie Andrews Jenner

Courtesy Frank Barry

Courtesy Jim Shannon

Courtesy Jim Shannon

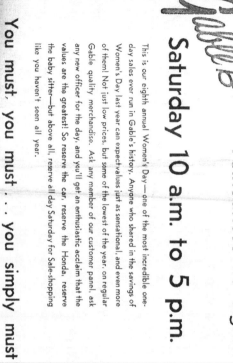

Courtesy Altoona Mirror

Doe. Rabbits. Squirrels. Chipmunks.

Anne Dixon brings them to life on her easel, one careful brush stroke at a time. These days, she paints "anything with fur and feathers." That's how she likes to put it.

Wolves. Bears. Bobcats.

The creatures she draws are incredibly lifelike, amazingly detailed...shown in the midst of lovingly captured natural habitats. One look at her work, and you can see what a professional she is. You can tell she has been committed to her art for a very long time.

Eagles. Bucks.

She has been practicing this work since the early 60s, in fact. And she got her start in a place that once had great need for her skills.

Trout. Rattlesnakes. Butterflies.

Even though she ended up doing something else altogether for most of her years at Gable's department store.

Portrait of the Artist as a Young Woman

Anne Dixon—whose last name was Wahl in those days— went off to the Art Institute of Pittsburgh after graduating from Altoona High School in 1963. She had a natural talent and love for illustration and decided to put it to use in the world of advertising art.

Courtesy Anne Dixon

163

According to Anne, the education and training she received at the Institute prepared her well for the career she'd chosen. "It was a great school," she says. "We had classes in anatomy and everything related to advertising art. I learned and studied and practiced hard, so I'd be ready for anything that came my way in the field."

After graduating from the Institute, Anne found work in La Jolla, California—then returned to Altoona in 1965, where she found a job as an advertising artist at Gable's.

Working under Advertising Director Fred Deichert, Anne created illustrations for the store's plentiful newspaper ads. The techniques she'd learned at the Institute helped her produce quality drawings of many varied products on a daily basis.

"I always painted on art boards," explains Anne. "And I used lamp black, which is a special kind of paint that came in a tube.

FRED L. DEICHERT JR.

"Mr. Deichert had a schedule of what was going to run in the ads for the week, and I drew it all on the boards. Different departments—the dress department, for example, or jewelry or cosmetics—would bring their featured items to the office, and I would illustrate them. If the items were too big to go anywhere, like washers or dryers, I would go down and sketch them, then go back to the office and draw them to size."

When it came to drawing items of clothing, Anne didn't need to use models. She just saw the clothes on hangers or tables and filled them out with her knowledge of anatomy and her imagination.

Courtesy Anne Dixon

After completing the product illustrations, Anne handed them off to Mr. Deichert, who put them together with ad copy and other materials and sent them off to the newspaper for production. The advertising team at the *Altoona Mirror* pulled it all together, placed the finished ads on the pages of the newspaper, and made sure everything was printed properly.

Anne says it was a fun job, and she did it well. It was exactly the kind of job she had trained for, and the people she worked for seemed to be happy with the results of her efforts.

Why then, after two years, did she end up as a sales clerk selling juniors' sportswear on the second floor of the store?

Blame it on the Mats

According to Anne, her days in the advertising department at Gable's ended because of "mats."

Like modern-day clip art, mats were finished artwork of a generic nature. Instead of paying an in-store artist like Anne to draw products to order, a thrifty company could simply plug mats of similar products into their ads. The mats weren't exact reproductions of the actual products featured in the store, but they showed the same *types* of products that customers could expect to find.

And that was the route that Gable's decided to go in '67. "Instead of paying me as a full-time artist, it was easier to order pre-made mats that resembled the clothing, rugs, appliances, or whatever was on sale at the time," says Anne. "Suddenly, there was no longer a job for me in advertising at Gable's, so I took the only job I could find in the store at the time, selling juniors' sportswear on the second floor."

Working as a sales clerk wasn't Anne's ideal job, but her sojourn in sportswear lasted only a few months. At that point, she found a new job—one that, though it wasn't the ad illustration she'd done before, would at least draw on her creative talents and Art Institute training.

Gable's was putting her on Display.

Breaking into Windows

As a designer in the display department, Anne went to work filling Gable's windows with enticing exhibits. Her boss, Jim Pennypacker, handed out assignments based on each week's sales, and Anne and her co-workers—Jim Shannon and Isabelle Nardelli—worked as a team to fulfill them.

It was a job she loved from the start. "Doing the windows was wonderful," she recalls. "We would be so creative. It was great. It was the best department I ever worked for."

Anne and her teammates brainstormed to come up with themes for each window, often based on seasonal activities such as going to the beach or enjoying autumn leaves, popular entertainment like the film *Bonnie and Clyde*, travel to places like Mexico and Paris, or special events like the U.S. Bicentennial. Then, they would size up the space and devise a design.

"We had a planning session," says Anne. "We would go down to the window in question and stand around, trying to figure out what to put where. We would consider the placement of mannequins and props. The color of the clothing and season of the year were factors too. We took those into account when selecting the various elements of the display."

All Courtesy Jim Shannon

When the planning was done, the team began setting up the window. Various pieces of merchandise such as clothes, furniture, toys, and housewares were supplied by the departments within the store. As for props and backdrops, the team pulled them out of storage or developed new pieces to accentuate the settings. "At the time, the display department occupied the whole backside of the Twelfth Avenue building," explains Anne. "I mean, it was *big*.

"The department had these huge bins filled with things you could use in the windows—grass mats, palm trees, whatever. You name it, we had it. And if we didn't have it, we made it.

"That was where the workbench area came in. It was huge too. It wrapped around the corner of Twelfth Avenue and Thirteenth Street on the top floor.

"We had this *massive* workbench and smaller cupboards where we kept our tools. And we kept everything neat and made sure it was all cleaned up by the end of the week, ready to start the next week. We would come in Monday, and it would all be sparkling and ready to go.

"We did it like that because we cared," says Anne. "That place was our second home, and we wanted to keep it nice."

"The finished displays were up to us. Mr. Pennypacker gave us a lot of creative freedom. He knew whatever we did would be done well and done right, and it would be appealing to the public eye. That's what I loved most, that freedom to create."

Anne also loved the excitement and attention her team's displays got from the public, especially during the Christmas season.

Break Out the Red Ryder Air Rifle

After arranging the contents of each window, the display team examined and perfected their work. "We would go around and stand outside and look at it to see if we needed to add anything, take anything away, or move anything.

Gable's windows were a major attraction at Christmastime, and it was up to Anne, Jim, and Isabelle to wow shoppers and put them in the holiday spirit.

"The Christmas displays were special," says Anne. "We went all out to top ourselves and dazzle the crowd."

According to Anne, the displays were curtained off while the team worked on them, then dramatically unveiled when they were done. On the night of the unveiling, throngs of people gathered on Eleventh Avenue, waiting for the Christmas lights to come on and the window displays to be revealed.

"We had people in each window, ready to unhook the curtains," remembers Anne. "And one person manned the light switch. He or she flipped the switch, and all the Christmas lights flared to life.

"That was the signal for the people in the windows to unhook the curtains so they all came down at one time. The crowds outside cheered and applauded and pushed forward, admiring what we'd done.

"It was just like in the movie *A Christmas Story*. There were lots of kids with their little faces pressed up against the glass, staring at the toys and decorations.

"It felt so good to help make all that happen," says Anne. "To be an important part of that holiday tradition that everyone loved and looked forward to."

Christmas tended to bring out the best in the display department's work. Anne's all-time favorite window at Gable's was a Christmas project, in fact. "It was called 'Silent Night,' and Jim Shannon designed it," she remembers. "He blocked in the whole window with plywood and cut a big oval out of it, which became the letter 'S' in the word 'Silent.' The letter 'N' in 'Night' also was an extension of the oval, with the rest of 'Night' in gold lettering atop the plywood screen. Inside the oval, there was a nativity scene with Mary, Joseph, and the Christ Child. It was just beautiful."

All Courtesy Jim Shannon

MISS PRESIDENT - 67'

Wild Things

Looking back on her four years in Display, Anne has no regrets. "I think we did excellent work," she says. "We were proud of what we did because it was something we loved to do."

She finally left Gable's to move to New Hampshire with her husband, Jim, whom she'd met at Gable's, in 1969. Eventually, she and Jim moved back to Altoona, where they live to this day…and still get together with her former colleague Jim Shannon and his wife. Their work together paved the way for a lifelong friendship.

The creativity of working in Display also helped Anne's lifelong development as an artist. Through the years, her love of design, drawing, and painting grew stronger, and she eventually became a professional wildlife illustrator.

Anne went on to paint covers for numerous wildlife-oriented publications, including *Fly Fishing Guide, Trout Unlimited*, and the magazine of the New Jersey Division of Fish, Game, and Wildlife. She was inducted into the Library of Congress in 2009.

Her illustrations encompass plenty of local flora and fauna, as well as more exotic beasts and settings.

She is equally at home painting Blair County wildlife and animals of the African savannahs.

Lions. Leopards. Giraffes.

She still spends many hours at her easel, finding peace in the rendering of fur and feathers… the capturing of grace and grandeur in paint.

Elephants. Antelope. Rhinos.

She dabs and swirls her brush on the canvas, smiling as she brings to life the creatures great and small, envisioning distant environments where she has yet to set foot.

Tigers. Flamingos.

And in the back of her mind, once in a while, she remembers flipping that switch at Gable's, turning on all the Christmas lights at once…

Buffalo. Wildebeest.

…and the oohs and ahhs of the crowd on Eleventh Avenue…

Dragonflies. Crocodiles.

…and she thinks, with a twinkle in her eye, wouldn't that make a hell of a painting one of these days?

MEMORY DEPARTMENT

I worked at Gable's from June until November of 1968, between high school and when I went into the Air Force. I was only there five months, but I got a retail education that I never forgot.

I worked in the sign department for Grace Waite. She was spectacular. I still remember how she'd take a brush, dip it in a can of paint, and paint the Gable's logo freehand. She painted out that word "Gable's" exactly the way you see it on signs and bags. Grace was very, very, very talented.

When I worked in the sign department, I helped create price cards and banners and stuff like that. I used what we called a card stamp machine for the price cards. With that machine, you set up the letters you wanted, then pulled the lever down, and it printed what you'd selected on the card.

There also was a device called a proof press, which we used for signs and banners. Anything that required hand drawing, Grace did freehand.

The departments would come by and put their orders in, and we completed them. We put the finished orders in the slots for each department, and they sent someone to pick them up.

The sign department was upstairs, so I spent most of my time in the upper floors. The president and executives and office workers were there, and we were pretty much detached from the rest of the store. At the start of my shift, I would come in and go right up on the elevator. The only time I came down was to go to lunch or leave for the day.

Still, I made quite a few friends while I was there. Gable's was a great place to work, and the employees really helped each other out...especially Grace. She was like a mother hen to me. And she was so talented, it was exciting just to watch her work.

David Winstead

Photo by Gelon V. Smith

169

Photo by Gelon V. Smith

In 1965, I went to work at Gable's, starting in the paint department. That was a fun job. I found out the difference between lead-based and water-based paint real fast when I had to unload a tractor trailer full of it. Lead-based paint is twice as heavy as water-based.

Next, I worked stocking candy. I brought the candy down from cold storage to the candy department, where they sold more candy than you can imagine. They had the finer chocolates on one side and other types of chocolates in the middle. We sold case after case after case of it. I had a lot of fun in that department...especially because it's where I met my wife, Anne.

She was working on displays in the window right behind the candy department. I took a liking to her and brought her little bags of candy to keep her happy. We started talking, and a couple years went by, and we eventually got together and got married.

After the candy department, I ended up working in the dress shoe department. The environment over there was a lot of fun. The customers who came to that department were serious shoppers.

I finally left Gable's in 1968 and moved to New Hampshire with Anne. It's a beautiful part of the world, and we loved it up there. It was a very happy time in our lives.

Years later, after several job changes and moves, I ended up working for a big corporation down in south Georgia. Interestingly enough, it was M&M Mars! After working in the candy department at Gable's, I ended up working at one of the biggest candy manufacturers in the world.

Jim Dixon

Courtesy Jim Shannon

My father purchased our first console color TV from Gable's, back when I was a teenager. We had some problems with it and couldn't get them to come over and do something about it. Dad got fed up and had me help him load the TV in the back of his beat-up old pickup.

We went up on Eleventh and Twelfth Avenue to take the TV back to the store. I was mortified that we went there like that, in work clothes instead of dressing up. I kept hoping that none of my school friends would see me.

But it all worked out. Gable's made it right. Everything turned out good, and my dad was happy the TV came back fixed.

None of my friends saw me, and I was relieved. You were supposed to dress up to go to Gable's, not walk in wearing sloppy work clothes. I felt really self-conscious about that.

George Rowles

Chapter Eighteen

The Powers That Be

1969

On a sunny morning in 1919 or so, William F. Gable sits at his desk in his office at Gable and Co. on Eleventh Avenue. He's writing in a ledger or reading a report or sketching improvements to the store…and he pauses. He lowers his pencil or papers and stares off into space, maybe thinking about how far he's come, or how his life has changed, or what he has yet to accomplish.

Or who else might sit in that chair someday. Robert or George, certainly. Nothing makes him more proud than to know his sons will someday run the firm. Or a nephew, perhaps. As long as the store stays in the family.

Maybe, if things go well, and the company continues, another generation will sit there someday. A grandson might succeed one of his sons.

William nods. That could be all right. A grandson. Someone who will value and perpetuate what he has built here. Someone who will carry it onward into the future, creating a legacy for *his* sons and grandsons.

William smiles and gets back to work. He hopes he's there to see it… but if he isn't, at least it's good to think about now. He and his descendants, tending the same business.

And one of those descendants, 50 years later, is William's grandson.

Robert Southwick Powers is the new president of Gable's.

Powers to the People

The news hit on Saturday, Feb. 1, 1969. It was the biggest story since Sid and Larry Good bought William F. Gable and Co.

W. Stanley Truby, president of Gable's since 1961 and an employee of the firm since 1922, was retiring. He was the first president without Gable blood, though his sister had been married to George—and he was stepping away. He was handing the reins to someone who had *plenty* of Gable blood in his veins.

That man, Robert S. Powers, was the son of Edna Gable Powers, the daughter of William F. Gable himself. Bob Powers had been waiting in the wings for a long time, preparing for this very opportunity...and now it was his.

He had started working at Gable's in 1939 as a salesman in the men's furnishings department. In April 1968—shortly after the sale of Gable's on March 31—he had become a director of L.S. Good and Co. Then, on Feb. 1, 1969, the board of directors of L.S. Good voted to make him president of Gable's, and he accepted the offer.

That Monday, when Bob went to work for the first time as president, he walked into that same corner office on the top floor where his uncles, Robert and George, had once worked. Did his heart race a little as he walked through the doorway, taking up the mantle of his predecessors, all the way back to the legendary founder, William? Did the hairs on the back of his neck stand up as he settled into the chair behind the desk? Did he smile and nod as he placed his hands on the desk, feeling the same wood beneath his fingers that Robert and George had once felt? History records none of these things.

But, yes. *Of course he did.*

Why Not Move It To December?

It soon became clear that Bob Powers would not be a passive president. Huge changes were in the works at Gable's department store.

Six months after Bob's ascension to the presidency, the company marked its 85th anniversary celebration...in *August*, this time. The event, which had already moved from March to June, had shifted two months later, "for the convenience of customers," according to Bob.

"In August, we can offer a varied assortment of new fall merchandise—including back to school items—at amazing values. We also will avoid the snowstorms which plagued sales in past Marchs," explained Bob.

In spite of the change of dates, this anniversary sale would be a great one, said Bob. Gable's would offer "an extensive collection of brand names—fashions selected for newness in the hard lines and fashions with intrigue in the soft lines."

The anniversary event also was the perfect time to kick off a major overhaul of the store. For one thing, Bob announced that full electric heating and air conditioning would be installed throughout both buildings for the first time in Gable's history. It was an upgrade that was long overdue, one that would greatly improve the comfort of shoppers in every season of the year.

In addition to the heating and air conditioning installation, new departments would be added to the store. New employees would be hired to staff them, boosting Gable's personnel by 25 percent...and these new workers would be the cream of the crop. "We want both men and women who are energetic and enthusiastic when it comes to serving a customer. We're trying to create a right attitude," said Bob.

The carefully chosen new staff would be well-trained in the store's special new service programs to provide excellence in all ways. "They're not just clerks; they're salespeople who have the customers' wants in mind; they will treat each customer as an individual."

Shiny, Happy Gable's

Then there was the biggest change of all, or at least the most outwardly visible. The exterior of both Gable's buildings would be enclosed in "anodized aluminum" sheathing. Work on the new façade, complete with a nearly two-story-high Gable's script logo, would begin in early 1970.

By the time all these upgrades were finished, Gable's would be "the most beautiful store in the east," according to Bob. "Gable's is going to be the showplace of Central Pennsylvania," he said.

There would be more merchandise for sale than ever before too. In fact, a new warehousing floor was opened to accommodate the vastly increased stocks. The warehousing space was located off the Eleventh Avenue alley and permitted stocking and delivery of homeware items.

Between the increased stocks and renovated store buildings, customers would find an enhanced and inviting shopping environment. "Remember this: Large assortment, pleasant surroundings, eye-catching displays. They all spell Gable's," said Jack Mitchell, vice president of merchandising.

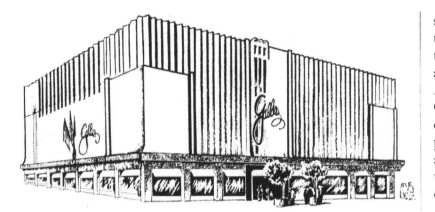

The shiny, renovated store would be well-positioned to face the challenges of the 1970s and beyond… and would help downtown Altoona to do the same. Gable's would spend a million dollars on the project to prepare for the future and affirm its commitment to the redevelopment of the downtown business district.

The director of the Redevelopment Authority, William C. Bellamy, applauded the effort. "We're delighted at the further evidence of faith in the downtown's future made by Gable's store," he said, "since millions of dollars have now been invested by downtown Altoona stores, which believe in the future of the city. This announcement continues the free partnership between public and private interests."

Overpowering Gable's

Meanwhile, off in Eldorado, the Logan Valley Mall kept growing, gradually becoming more and more of a threat to downtown retail. Would this force to be reckoned with be overpowered by Gable's and its new president? Or was Gable's decision to double down on its current location an error in judgment?

Sitting at his desk in his top floor corner office, Bob Powers must have asked himself much the same questions. Was he doing the right thing for the store, and himself, and his family?

Maybe he even wondered if his son, Jamie, would occupy the president's office and desk after he did. Maybe he wondered too if a grandchild would someday take the reins and leave his own mark on the company.

History doesn't record if Bob actually asked these questions, or if his grandfather William asked them fifty years earlier. But what do *you* think?

All Courtesy Altoona Mirror

174

Everyone, every day, does display advertising. That's what Jim Shannon says.

Back when he gave lectures on display advertising at high schools, he would ask the students if they had ever done display. Nine out of ten times, not a single hand would go up.

"I told them I was surprised, because I knew for a fact that they did display advertising all the time," says Jim. "Every day, when they woke up and decided what to wear based on whom they wanted to attract, they were practicing display. Each and every one of them was a walking billboard. *All* of us are."

If Jim sounds like an evangelist when it comes to display, it's with good reason. He worked in the display department at Gable's from the late 60s through the mid-70s, serving as display director during the last years of his career.

Courtesy Jim Shannon

He has done a lot since, but he has never lost his love of display...or Gable's...or his fellow display workers. *That* is the display he creates every day of his own life—scenes of a man at peace with his past, a man who has never forgotten the sweetness of yesterday.

Or given up on the tingle of tomorrow.

A Gofer on Display

It all started in 1966, when Jim joined Gable's as an intern from Penn State Altoona. A retailing and merchandising student, he interned in the men's clothing department.

When the holiday season rolled around, however, Jim was offered seasonal work in the display advertising department. He jumped at the chance.

The next thing he knew, he was working for Display Director Jim Pennypacker with Anne Wahl and Isabelle Nardelli. The team hit the ground running, because the days were beyond hectic with Christmas on the way.

"During the Christmas season, every display case and post on every floor of the store had to be decorated," recalls Jim. "Then there were the windows, all 18 of them. You might say there was a lot of hustle and bustle in the display department at the time."

Isabelle Nardelli

Fortunately, the members of the display team meshed perfectly. "We got along well together. We were like a fine watch," says Jim. "Our way of looking at things was complementary."

At first, though, Jim's role on the team wasn't very creative. He mostly worked as a "gofer," hauling display components through the store buildings. "The display department and storerooms were on the fourth floor of the Twelfth Avenue building. The main display windows were on the ground floor of the Eleventh Avenue building. So all the props, equipment,

Courtesy Jim Shannon

mannequins—everything had to be transported from the highest point on Twelfth Avenue to one of the lowest points on Eleventh Avenue. It was even more challenging because there was only one overpass between the buildings that wasn't open to customers, spanning the alley. That's why I was so valuable to the team at first. I was a young guy with a strong back, and I didn't mind hard work."

But after a while, the rest of the team started including Jim in the creative process...and it turned out to be a perfect fit. "We all fed off each other. One would come up with an idea, and the others would embellish it."

Display Step by Step

As the creative side of display took hold of Jim's imagination, the practical side taught him what he needed to know to succeed in the field. Every day was an education in the system and processes involved in display advertising at Gable's.

As Jim discovered, the initial planning related to display advertising came out of merchandising meetings. At those meetings, Mr. Pennypacker got the details on what merchandise was going to be featured in the different departments of the store and when. He also found out about any

Courtesy Jim Shannon

special sales or store-wide promotions that were scheduled. Based on that information, he developed what were called "window sheets"— paper forms on which the schedule of each window's contents was mapped out.

After Pennypacker finished the window sheets, he gave a copy of each to the buyer or merchandiser involved. Then, he gave copies to Anne and Isabelle, who picked up the merchandise needed from each department the next day. "If we had clothing on a window sheet, it would go to the alterations department for cleaning, if necessary," says Jim. "Then, our team went to work designing the window around the merchandise.

"The colors of the merchandise, the style of the merchandise, all these things would factor into what the window design would be. We would decide on what to use for backgrounds, like seamless paper.

"We had all different types of props and floor coverings. Everything had to fit together to make a great design. For example, we might have a background with an autumn rust color, with leaves falling a certain way because the mannequins would be dressed and positioned a certain way.

"We also had to incorporate window copy, the printed signs describing the merchandise and pricing details.

Window copy signs were prepared by the sign department, which printed them on a special press," says Jim.

With everything gathered together, the team set about assembling the displays. "One of us would be dressing mannequins. I would be picking up the props, and someone else would be preparing the props, getting them window-ready. Another person would be accessorizing the mannequins with jewelry, handbags, and shoes. We often used hats too, which were still in vogue back then, mind you."

Sunburned

As a display took shape, the team considered adding cosmetics on risers. Perfumes in their colorful, contoured bottles were especially good as visual

accents… except for one problem: the sun.

"In the summertime, the temperature in the windows would sometimes exceed 100 degrees," explains Jim. The hot sunlight could cause a noxious reaction in perfumes, so the team had to use lookalike fluid-filled bottles.

"Perfume manufacturers sent us what were called dummies," remembers Jim. "They looked like brand-name perfumes, but they were really just colored alcohol in labeled bottles."

Perfumes weren't the only problematic items when it came to the sun and high temperatures. "We always had to watch what we put in those windows. For example, we couldn't use anything made of wax, like candles. If we were going to do something with wax, we had to put it in one of the small entrance windows. Even then, we had to keep an eye on it."

Clothing used in the windows faded so much, it could not be resold as new. Props and backdrops faded as well, and had to be replaced.

Melting and fading from direct sunlight was such a problem, the window displays had to be changed often. Even without the need to update displays for sales and special events, the windows would have had to change every two weeks or so because of damage from sunlight, Jim says.

Case by Case Basis

In addition to the windows, the display team was responsible for the many cases and alcoves throughout the store. Usually Jim, Anne, and Isabelle worked on these on Saturdays, after the windows had been squared away for the week.

"The cases were on the ground floor of the Eleventh Avenue building," remembers Jim. "The alcoves were by the main elevator in men's furnishings. We also had a large alcove in the men's sportswear area, where a full-sized mannequin could be set up."

Then there was the ledgetop space on the Eleventh Avenue ground floor. "The ledgetop was only accessible by crawling up the bannister of the stairs going to the second floor, then pulling yourself, your props, and your merchandise over the ledgetop. You always had to work backwards up there, starting at the far wall and working toward the stairs, so you didn't paint yourself into a corner.

"When you were working on the ledge, you had quite a view," remembers Jim. "You could see the entire first floor of the Eleventh Avenue store. It was all very open because this was before the ceilings were lowered.

"You could see the remnants of the pneumatic tube system, and the remnants of the ceiling fans, which were the only air conditioning at Gable's for many years. I'll never forget that spectacular view."

The "Crappy" Care Package

As much as Jim loved Gable's, he eventually had to go back to school full-time to finish his college degree. He never lost touch with the display team, however, and got together with them on weekends when possible.

After graduating from Penn State, his love of display led him to a job as the trainee manager of display at Kaufmann's Department Store in Pittsburgh. Compared to Gable's, the display department was massive, with more than two dozen employees. "They had a display director and assistant display director, a manager of props…even someone who worked on artificial flowers 100 percent of the time," recalls Jim.

He learned a lot at the big city store, further honing his skills in the display field. He was ready for bigger and better things.

But then, in January of 1968, he was drafted and shipped off to Germany. It could have been worse, though, as the Vietnam War was in full swing.

And his teammates back at Gable's kept in contact and helped him over the rough spots. "When I was injured with a double hernia, they sent me a care package," he remembers. "There were poems, display props, even a nylon leg from the cosmetics department. Also a poem about Santa Claus delivering presents in the rain. And then there was the papier-mâché excrement with dead flies glued to it. The team's sense of humor was always there."

The Prodigal Jim

Jim came home from the service and returned to work in the display department at Gable's in February of 1970. Pennypacker hired him as assistant display director, but the old team wasn't the same anymore. Isabelle had taken a job at Gimbel's Department Store in Pittsburgh. Anne Wahl—who'd gotten married and become Anne Dixon—had moved to New Hampshire.

Jim got married too, in October 1970. His wife, Judy, also had been a Penn State student and Gable's employee, though she had moved on to work at the Bon Ton Department Store, which became Monarch's.

During Jim's stint as assistant display director, he had one artistic accomplishment that made an intimate connection with almost every Gable's customer. In fact, everyone with a Gable's charge account carried his work with them every time they visited the store.

"I designed the first plastic credit card for the company," says Jim. "It replaced the old metal charge plate in 1970.

"The plastic card was standard-sized, in line with cards from other businesses. I designed it with blue, gold, and white stripes, like Gable's shopping bags. Those colors had been in use at the store since the 50s. Everyone in Altoona could immediately identify that look as belonging to Gable's. If you saw someone with those colors on a bag, you knew they were shopping at Gable's. Same for the card.

"Numerous other ideas for the design were presented, but mine was the one that was chosen. It was used until L.S. Good decided to change it to the maroon background with the Gable's name on it," says Jim.

In spite of his success on the job, Gable's wasn't quite so great for Jim this time around. As a married man, he wasn't as happy with the pay as he'd once been. He also grew dissatisfied with the lack of health insurance and retirement, so he started fishing for a new job elsewhere.

When a job at a petroleum farm in East Freedom fell through in 1972, Jim was hired by Tom Wolf of Wolf Furniture as assistant decorator for all their stores. After five months with Wolf, however, Jim heard about a new opportunity at his old stomping grounds: Mr. Pennypacker was leaving Gable's for a job at an L.S. Good store in Michigan.

As a known quantity with extensive Gable's display department experience, Jim was a shoe-in for the job. President Powers hired him back, and he became the director of display at Gable's department store.

Jim was running the show now, attending meetings and handling budgets and scheduling, but all that didn't keep him from getting back in the creative spirit. The design techniques and artistic flair came right back to him. He still had some tricks up his sleeve.

Strobe This, Peel That

Yes, there were groovy black light strobes in some of Gable's windows. They were just one of a multitude of flashy flourishes that Jim used to grab attention for the merchandise on display.

"The black light strobe fit with the style that existed in the 70s, when bellbottoms were the

rage," remembers Jim. "In display, you always have to go with the times and styles."

The black light strobes were difficult to make, given the technology of the times. "Black lights were fluorescent, and it was hard to have fluorescent tubing in a strobe light," says Jim. "But someone found a way to make it for us, and we used it at Gable's."

Another of Jim's special touches was the use of peel-away paint applied to the windows. "Since the name brand Peel Paint

was so expensive, at $150 per gallon, I came up with my own concoction. I added Elmer's glue and magic color paint chips, and I had it mixed in the paint department on the fourth floor.

"When the peel-away paint was ready, I slopped it on the window, then drew on it. Next, I scored the lines I'd drawn, remembering that I'd be taking away what I didn't want to be seen. Finally, I'd peel off sections, leaving the rest of the image intact."

The peel-away technique added an extra dimension to displays, projecting design elements in a layer on the glass that served as a framework for the mannequins, props, and other components behind it. Jim especially enjoyed the results when he used peel-away on display windows marking the U.S. Bicentennial in 1976.

In fact, the whole Bicentennial celebration was a highlight of his time as display director of Gable's. It also was the last major event of his Gable's career.

Store and Stripes

To mark the Bicentennial, Jim broke out plenty of red, white, and blue. As the Fourth of July, 1976 drew nearer, patriotic decorations filled the windows, cases, alcoves, and walls.

But Gable's Bicentennial celebration was unique because of the focus on local craftspeople and historians, not just a parade of bargains. "We invited seamstresses, quilters, silversmiths, and all kinds of craftspeople to come to the store to create and sell their wares," remembers Jim. "We brought in historical societies, too. The emphasis was on the arts and crafts of colonial times.

181

All Courtesy Jim Shannon

"We didn't charge them any kind of fee or percentage of sales. We set them up, showed them hospitality, and provided display backgrounds. All they had to do was show up on schedule. If they sold anything, it was between them and the customers," says Jim.

A fashion show with a Bicentennial theme also was part of the festivities. Jim projected slides of national parks and monuments on a screen behind the models—one of whom was his infant daughter, a babe in arms at the time.

"We had lots of fashion shows that year," recalls Jim. "For a while in 1976, there was a fashion show every other week. They required a lot of work too. We had to set up runways, backdrops, lights, props, you name it. But people loved them."

Goodbye, Farewell

Between the many special displays and decorations, the marketplace for craftspeople, and the patriotic fashion shows, the Bicentennial was a big success for Gable's and Jim. But by the time the echoes of the fireworks had faded, he was getting restless again. His earnings and benefits still weren't meeting the needs of his young family.

When a former co-worker told Jim about the great pay and benefits he was getting with the railroad, Jim decided to try

that route if the opportunity arose. A job did come up in 1977, and Jim left Gable's again. "The railroad job was too good to pass up. I would take a cut in pay, but I would more than make up for that in benefits," says Jim.

This time, when he left Gable's, he never went back. He started at the railroad as a laborer, then became a machinist, and eventually rose through the ranks to become a senior industrial engineer.

But he never completely severed his ties with his co-workers at the department store, right up until it closed in 1980. Even then, he played a role in the story of Gable's. Informed by friends of the impending closure of the store in 1980, he spread the word to the media. "I had the dubious honor of being the first to notify WFBG that Gable's was going to close," he says. "The next morning, the press was at the doors of the store to meet the president, who confirmed the story."

To this day, Jim keeps up with his friends from Gable's. He and his wife, Judy, still visit and vacation with Anne and Jim Dixon and see Isabelle Nardelli during the holidays each year.

Looking back, he still fondly remembers his years at Gable's. "I don't think there was a bad time had by any of us working together. Everyone in the other departments of the store knew everyone in display and was very supportive of us. It was a family store, and the workers were the Gable family.

"I'm just sorry it wasn't more profitable than the railroad, or I never would have left."

MEMORY DEPARTMENT

In the 60s, the store was busy and exciting. The lovely part about retailing, especially in Gable's, was that every week, a buyer would have a meeting with his or her sales staff. They would talk about what merchandise was going in, what the selling points were, its features, and how good it was. So, whenever there was a customer, the sales clerk would say, for example, "Look, you have double-stitching on this item." They knew about the features. It was generally one-on-one. Customers love that.

When it was really busy, there was always one person at each register, and more than one register per department. You didn't have centralized checkout like you do today. The person at the register would ring you up, and meantime, there would be

salespeople on the floor. It was called "customer relations," and people loved it. People learned each salesperson's first name. They would say, "Where's Rose today? I wanted to see Rose."

The salespeople were very well-educated about all the merchandise in the department. It was one of the features of the Gable's store that made it such an enjoyable place to shop.

If you find someone who remembers the store, they will say they miss it, but it's not the

Courtesy Jim Shannon

store per se they miss. It's the personal contact they had with the personnel. Today, in retail, just *try* to find a salesperson when you need one.

Jim Shannon

Gable's memories for me were the sights and smells of the store. There was a fresh roasted nut stand as you came in off Eleventh Avenue, and there was a shoe repair shop in the basement. Of course, I remember the display windows at night, especially during Christmas holidays. Then there was Gable's pet shop, which was the first place I ever saw exotic birds and monkeys.

Once, I dated a girl who worked in the Record Shop. The first eight-track tape player for the house I owned came from there.

George Rowles

183

My husband and I bought our very first bedroom furniture at Gable's after we got married back in 1971. I gave it to my daughter when she got married, and it still looked great! It was good quality furniture, made in the USA!
Marge Caputo

When my dad went to work at Gable's on a Sunday, he would take me with him. We would park on Twelfth Avenue by the main entrance, and there was a doorbell in the upper left hand corner on the door frame. He would pick me up so I could ring it, and a maintenance or security employee would come and let us in. The button is still there to this day.
Bucky Deichert

I was on Gable's Junior Fashion Board from 1976 to 1977. We did five fashion shows a year, and at Christmas, we dressed as elves and served the kids during Breakfast with Santa in the basement restaurant.
Sherri Naugle Herleman

Courtesy Jim Shannon

Courtesy Jim Shannon

My wedding gown was purchased at Gable's in February 1974. Forty-two years later, I still have my gown and the Gable's bag it came in! And I'm still married! I loved shopping at Gable's.
Robin Garber Ritchey

My father was employed at a business "intown" (meaning in the Downtown Business District of Altoona), and he would frequently walk to Gable's on his lunch break. It was Easter time 1973, and rather than give their children the typical Easter critters (bunnies, chicks, or ducks) my mom and dad decided that they would get us gerbils. Well, our dad purchased two gerbils for us kids from the pet department in Gable's store. My brother and I were thrilled! I was nine years old, and my brother was seven, and we were about to get a crash course on the birds and the bees. You see, as luck would have it, dad had brought home a male and a female. We had plenty of gerbils after those two (their names were George and Tillie) had reproduced over and over.

When we ran out of friends and neighbors who wanted gerbils of their own, our parents decided, in an agreement with the Gable's department store, to return George and Tillie to the store, where they would become the store's breeding pair, living out their lives in the pet department and doing what they did best! My brother and I, of course, always raced up to the pet department first thing to check on them each time we went into the department store. I guess we just eventually grew content that they were happy and well cared for, and so were my brother and I, and we all lived happily ever after! Including George and Tillie's offspring, whom we kept as our pets after the adults were relocated to the store. We made sure they were the same gender that time!
Nancy Carney

Chapter Nineteen

Another Brick in the Wall

1971

The original exteriors of the Gable's buildings would probably never be seen again. Those classic lines were being hidden away forever. The rows of windows above the first floor—*all those windows*—would be permanently sealed in the dark. So much for "The Daylight Store."

Everybody knew all this as the brick walls rose around the store buildings on Eleventh and Twelfth Avenues…as layer by layer, they accrued, like sand dunes in a desert. Everybody knew exactly what was happening, but nobody stood in the way. After all, it was modernization, wasn't it? An *improvement*.

More than that, it was part of the redevelopment of downtown Altoona. It was the leading edge of an effort to reshape the downtown area so it could compete with suburban shopping malls and business parks.

Who could argue with a project like that?

Laying the Groundwork

The $500,000 project had been announced by President Bob Powers in 1969. Clifford Hayes of Campbell, Rea, Hayes, and Large was the architect. J.C. Orr and Son, the same outfit that had built the Arcade Parking Center, was the contractor.

Though the project was planned for early 1970, it didn't get rolling until the following year. It was then, in April 1971, that the way was cleared for work to begin. The last delay was removed on April 15, when Altoona City Council adopted a new ordinance allowing Gable's to encroach on city rights-of-way. This was necessary because the new walls would be built outside the old ones, requiring ten inches of additional space all around.

With the ordinance granted, work got underway on Tuesday, June 1, 1971.

Workmen started by putting up temporary structures to protect the public along Eleventh and Twelfth Avenues and Fourteenth Street—scaffolds, canopies, covered walkways, and the like. Several metered parking spaces along the affected streets were blocked off for the duration of the project as well.

If everything went smoothly, it would all be done in time for the Christmas shopping season. In the meantime, Orr and Son said they would keep any inconvenience to a minimum.

The construction zone "may be somewhat of a mess while steel is being erected," said Joseph H. Orr Jr. of Orr and Son. He didn't expect any interference with traffic on Eleventh or Twelfth Avenues, however.

Meanwhile, renovations were continuing inside the store too, as part of the overhaul launched during the 85th anniversary year in 1969. Workers still needed to finish lowering ceilings, relocating several departments, and installing carpeting and lighting fixtures.

By the time it was all done, Gable's would be like a brand-new store, inside and out. It would be remade for the 1970s and beyond...assuming it survived that long.

The Great Walls of Gable's

As the days and weeks unfolded, Orr and Son's workers implemented the plan to conceal Gable's original exterior. They started with the Twelfth Avenue building, jackhammering the sidewalks along the base of the walls to cut space for the insertion of footers and steel beams.

Next, they built and scaled tubular scaffolding to cut away cornices that would have gotten in the way of the new façade. They poured footers and raised the steel beams that would serve as the supporting framework of the walls.

Originally, the walls were supposed to be clad with anodized aluminum—but plans changed as the project advanced. Instead of aluminum, the new sheathing would consist of "hand-molded Colonial brick, accented with limestone columns."

Flemish-type projected headers on the bricks would give the walls a more textured appearance. Aluminum would still play a role in the design, however, as canopies made of the metal would be installed over all-new entrances.

To cover the 25,555 square feet of storefront on both buildings, the crew would need approximately 230,000 bricks. The amount of mortar must have been equally astronomical...and the backbreaking labor of loading, lifting, and laying them? You do the math.

It was a massive undertaking in every way, a demonstration of retail and municipal might rallying to restore the vitality of the downtown business district. And it was carefully calculated and executed to not interfere with the flow of commerce at Gable's or any other downtown establishments.

Photo by Fred Deichert

Photo by Fred Deichert

Would these great walls be worth it in the end? Would they keep the customers coming through the doors, spending freely in the store as they had for decades? If not, it wouldn't be for lack of trying. Whom do you think the whole project was aimed at, after all?

"Most important is the fact that this investment is being made for the convenience of our customers, who are—and have always been—responsible for the success of the store," said Bob Powers. "We want a convenient store for the pleasure of our customers. A complete store, with a complete stock and complete shopping pleasure for our customers."

City officials had a bigger picture in mind, one in which Gable's inspired other businesses to pony up for renovations. "It shows the Gable Co. faith in downtown Altoona, and will be an encouragement for other businessmen who plan to rehabilitate their downtown stores," said Assistant Executive Director Jack Harkless of the Redevelopment Authority.

Built Like a Brick House

Once the project got started, it quickly gained momentum. Workmen faced the steel beams around the Twelfth Avenue building with limestone columns. They installed the new entrances with their aluminum canopies. And they laid the brick, of course—enough brick to build the Great Pyramids of Giza, or at least that's how it seemed.

Photo by Nadine Shade

Orr and Son finished the Twelfth Avenue building in September and moved on to the Eleventh Avenue structure. The same design and materials were used, ensuring that both buildings would match perfectly.

Again, sidewalks were jackhammered, footers poured, scaffolding built. Steel was raised, limestone columns erected, brick laid.

Little by little, the original exterior of the classic building disappeared behind brick walls. Drivers

and pedestrians paused on their way past, taking long, last looks at the vanishing features, the changing face of the monument to their shared history.

With one building completely encased and the other close behind, did the looky-loos have second thoughts about the project? As the reality and permanence of the change hit home, did they experience regrets? Who can say?

But wouldn't you, if you were them?

Wall to Wall Change

The full renovation of Gable's, inside and out, wasn't finished until the spring of the following year. A ribbon-cutting ceremony marked the completion on May 9, 1972.

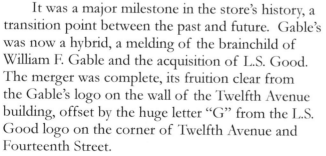

It was a major milestone in the store's history, a transition point between the past and future. Gable's was now a hybrid, a melding of the brainchild of William F. Gable and the acquisition of L.S. Good. The merger was complete, its fruition clear from the Gable's logo on the wall of the Twelfth Avenue building, offset by the huge letter "G" from the L.S. Good logo on the corner of Twelfth Avenue and Fourteenth Street.

Gable's had become something new. The new era was underway, the old guard gone or on its way out.

As if to emphasize this point, Robert Gable died on Dec. 29, 1971. The former company president bowed out just a few months before the grand premiere of the newly renovated Gable's.

Ironically, his tribute in the *Altoona Mirror* lauded him for embracing change...the very thing his passing helped to underscore. "He was a man of vital imagination and a man of action, and for him the word 'change,' so popular today, had a very positive meaning," according to the *Mirror*. "It was not change for change's sake that intrigued him, but new and better ways of doing things, new methods."

Photo by Philip Balko

The original family triumvirate that had dominated Gable's during its formative years—Robert; his brother, George; and their father, William—was now gone for good. Time had swept them away, leaving the power in new hands.

And those hands had spent a million bucks building walls and renovating the store's interior.

Photo by Fred Deichert

Writing on the Walls

Downtown Altoona looked a lot different, all of a sudden. Instead of the whitewashed, window-laden façades of classic Gable's, twin brick-walled structures occupied the heart of the business district.

It was all so new and different, but was that a good thing? Had the business leaders and municipal officials been wise in covering the familiar structures with unfamiliar shells?

The old-fashioned architecture of the original buildings was yesterday's news, wasn't it? People wanted shiny, streamlined structures nowadays that spoke of new aesthetics and technologies. To salvage something from the past, the least they could do was disguise it as something of the future. Encase it in brick walls, hiding their grandparents' block and wood and glass where it wouldn't do any harm.

As if that could stave off the storm that was coming... the shakeout that would settle things once and for all. Suburbs versus downtown. Old-time department stores versus newfangled malls.

As if the classic lines and *all those windows* they were locking away forever weren't treasures themselves. As if those very things, managed creatively, could not have been the saving graces everyone was seeking back then.

As if the writing wasn't already on the walls even as the workmen erected them.

Photo by Nadine Shade

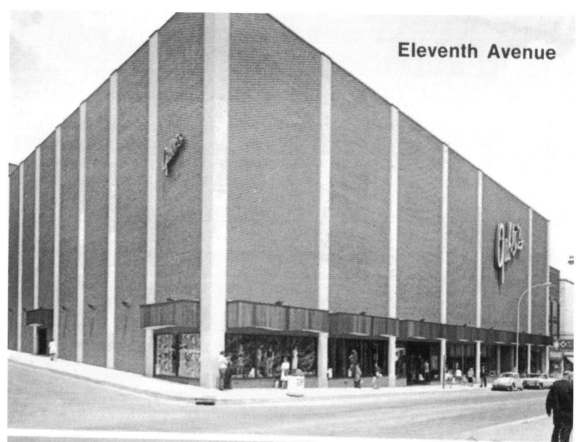

Eleventh Avenue

Twelfth Avenue

Courtesy Jeffery Holland

Memory Department

I remember in the 70s, when I was six or seven years old, that Gable's would give out keys to a treasure chest when you bought something. The chest was located on the second floor by a staircase. I would sit on the staircase and watch people bring their keys and try to open the lock to get a gift envelope from the chest.

Bucky Deichert

Around 1977, I worked at the candy counter in the mezzanine for a while. When I started, they told me to eat all the candy I wanted. I thought, *wow!* But after two weeks of sampling the candy, I couldn't look at it and did not sample any more of it. They sure knew what they were doing!

Kathy Carey

I remember walking across the street in our choir robes from First Lutheran church and singing Christmas carols on the stairs in Gable's. We sang four or five songs, and the applause afterward was awesome. This was in the 70s.

Gable's always had beautiful Christmas decorations. It's sad to see every time I come home to Altoona and see Gable's as an office building versus a flourishing department store. I miss the old downtown, don't you?

Sharon Adams

The rock band Piranha played in Gable's for their fashion show in 1977!

Lane Williamson

The display department helped with the floats for the annual Christmas parade. The carpenter at Gable's helped with constructing one of my designs for a float. We built an eaved roof with a chimney, and Santa waved at everybody from inside of it, rather than riding a traditional sleigh.

Jim Shannon

There was a dress code at Gable's back in the day. In the men's furnishings department, the salesmen had to wear slacks, a shirt, and a tie every day. In the suit department, they pretty much wore suits every day. Women had nice slacks, nice tops, and some of them wore blazers or nice dresses. Back then, people wore dresses and skirts and blouses in the workplace.

Jamie Powers

All Courtesy David Seidel

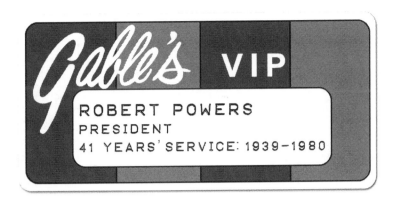

Could there have been a better steward of Gable's department store than Bob Powers?

After working at Gable's since 1939, Bob knew and loved every inch of the store. He was a grandson of the founder, William F. Gable himself, and a true believer in his retail management techniques. Like William and his sons, Robert and George, he was committed to public service and giving back to the community. He was a business school graduate, a Navy veteran, and a family man with deep roots in Altoona and Blair County.

That was why, when W. Stanley Truby retired in 1968, it seemed only natural that Bob would replace him as president. Having a man in the corner office with Gable blood, Gable style, and an appreciation for Gable's rich history seemed like an excellent plan that would pay great dividends.

And it did, at least until 1980, when there was suddenly no store left for him to be president of.

Powers' Source

Bob was born on May 19, 1920, to James Henry Powers and Edna Gable Powers, one of William F. Gable's daughters. Raised in Pottstown, Pa., he graduated from the Hill School, a prestigious prep school in the area.

After that came the move to Altoona and his first stint at Gable's. He joined the firm as a salesman in the men's furnishings department in 1939—then stepped away to serve in the U.S. Navy during World War II.

Stationed in Panama, Bob was a chief petty officer and radio man, working with short wave radio. He served from 1942-1944, then got his discharge and came back to Pennsylvania.

Following his Navy tour of duty, Bob attended the School of Retailing at the University of Pittsburgh. During his summer breaks, he returned to Altoona and worked part-time at Gable's.

After graduation in 1946, he went to work full-time at the store. He also got married and started a family.

All Courtesy Jamie Powers

He and his wife, Caroline, would eventually have five children: Pamela, Jamie, Stacy, Caroline, and Robert Jr.

Bob's post-Navy Gable's career would continue uninterrupted until the closing of the store in 1980. During this span of 34 years, he worked his way up from a sales job to the top of the company.

Rise to Power

Bouncing between various positions, Bob became Gable's credit manager in 1951. He moved to assistant treasurer in 1961, then full secretary-treasurer in 1964. After that, in August 1967, he was promoted to executive vice president.

In April 1968, shortly after the sale of Gable's on March 31, Bob became a director of L.S. Good and Co. It was a condition of the sale, meant to ensure a role at L.S. Good and Gable's for a member of the Gable family. The four key stockholders behind the sale— Gertrude (Gable) Patterson, Virginia (Gable) Norton, Florence (Gable) Parsons, and Ann (Gable) Ford, all sisters of George and Robert Gable—had agreed to accept L.S. Good's offer as long as Bob was made a Good director, promoted to president of Gable's, and guaranteed a pension.

On Feb. 1, 1969, L.S. Good held up its end of the deal. The Good board of directors offered the presidency of Gable's to Bob, and he accepted.

The Powers era had begun...or, rather, the Good/Powers era. Bob might have been president, but L.S. Good still owned the William F. Gable Co.

According to L.S. Good, Gable's would enjoy a great deal of autonomy. Syd and Larry Good said that was how they ran the other stores in the company, and they weren't planning to change that with Gable's.

But in the end, whatever autonomy the Goods offered was limited. L.S. Good could still do whatever they wanted with Gable's... and Bob's plans and actions still had to meet with their approval.

None of that changes one simple fact, though: Bob presided over some of the biggest improvements in Gable's history.

The Height of His Powers

During Bob's first years as president, he led the million-dollar renovation project that dramatically upgraded the interior and exterior of Gable's. Faced with the rising threat of the Logan Valley Mall and other suburban shopping centers, Bob and the Goods created a rejuvenated store, a redesigned "vertical mall" with air conditioning, drop ceilings, new carpeting, and extensive updates that could hopefully hold its own against the competition. The buildings, with their streamlined, modern-looking brick-and-limestone casings, became the inspirational symbol of redevelopment in the 70s in downtown Altoona.

Courtesy Anne Dixon

In the years that followed, Bob worked hard to keep Gable's viable by keeping merchandise quality high and prices low in spite of economic pressures like inflation and the energy crisis. He advertised heavily and continued traditional special events like the Anniversary Sale.

Bob also worked with business organizations to share ideas, network with resources, and encourage favorable conditions in the business climate that benefitted all retailers. He served on the boards of the Pennsylvania Retailers Association, the Keystone Group, the Altoona Chamber of Commerce, Altoona Enterprises, the Altoona Parking Authority, and the downtown Altoona Merchants Association.

Perhaps most importantly, he continued to emphasize investing in human capital instead of a profit-focused approach to management. For example, when revenues dipped, he found ways to cut overhead costs instead of cutting wages and jobs. Switching off one panel of lights on each floor of both buildings reduced the electric bill by $10,000 over the course of a year, enabling Bob to redirect the savings to pay staff.

His efforts seemed to pay off. According to his son, Jamie, Gable's was still in the black in the late 70s, with more than 800,000 deposits in the bank. Of L.S. Good's 14 stores, only Gable's was still profitable by 1980, says Jamie.

Power Loss

But somehow, when financial woes swept through Good, the hammer fell on Gable's first. William F. Gable and Co. was forced into bankruptcy, and the store closed, four years shy of its hundredth anniversary.

And all of it happened on Bob's watch. He ended up with the dubious distinction of being the last president of Gable and Co. Imagine how that must have felt, as he tied up one loose end after another to shut down the store and company. Imagine, years later, how it must have felt to look back, always knowing he'd been the one in the corner office when his grandfather's creation went down for good...even though he'd done everything he could to save it. Even though the blows that had wrecked it had been beyond his control, inflicted by the owners and their associates.

How heavy a burden that must have been to bear. If he were here today, what could we say to him to lighten that load? "We know you tried your best"? "You did everything you could"?

Or how about this? "You would have made your grandfather proud." Because perhaps Bob's greatest achievement was keeping up the legacy of William F. Gable, treating people with respect and equanimity.

"He believed that if you took care of your employees, they took care of your customers," remembers Jamie. "And if you mistreated the customer, you were in serious trouble. Because that whole store was all about the customers. The customers were always right, no questions asked.

"That was always Gable's philosophy, and Dad never strayed from it," says Jamie. "He believed in honoring his fellow man, just like William, Robert, and George Gable did."

Powerful Moments

One of Bob's ambitions had been to lead Gable's to its hundredth anniversary in 1984. Only then would he retire and hand the dynasty to Jamie.

Bob didn't reach that goal, because Gable's collapsed in 1980. His retirement came early, and the company fell short of its centennial celebration.

But he still managed to mark the occasion with the rest of his Gable's family. Bob, Jamie, and many other former Gable's employees and VIPs got together in 1984 for one last anniversary party for the store—a hundredth birthday party in the Logan Room of the Penn Alto Hotel in memory of the late, great Gable's. It was called "An Evening to Remember," and was attended by 150 colleagues from the William F. Gable Co.

Did Bob hug one comrade-in-arms after another that night? Did he laugh with his fellow Gable's folk at all the stories and jokes about the old days before the closing of the store? Did he raise his glass again and again, so many times it made his arm ache, in toast after toast to the glory of Gable's?

As the last surviving president of the company, did he have tears in his eyes more than a few times that glorious night?

What do *you* think?

Chapter Twenty

The Quiet Countdown

1973-1979

As the 1970s drifted past, did anyone realize they were counting down the years until the end of Gable's? Or were they lulled into a false sense of security by a period of calm and stability at the store?

The latter is closest to the truth. Why worry if things were going smoothly?

In the wake of the internal and external renovations of 1969-1972, things settled into a state of peace and quiet at Gable's. To the typical customer or employee, it must have seemed like business was going fine, and their beloved store was sailing in calm seas.

But dangers were building under the surface. Storm clouds were massing just over the horizon.

The end was near.

Maybe it's for the best that most folks didn't know until it was too late. At least they had those last few years to enjoy their time at Gable's. At least they had time to make some more memories before their favorite store was gone for good.

The Century Mark

As Gable's cruised through the 70s, people knew they could rely on certain things: Dave Little would give them a hearty greeting when they walked in the door; the malts and bobwhites in the basement snack bar were out-of-this-world delicious; the window displays at Christmastime were marvelous; and there would be an anniversary sale every year, complete with hoopla and fantastic bargains galore.

The sales were held later now, in August instead of the traditional March 1, but they seemed a little more special each year. Because each fresh anniversary took Gable's closer to the fabled century mark—the 100th anniversary of its founding.

The final decade-long countdown to the 100th was inaugurated on Aug. 15, 1974, when the 90th anniversary sale kicked into gear. Once again, the usual horde of bargains and attractions was featured, and the Treasure Chest of Prizes was part of the party. Shoppers could get a free key in any department, then try it in the locked chest on the third floor of the Eleventh Avenue building. If the key opened the lock, the lucky shopper who possessed it would have more than 700 prizes in the chest to choose from, including a $500 paid-up charge account.

A year later, on Aug. 14, 1975, the 91st anniversary celebration commenced. This time, the 24-day sale would feature "a whole new world of values in all merchandise lines," according to President Powers. "It is truly a million-dollar promotion."

Raymond Crouss, vice president and general merchandise manager at Gable's, said it would be the biggest anniversary sale ever. "I think we have succeeded in putting together an exciting sales event," he said. "The store is just full of back-to-school, back-to-work, and back-to-college values."

Offering so much merchandise at bargain prices was a factor of Gable's relationship to its latest owners, according to Powers. "Being a member of the L.S. Good & Co. group, which now comprises 14 stores in the leading cities in five states, we have the ability to purchase quality merchandise at tremendous savings. We like to share these savings with our customers."

The emphasis, as always, would remain firmly on customer satisfaction. "Then, too, there is Gable's time-honored and written policy that our customers are always No. 1 in our table of organization. It is an assurance that each of our customers can buy from us with the utmost confidence," said Powers.

A Vertical Mall

The year 1976 was all about the U.S. Bicentennial, and Gable's had its share of patriotic festivities. One such event, American Heritage Bicentennial Week, ran from May 10 through May 14 and featured Senior Citizens' Day, 4-H Day, Armed Forces Day, Blair County Day, and Altoona Day. Each special day featured displays, presentations, demonstrations, and entertainment, revolving around a Bicentennial theme.

Patriotism was front and center every day in the lead-up to the grand finale on the Fourth of July. Red, white, and blue decorations filled the store, and window displays were dominated by the Spirit of '76. Local craftspeople were set up throughout the store, often in period costume, demonstrating and selling arts and crafts from the Colonial era. Fashion shows included patriotic imagery and tie-ins. The restaurant in the basement Budget Store served Bicentennial Sweet Specials for 59 cents each, and deep dish hot apple pie with ice cream was offered daily. What could be more American?

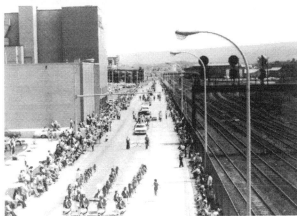

When the fireworks were all over, and Bicentennial fever had run its course, Gable's got back to basics. The anniversary sale was still the cornerstone of its retail year, and Gable's did not disappoint. The 92nd anniversary sale in August 1976 was huge, with loads of new merchandise in stock throughout the store. "We are extremely proud and excited about the new line of fall fashions in our multimillion-dollar inventory," said President Powers. "And we will again feature our traditional Treasure Chest, which will have more than 800 gift items. The prizes will include five $100 paid-up charges."

The 93rd anniversary also was a hit in 1977, bigger and better across the board. The 94th anniversary in August 1978 was massive too, and heavily promoted with lots of advertising and front-page coverage in the *Mirror*.

But that very coverage hinted at the troubles to come, mentioning that downtown retailers were facing "increasing competition from malls and chains." According to the *Mirror*, Gable's had risen to the challenge with its big renovation project in 1969-1972, introducing its new exterior as well as air conditioning, new lighting, carpeting, and drop ceilings. Gable's had become "a vertical mall," containing such amenities as "a beauty salon, shoe repair shop, restaurant, photography studio, and just about anything a shopper needs in the way of clothing, furniture, and household wares."

All Courtesy Jim Shannon

Photo by Red Hildebrand

But the "vertical mall" didn't have as much life left in it as people thought. Gable's days were numbered, and the sound of its downfall was just starting to rise.

By 1979, it would be impossible to ignore. The full implications of what was coming would not be obvious at first, but everyone would suddenly realize the state of Gable's was not as steady as they thought it was.

L.S. Good Sells Gable's...or Does It?

How's this for a bombshell? "L.S. Good Sells Gable's." That was the headline on page 21 of the *Altoona Mirror* for Saturday, March 10, 1979.

Talk about a bolt from the blue! There had been no previous news of such a sale leading up to the story. As far as anyone outside Gable's upper management knew, it had just been business as usual at the store. In fact, they'd just marked the store's 95th anniversary date nine days earlier on March 1—just five years from the century mark.

And now *this*. Just like *that*.

Here's how the lead paragraph read: "The William F. Gable Co. at 1318 11th Ave., the city's largest department store, has been purchased by the trustees of a New York holding company, according to records in the office of Blair County Register and Recorder James F. Shuman."

Then came paragraph two: "The Main Realty Holding Trust, with offices in Great Neck, Long Island, has purchased Gables for $3,851,000."

Next came more information about the trust that had apparently bought Gable's from L.S. Good. "The Main Realty Holding Trust is a group of individuals who handle the funds of a union pension system, possibly the Teamsters Union. The funds for the union pension are administered through the Leigh Company, 287 Northern Blvd., Great Neck."

Didn't leave much room for misunderstanding, did it? And the details that followed just hammered home the truth of the tale. "According to attorney (James) Routch in Hollidaysburg, the L.S. Good Company of Wheeling, W. Va., which owned the stock of the Gable Co. for several years, and which in January purchased the building, needed to improve its cash flow and thus decided to sell 2 of its 10 stores, the stores in Altoona and Binghamton, N.Y."

Seemed pretty cut and dry, right? Gable's had been *sold*. Ownership of the store had changed hands.

Or had it? Two later paragraphs added an element of confusion. They didn't seem to fit with the rest of the story. "Mr. Routch said Gable's in Altoona will now be leased back to the L.S. Good Co. so that actual management operations of the store won't change.

'Nothing is changing except the ownership,' attorney Routch said."

Which begged the question, *Huh?* Based on those two paragraphs, it seemed as if the store had been sold, then somehow leased back to L.S. Good, which would continue to operate it.

Clearly, the elements of the *Mirror* story didn't all jibe. So which were true, which were false, and where exactly did the facts of the situation lie?

Imagine the gossip that must have run rampant through Altoona and all of Blair County after that story hit the paper. Imagine how wild the speculation must have gotten as folks tried to figure it out for themselves. Imagine how many questions they asked over the phone or in person at the Gable's department store as they tried to get to the bottom of the contradictory news coverage.

Imagine all that, and you'll understand why the *Mirror* issued a reassuring clarification two days later.

At least, it was *supposed* to be reassuring.

Gable's Not Sold, Just the Building(s)

Maybe the word "reassuring" is a bit strong when considering the headline in the follow-up story in the *Mirror*. "Gable's Not Sold, Just the Building." What about the first line of the story that followed? "Rest assured, Gable's has not been sold!"

Not exactly a great comfort, was it? It was more like a "good news, bad news" piece. The good news is, Gable's department store has not been sold. The bad news is, the buildings in which the store is located *have* been sold.

Just five years out from the company's hundredth anniversary, the buildings had been sold right out from under the store. Would this news be more likely to make you sigh with relief and relax, or keep worrying about the fate of your favorite department store?

President Powers was in favor of relaxing. "We've been in business 95 years," he said. "We have every intention of continuing indefinitely to serve the Altoona market." Sidney Good, chairman of the board of the William F. Gable Co., agreed.

But still…they had *sold the buildings*.

According to the new article, the buildings housing Gable's department store had indeed been sold as indicated in the original *Mirror* piece, but the stores and their contents remained the property of L.S. Good and would stay that way. L.S. Good had signed a new 20-year lease with the new owners and would continue to operate the store in its existing buildings for at least that long. The owners of Gable's expected "to be serving customers in downtown Altoona in 1999 and beyond."

So nothing was changing, really. President Powers said that "the policies and merchandise which have existed down through 95 years of operation will continue to be in effect for the next 20 years at least. Gable's plans to celebrate the turn of the century with Blair County."

Furthermore, this was a *good* thing, a commitment to Altoona. That's what Powers and Attorney Routch emphasized. Gable's was staying put for the next two decades, at least.

There was nothing to worry about. Nothing to see here. Nothing was changing or about to change for the worse, not really. We now return you to your regularly scheduled program.

Otherwise known as "the last days of Gable's department store."

Not that there were many of them left, as it turned out.

Courtesy Jim Shannon

ALTOONA MIRROR, ALTOONA, PA., THURSDAY, JUNE 13, 1974 ....Mirror Classified Ads....Phone 944-7171

a special friendship

THE GABLE STORE IN 1884

THEN

When "Gable and Company" opened the doors of its tiny 20x40-foot store on March 1, 1884, The Evening Mirror, as it was then called, was almost ten years old.

The Altoona of that time was a far cry from the city that I have on the 100th year celebration of the Altoona Mirror. Instead of miles of well-paved streets, the long blocks of 11th Avenue between 12th-13th Street were the only bit of paving the city could boast. The remainder of the streets were ordinary mud roads, and it was not an uncommon sight, even on 11th Avenue, to see wagons stalling hub deep in the muck.

But the city grew, as did the Gable store and the Altoona Mirror . . . so much so that in October, 1884, seven months after Gable's opened, the store moved to larger quarters where it continued to grow at such a rapid pace that in 1892 it was again necessary to find newer and larger facilities. This time it located at 1320-22 11th Avenue, which was a small portion of the present site.

Its friend, the Altoona Mirror, was also growing . . . from its birthplace at 11th Avenue and 12th Street it too outgrew several sites before it finally located at its present site, 1000 Green Avenue, in 1912.

FIRST MIRROR PLANT 1874

12th AVENUE BUILDING OF GABLE'S, REMODELED 1972

NOW

Needless to say this final locations were not the end of the growth. In the intervening years, Gable's has grown to be Central Pennsylvania's largest department store with the merchandise in any one department surpassing the total contents of the store on opening day 90 years ago, with a 14-store buying power of almost 100 million dollars.

Its friend, the Altoona Mirror, has grown too . . . from a little 4-column 4 page newspaper with a circulation of 625 to a newspaper with a press capacity of up to 80 pages and a circulation of over 36,000. And with the help of the community we will both continue to grow.

GREEN AVENUE SECTION OF THE PRESENT ALTOONA MIRROR

11th AVENUE SECTION OF GABLE'S, REMODELED 1972

In tribute to the 100th Anniversary of the Altoona Mirror, we can think of no better way to say "thank you"...It hasn't been just the growth of a business, but it has been the growth of a special friendship . . . between a department store and a newspaper.

Gable's

Courtesy Altoona Mirror

Courtesy Jim Shannon

Courtesy Jim Shannon

MEMORY DEPARTMENT

Every year, the first Friday after Thanksgiving was known as "One Hundred Thousand Dollar Day" at Gable's. We called it that because that's what it used to be in the old days, though we actually did around 500 to 600 thousand dollars in business by the late 60s and 70s. Everybody on staff wore special ribbons that day, and we promoted the heck out of it. We ran 14-15 pages of advertising in the *Altoona Mirror*...5-6 pages in the Johnstown *Tribune-Democrat*...and 6-8 pages in the *Centre Daily Times*. We ran commercials on every TV station and all the radio stations in the region, too.

Then, on the Sunday after Thanksgiving, 50-75 managers and key employees would come in and work with the display department to decorate the entire store for Christmas. That's when it was done every year at Gable's department store.
Jamie Powers

I cried every year because my father made me go to breakfast with Santa in the restaurant, and I was deathly afraid of Santa Claus at that age. Santa would come around to each table and say "Merry Christmas" to us, but it was only kids and no adults at the table. I had no one to run and cry to so I had to sit by myself in total fear!
Bucky Deichert

Gable's was where I got my first job right out of college. I worked in the cosmetics department. Actually, I was the last one hired, so when they were going to close, I was the first to be laid off. I remember the Christmas party they had at the Penn Alto Hotel.
Sue Masic

I remember being in Gable's and getting a free blood pressure screening. Shortly after mine, a man was told that he needed to contact his doctor immediately. The man said he would go home and do it. The person who took his blood pressure told him he didn't have time, and he needed to do it now. The man consented. For some reason, I have always remembered this.

I also remember being in Gable's when I heard two employees talking about the fate of President Nixon. I looked at them both and said he'd be gone by the end of the week. Sure enough, he was.
Stephen Berman

I remember going to the pet department at Gable's. They had a toucan, a mynah bird, chimps, and spider monkeys. My two favorite aunts in the world would take me to Gable's every Saturday. I loved the toy department, too!

Kelly Bowers

My grandmother was a loyal Gable's shopper. I was one of six children, and for our birthday, she would shop for our new dresses and have them sent to each one of us by the Gable's delivery truck.

Charleen Lowery

I loved Gable's as a kid. Mom would park at the Station Mall, and we would take the bus over so she didn't have to deal with parking. The basement was my favorite part, because occasionally we would get a drink or a little snack at the restaurant counter, but I was always allowed to ride the mechanical horse ride outside the bathrooms. Mom would put a coin in and let me ride when she went to the bathroom. That was the one place where I didn't "check out" the ladies' room. I would ride the horse instead.

Melissa M. Tonkin

My mom, Cynde, used to be a model for the store. I also modeled there until I was 13, when the store closed. I also was in the Gable's commercials which aired on WTAJ-TV. I have pictures of my mom as a model at Gable's, as well as pictures of me on the runway. It was awesome to model with my mom! I remember how fun it was to be the first to wear the latest fashions straight from the New York runway to Gable's runway!

Jennifer Snyder

Cynde Kensinger-Clapper

Jennifer Snyder

Chapter Twenty-One

Powers and Principalities

1979-May 1980

Bob Powers took a good, long look at the growing addition to the
Logan Valley Mall. He slowed down a little as he drove past, observing
the workmen as they labored on the job site, building the home of Gable's
newest competition.

Hess's, an Allentown-based retailer, was coming to town, joining Sears
and JC Penney as anchor stores in the expanded mall. The new store would
make the mall more attractive than ever to local shoppers, giving them more
reasons not to go downtown to patronize Gable's and company.

Courtesy Altoona Mirror

205

President Powers liked to think Gable's could compete, but he must have had his moments of doubt as he watched the new challenger rise. How much retail trade could one town the size of Altoona support, anyway? It wasn't exactly Chicago or New York City.

Power Struggle

Gable's was already in unknown territory these days, since L.S. Good had sold the store's buildings out from under it back in March. The way the sale had gone down had created a crisis of confidence in the store...and the impression that it might be on shaky ground. Had a day gone by in the weeks since the story broke without Bob hearing a question or rumor about Gable's being sold for real this time? Not just the buildings, but the store inside?

Now Hess's was determined to give it a run for its money. Company officials wanted to make it "the dominant department store" in the Altoona area, according to the *Mirror*.

"Yes, you have Sears, Gable's, and Penney's, but we feel we're a little of all of them put together under one roof," said Hess's President Irwin Greenberg.

Though Greenberg didn't offer projections on how much money the new store would bring in that first year, he said it would "possibly be profitable from the start." According to Greenberg, most of the other 17 Hess's stores took off "better than expected."

As usual, Gable's had a target painted on its back...and, as usual, Bob Powers was ready to fight off all comers. By the time the new two-story Altoona Hess's opened in September 1979, his battle plan would already be well underway.

He and his team weren't denying that Hess's would make life interesting. Gable's Vice President Ray Crouss told the *Mirror* his store would feel the impact of the opening of Hess's and the expanded, 90-store mall. Crouss also predicted, however, that customers "would gradually find their way back downtown." Gable's wasn't about to throw in the towel.

So why did Bob have a sinking feeling in his gut as he drove past the expanding Logan Valley Mall? Why did he keep thinking about that headline from back in March, the one that turned out to be so misleading?

L.S. Good Sells Gable's.

It was fear talking—no more, no less. Bob turned his back and drove away from the Mall, heading back to his downtown citadel.

Courtesy Altoona Mirror

Pasquerilla's Properties

In the days leading up to Hess's opening, Greenberg boasted that they'd received a huge number of credit card applications, showing "the biggest acceptance in any of our markets."

Hess's opened for a "sneak preview" to intensify shopper interest on Sept. 17 and 18, then threw the doors wide for its grand opening on Wednesday, Sept. 19. Customers poured in after the ribbon-cutting ceremony with Greenberg, Hess's Chairman Philip Berman, Miss Pennsylvania Carolyn Black, and Frank Pasquerilla, president of the Logan Valley Mall's developer and owner, Crown American Corp.

The parking lot around Hess's and the rest of the new addition quickly filled with cars. The expansion had generated great interest, nearly doubling the mall's size and transforming it into a "supermall." Modern architectural features, including a tubular elevator, a spiral walkway, and a fountain layout, had added to the excitement.

Now, on Day One, the place was bustling. Pasquerilla said the crowds would keep coming, but the mall wouldn't drain all business from local retail centers. He expected the Station Mall to experience a drop-off at first, but he said it would get back a lot of what it lost.

"The bulk of our growth here will be from attracting more shoppers from the area," said Pasquerilla. He claimed the Logan Valley Mall would bring in more shoppers from surrounding areas, like northern Cambria, Clearfield, Bedford, and Huntingdon counties.

But he didn't have much good to say about the downtown business district as it now stood. He didn't seem to have a lot of faith in its long-term prospects. "I think there's a definite future for downtowns, but I think they have to make themselves into service centers with hospitals and banks. Everybody looks to the retailers, but these areas have to become employment centers first."

It seemed clear that Pasquerilla's faith was in suburban properties, not downtown ones. He was gambling on the Logan Valley Mall and Hess's, and he was playing the game to win.

Courtesy Altoona Mirror

Sunday Morning Coming Down

It didn't take long for Hess's to have a major impact on the marketplace. The store drew plenty of traffic and seemed poised to rack up big numbers during the Christmas shopping season.

To help guarantee and improve those numbers, Hess's executives made a controversial move. Encouraged by shopper surveys at their stores in the Richland and Nittany malls, they announced that the store would be open for business on Sundays...*every* Sunday, starting with the first one after the grand opening, Sept. 23.

A similar move had been made in Altoona the previous year, when all local department stores—except Gable's—had stayed open from noon to 5 p.m. on Sundays during the Christmas shopping season. After the holidays, they'd all gone back to closing on Sundays, and Altoona had gone back to business as usual, but that was over now. Hess's was going to stay open *every* Sunday, with no end in sight.

The announcement caused a stir in Altoona, to say the least. The other department stores in town refused to follow Hess's example...though only Gable's ruled out revisiting the issue.

Executives at Sears, JC Penney, Hills, Gee Bee, and K-Mart said they wouldn't open on Sundays for the time being, but they might yet reconsider.

After all, the state's Blue Laws, which had prohibited Sunday store openings, had been overturned. There were no longer any legal restrictions, and businesses in other communities had done well with Sunday sales.

"We'll just have to see if Hess's decides to stick with it," said Wayne Ward, operations manager at Hills. "We don't want to open, but as far as customer convenience goes, we may have to."

Local merchants might have been on the fence about Sunday hours, but the Ecumenical Conference of Greater Altoona had no such indecisiveness. The situation was black and white to the conference.

"There are two major issues here," explained Eileen Becker, conference spokesperson. "First, our society does need periodically to come to a halt and allow all segments to pursue other interests than business. These may be religious, civic, cultural or recreational. And second, to quote from a recent editorial in a retail trade magazine, 'The hundreds of employees of large and small retailing are not second-class citizens, they have every right to be included in the social system. They should not be called upon and saddled with working Sundays.'"

The Ecumenical Conference felt so strongly about Sunday hours that the group threatened a boycott of local merchants who opened their stores for business.

Hess's wasn't intimidated by the threat. "We're not going to tell people how to run their lives, and we don't expect to be told how to run our business," said Hess's Vice President Fred Bentelspacher.

"If it's all right to open 7 or 8 or 10 Sundays before Christmas, what's wrong with 15 Sundays before Christmas?" said Bentelspacher. "We'll just let the people in the marketplace tell us if they want us to open Sunday."

Another Pleasant Valley Sunday?

Hess's executives kept their promise and opened for business on Sunday, Sept. 23. To provide access to the store, the Logan Valley Mall kept its common areas open too.

In spite of the Ecumenical Conference's opposition, the day went off without a hitch. Customers showed up much the same as on any other day and bought merchandise. Hess's made money, and the sky didn't fall.

And that was all the other stores needed to see. Gee Bee executives soon announced they also would adopt a policy of opening every Sunday, starting Sept. 30.

In the weeks and months that followed, other department stores in the Altoona area fell in line too. One by one, the stores reversed their Sunday closure policies, leaving Gable's and a handful of downtown merchants as the only holdouts clinging to tradition.

Bob Powers resolved to stand firm, though it couldn't have been easy. When the Ecumenical Conference's boycott failed to materialize, it was harder to see any downside in adopting yearlong Sunday hours. Gable's, which had staked out the moral high ground, must have looked like a loser, while all the other big retailers in town reaped the rewards of Sunday business.

As competitive as the retail climate in Altoona was just then, could Gable's afford to sacrifice any edge in the battle for survival?

The answer became clear on Sunday, Dec. 9, 1979, when Gable's, McCrory's, Schulman's, Stag Sportswear, and Ye Olde Hobby Shop opened for business. According to Gable's Merchandise Manager Ray Crouss, the change would only last through the holiday season at William F. Gable and Co...but it remained to be seen if Crouss might change his tune later.

"I think it's unpatriotic," said Leonard Whiting, owner of H&H Tires and Appliances. "They're not getting any more business; they're just spreading out the available business over seven days."

But Crouss seemed happy with the results at Gable's. "The only comments we got all through the store were from people who said they were happy about it," he told the *Mirror*.

With so much happiness evident, how long could Gable's continue to resist? The answer was, for as long as the store stayed in business…though, as it turned out, Sunday hours would soon be the last thing on anyone's mind at Gable's.

After all, they had a brand new Gable's store in the works.

The Second Gable's Store

If you can't beat 'em, join 'em. That seemed to be the thinking behind L.S. Good's latest plans for Gable's.

Competition from malls was taking a bite out of sales—so Gable's was getting into the mall business. The company hoped to open a second store—the first Gable's outside the mother store—in the new Ferguson Mall planned for the State College area. The new store would operate as a branch of the original one, sharing the management and buyers based at Gable's in Altoona.

According to the Jan. 4, 1980 edition of the *Altoona Mirror*, negotiations were in progress, but Gable's II wasn't a done deal yet. "We're in discussions, but I'm not prepared to comment on how far along those discussions are," said President Sidney Good.

One key problem was the land set aside for the mall—a 100-acre parcel owned by the Dreibelbis family along Route 322 west of State College. Oxford Development Co. of Monroeville, which had built the Monroeville Mall, the South Hills Mall near Pittsburgh, and the Grand Central Mall in Parkersburg, W.Va., couldn't seem to get the Ferguson Mall off the drawing board. A group of Ferguson Township residents was holding up the approval of the project by the township supervisors, challenging the rezoning of the parcel from residential to commercial. The group—A Community Organization for Responsible Development, or ACORD—had taken the matter all the way to the state Supreme Court, which had denied a stay request and appeal petition…but ACORD refused to give up.

So did Sid Good, though the proposed Gable's store would face competition from a new Hess's planned for the Nittany Mall in State College. "Obviously, we wouldn't be putting up a store there and putting the Gable's name on it if we thought it was doomed to disaster," said Sid.

Courtesy Altoona Mirror

As the battle dragged on in the following months, "doomed" did become the operative word from Good and Gable's perspective…as in "doomed not to happen." The 400,000-square-foot mall project looked less and less likely as ACORD continued to gain traction. Though the Ferguson Township supervisors had been prepared to decide on the project in late February, ACORD got an injunction from Centre County Court judge Richard Sharp to force a delay. Meanwhile, the regional planning commission rejected plans for the mall and considered proposals to reverse the rezoning, which would end all chance for mall development on the site.

Finally, Oxford Development had had enough. The company cancelled the project in mid-May 1980, and L.S. Good's plans for a Gable's branch became moot.

By then, unbeknownst to the public, those plans didn't matter anyway.

Two weeks after the cancellation of Gable's State College, a surprise announcement rocked the company—and community—to the core.

A Shocking Chapter

Was there anyone in Altoona, except perhaps some Gable's executives, who didn't gasp when they saw the front page of the *Mirror* on Thursday, May 29, 1980? Was there anyone whose eyes didn't widen with surprise, whose heart didn't race a little at the news?

There it was in black and white, the headline: *Gable's Parent Firm Seeks Protection From Creditors.*

Just imagine the talk around town that day as word spread. Or maybe you were there, and you remember it. Everyone talking about the same thing, the main thing that was on their minds—how the institution they had known and loved for so long was suddenly in dire danger.

It wasn't some vague threat anymore, some possible crisis for a time to be named later.

It wasn't the usual talk about how the mall was taking away business, and Gable's didn't seem as crowded as it used to be. It wasn't the usual wild speculation based on rumor and casual observation.

This was for real. This was Chapter 11 of the federal bankruptcy code.

L.S. Good and its nine affiliated corporations had filed petitions for reorganization and protection from its creditors under Chapter 11 in U.S. Bankruptcy Court in West Virginia. "The action was necessary since the company could no longer meet its financial obligations currently," said Sid Good in a statement from the company.

According to the *Mirror*, Good Co. had finished the fiscal year ending Jan. 31, 1980 with a $4,118,629 loss. The company also expected to show a loss in the first quarter of 1980.

If Chapter 11 protection was granted, creditors would be unable to take legal action as Good Co. reorganized. To resolve its financial woes, Good Co. would explore several avenues, including help from the federal Economic Development Administration.

Meanwhile, Sid said the company would conduct business as usual. "The company will continue to operate as usual and carry on its normal business. We don't anticipate any interruption of our service to our customers or to the community."

Bob Powers confirmed that Gable's would remain open and sounded confident that Gable's would be fine in the end. "The company will successfully resolve its financial difficulties, which will permit the Gable Co. to continue as a dominant force in the downtown community," he said.

It was a nice sentiment, suggesting that things would work out somehow. But of course he must have been worried. He, of all people in Altoona, knew the level of danger that Gable's faced...and maybe, in his heart, he sensed the outcome.

He said, in a statement, that he thought Good Co. had "an excellent chance" of fixing its money problems. But maybe, as he stared at the painting of William F. Gable on the wall of his corner office, he had a feeling that wouldn't go away...a feeling that no other Gable's president before him had experienced in quite the same way.

A feeling that Gable's wouldn't be fine in the end, after all.

Courtesy Altoona Mirror

Courtesy Altoona Mirror

Gable's VIP
JAMIE POWERS
REGIONAL MERCHANDISE MANAGER
8 YEARS' SERVICE: 1972–1980

Jamie Powers was next in line for the throne. If Gable's had not collapsed in 1980, he probably would have been the sixth president of the company.

His father, Bob Powers, had planned it that way for years. Bob intended to retire as president in 1984, the store's centennial year, with Jamie stepping up to succeed him. Once again, the leadership of William F. Gable and Co. would have stayed in the family, as William's great-grandson took the reins.

Unfortunately, the company fell in 1980 and never made it to 1984. As Gable's circled the drain, Bob and Jamie soon realized their hopes and dreams were dying with it. There would be no more presidents of Gable's, because soon there would be no more Gable's.

Jamie's eight years of working at the store would be the sum total of his Gable's career.

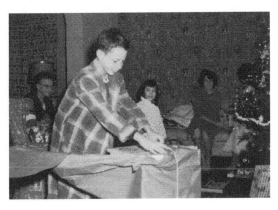

Origin Story

An Altoona native, Jamie grew up in Garden Heights, then moved to Hollidaysburg at the age of 12. He didn't stick around the area for long after that, though. He went away to prep school in Virginia, then attended Penn State University.

During his summer vacations from Penn State, Jamie returned to Altoona and worked at Gable's. He started as a manual laborer in the delivery department, sweeping the garage floor and cleaning the delivery trucks when they returned from their daily runs.

"We had six delivery trucks," recalls Jamie. "Every day, they went to different areas, delivering whatever merchandise our customers ordered.

All Courtesy Jamie Powers

Courtesy Jamie Powers

"Our trucks went all over Altoona, of course. They also went to Bedford, Williamsburg, Huntingdon, DuBois, Clearfield, Punxsutawney, and beyond. We sent trucks to Lock Haven and Williamsport once a week, and they would work their way back and be in Altoona by 4:30 in the afternoon."

According to Jamie, customers would phone in their orders based on newspaper ads or their own knowledge of the products stocked at the store. Then, personal shoppers would go through the store, department by department, and fill the orders.

Next, the personal shoppers took the ordered items to the packaging department, where team members boxed them up and put them in bins according to destination. Then the delivery drivers would load their trucks from the bins after returning from their routes each afternoon. That way, all trucks were packed up and ready to go for the start of the following day's deliveries.

Jamie remembers there was never a delivery fee, no matter what the trucks delivered or where they went. It was all part of Gable's commitment of customer satisfaction. "We'd even deliver a tube of lipstick, if that's all someone wanted. If an elderly person lived in Altoona and wanted a tube of lipstick, our drivers would deliver it to her free of charge."

The Gable's Mulligan

After working in the delivery department for a while, Jamie moved to a job in the appliance and furniture departments for his summer hours at Gable's. His responsibilities included operating a forklift, using it to move appliances and furniture in storage and on the sales floor. He also assembled furniture for customers as needed, especially outdoor patio furniture.

Next, he went to work in Supply, keeping departments stocked with bags, boxes, tissue paper, receipt paper, tablets, pens, and other supplies.

It wasn't until two years later, however, that his Gable's career and ambitions began in earnest. After studying business administration at Penn State, Jamie returned to Altoona. An assistant buyer's position in men's furnishings had become available, and Jamie applied for and was hired for the position.

The Man Who Would Have Been King

Jamie started full-time work at Gable's as an assistant buyer, then became a buyer after a year. Several years later, in early 1980, he made the big jump to company-wide merchandise manager for L.S. Good.

"I was promoted to merchandise manager for all 14 stores owned by L.S. Good," says Jamie. "That included stores in West Virginia, Ohio, Michigan, New York, Virginia, and of course, Altoona."

It was supposed to be the next step on Jamie's ladder to the presidency of Gable's. By the time he turned 34 in 1984, he should have been ready to replace his father as the head of the company.

But that's not the way it went down.

When L.S. Good filed for Chapter 11 bankruptcy protection in May 1980, Jamie's new job went away. He was demoted from managing merchandise for 14 department stores in six states to working as a sales clerk in the men's clothing department at Gable's.

And things went downhill from there. Twenty-three days after filing for Chapter 11, L.S. Good announced that Gable's would close. A liquidation firm was brought in to take charge of the final inventory and going-out-of-business sale.

At that point, there was no denying the new reality. Gable's was finished, and Jamie's hopes and dreams of following in his dad's footsteps as president were disappearing with it.

Life After Gable's

After the store's closing, Jamie moved to Houston and started a new, post-Gable's life. He worked for several companies in Texas before returning to Blair County for another work opportunity as an insurance agent and investment advisor at Prudential and Prudential Bache.

Next, Jaime worked for Family Vision and Hearing, becoming a vice president of the company. After that, he managed advertising services for AT&T Media Services and Adelphia Cable.

Following that job, Jaime went on to become advertising sales director at the *Altoona Mirror*, a position he held from 2003-2008. The work was a perfect fit, as Gable's and the *Mirror* had had a longstanding successful advertising relationship through the store's entire history. During his career at Gable's, Jaime had often worked on buying co-op advertising at the *Mirror*, and the experience had helped prepare him to switch to the *Mirror* side of the equation.

In 2008, he moved to a sales manager spot at Ogden Directories, a publishing company owned by the *Mirror* in Fort Myers and Naples, Florida.

Eventually, his career path led him to work for WTAJ-TV, which was ironic, since WTAJ got its start as Gable's television, WFBG-TV.

Today, he works in sales and lives a quiet life in Hollidaysburg. It's a far cry from the life he once thought he might have as president of the William F. Gable Co., but he's content.

And he still thinks back to the glory of Gable's and the love it inspired in so many shoppers for so very many years. He remembers what made Gable's special and continues to apply it to his own business dealings and relationships.

"Back in the day, the Gables made every employee feel like they were part of the Gable family. That's what made Gable's different from everybody else in retail. Every employee there was treated like they were a family member. Even today, people tell me 'I worked at Gable's, and I've never had a better job than that, and it was the greatest place to work,'" explains Jamie.

"The other thing we did that, to my knowledge, no one else ever did was, the Gable family had a philosophy that you never let the two percent of people who are going to take advantage of you affect the 98 percent of people who take care of you. The customers made our success possible, and we made sure they were always happy.

"If you bought a suit at Gable's, and it wore out after ten years, you could take it back to the store and say 'this thing should've lasted for twenty years,' and they'd take it back and give you a new one.

"If you had a refrigerator or stove for ten years, and you said that it should have lasted for twenty or didn't like how it heated up or whatever, they gave you a new one. No questions asked. I don't know of any retail company that did things like that.

"There will never be another Gable's, that's for sure...but hopefully, we can still learn from the example it set during its near century in business," says Jamie.

Courtesy Jamie Powers

Courtesy Jamie Powers

Altoona Mirror

VOL. 96 - NO. 7   PHONE 946-7411   Altoona, Pa., Friday, June 20, 1980   Founded June 13, 1874   ★   20¢ a COPY

Elderly Face Tougher Times — Social Security Needs Help

WASHINGTON (UPI) — Elderly Americans living on fixed incomes have less to look forward to economically, and the Social Security system supporting about 35 million retirees and survivors is nearly broke.

In their annual report, Social Security trustees Thursday said the program is running at a loss, and the difference will have to be made up by borrowing money from other accounts.

Without the transfers, they said the program will be "unable to pay benefits by late 1981 or early 1982."

Social Security Commissioner William Driver said he was optimistic Congress would agree

shortly to transfer money to the Old Age Survivors Insurance program from surpluses in Disability Insurance and Medicare programs.

Another report Thursday predicted the income of the elderly will grow more slowly than that of younger persons during the next 10 years.

The study, commissioned by the American Association of Retired Persons and the National Retired Teachers Association, said the elderly "will feel worst off" during the coming decade because "they will have a smaller piece of the pie. They will be standing still while the rest of the economy goes forward."

The study comes at a time when proposals

have been made to reduce cost-of-living increases for Social Security benefits or to tax half of those benefits.

The study, done by Data Resources Inc., of Lexington, Mass., said elderly income rose faster than inflation between 1967 and 1976, but said much of the gain was due to Congress raising many of the elderly out of poverty, actions unlikely to be repeated.

The solution, according to the organizations that commissioned the study, is for society to make it possible for the older persons to work longer and encourage them to do so.

In their report, the Social Security trustees

said payroll tax increases have failed to ease the program's economic problems because of inflation.

The Social Security payroll tax is now 6.13 percent on the first $25,900 of income. In 1981, it will be 6.65 percent on the first $29,900 of income, and will rise to 7.05 percent by 1990.

Thomas C. Woodruff, executive director of the President's Commission on Pension Policy, expressed concern about the report's long-term projections.

"We feel that prudent steps must be taken now to assure the long-range viability of Social Security," he said, adding his panel has recommended

moving away from a "pay-as-you-go system."

Americans apparently are becoming more prudent with their money. They reversed their saving habits during May and began putting more money away than they were withdrawing, the U.S. League of Savings Associations said.

Deposits exceeded withdrawals by $1.94 billion last month — a dramatic reversal from the trend during the previous two months when withdrawals exceeded deposits by a total of $1.8 billion.

Also Thursday, a panel of economists and business analysts predicted the recession will start to ease off early next year.

Gable's Going Out of Business — Final Sale Set

By TOM GIBB
Staff Writer

Downtown Altoona's keystone, Gable's Department Store, will close sometime in the next several weeks.

The closing, rumored over the past several days, was confirmed this morning by David Burnum, a consultant hired to oversee the large department store's going-out-of-business sale.

"I would say it could happen in four to six weeks," Mr. Burnum said.

Neither Robert S. Powers, store manager, nor Sidney Good, Good Co. president, was available for comment this morning, and the corporate vice president, Larry Good, refused comment.

The closing order came swiftly after Gable's parent firm, L.S. Good Co. of Wheeling, W. Va., filed for bankruptcy May 27 in U.S. Bankruptcy Court in Wheeling.

The store closing comes on the heels of a decision by L.S. Good Co., Gable's parent firm, to file for Chapter 11

bankruptcy and ask for protection from its creditors.

The Good Co., which owns 12 other department stores in Michigan, Ohio, West Virginia and New York, filed the bankruptcy May 27 and followed that up last week with a request that it be allowed to liquidate the Gable's store.

The request was granted by Bankruptcy Court Judge John Kamlowsky.

The closing will begin next week, Mr. Burnum said, when the store closes "for a few days" for inventory.

That inventory will be followed by a going-out-of-business sale which he estimated could last "four to six weeks."

"The only thing I have so far is the court order from Wheeling," he said. "I don't know exactly what the schedule will be. It all depends on how the sale progresses. Anything's possible."

The closing announcement sent shockwaves through downtown Altoona

and stunned both employees and shoppers.

Some employees reportedly were told of the closing Thursday night; others said they were told during a meeting this morning.

"We didn't know what to think," one clerk said as she tended her cash register this morning. "We thought the store was doing so well."

Whether anybody else might want to buy the store was left open to question this morning.

Gable's Department Store opened 96 years ago on March 1 at the corner of 11th Avenue and 12th Street.

Its founder, William F. Gable of Reading, arrived in the city on Feb. 12, 1884, on his 30th birthday.

Two weeks later, on the advice of his former employer, Dives, Pomeroy & Stewart, he bought into the John B. Sprecher business, which became Sprecher & Gable's.

Three months later, Mr. Gable's former employers bought out the remaining Sprecher interest and the

store became the William F. Gable Co.

By the turn of the century, the store grew to 35 departments and the personnel list jumped from 4 to 500. Expansion of quarters and an everchanging group of departments to meet buying trends has been the history of the store ever since.

Mr. Gable pioneered the anniversary celebration idea in 1904, and it was copied immediately by Wanamakers of Philadelphia. It became a common means of promotion for stores across the country.

Gable's Department Store — an 11th Avenue landmark for 96 years

President Says Talks 'Fruitful'

ROME (UPI) — President Carter and Italian President Sandro Pertini conferred today and found common ground on East-West issues and the Camp David Middle East accords in what Carter called "very fruitful, very friendly" talks.

Carter and Pertini met for 45 minutes at the Quirinale Palace, half an hour longer than originally scheduled. An Italian government spokesman said although Italy's position on the Middle East is a European one, he insisted it did not contradict the Camp David accords.

The Middle East was one of the many global issues Carter discussed with the Italian delegation. The United States has been concerned over a European Common Market declaration that the Palestine Liberation Organization should take part in the Egyptian-Israeli negotiations on Palestinian autonomy.

The Italian spokesman said Carter and Pertini found "compatibility of positions" on all key issues.

Carter later described his talks with Prime Minister Francesco Cossiga as "very fruitful, very thorough, very friendly and very constructive."

He then boarded his armor-plated limousine and went in a 16-car motorcade across Rome to the Victorio Emmanuele monument, a huge, gleaming white, neoclassical construction beside the Roman Forum that houses the tomb of Italy's unknown soldier.

"It's a great honor to pay tribute to brave men and strong allies," the president said as he laid a wreath on the tomb.

Courtesy Altoona Mirror

MEMORY DEPARTMENT

I remember the Gable's store so clearly, even after all these years.
On the first floor of the Eleventh Avenue Gable's building, there was men's clothing, then the shoe department, then furnishings, and then cosmetics. To the right of the cosmetics, there was a card and stationary department. To the left of that was fine jewelry, one of our leased departments. Then there was sportswear, then handbags.

Courtesy Jim Shannon

Next, there was a staircase that went up to our book department, and off to the left was our carpet remnant department.

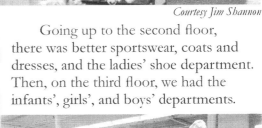

Courtesy Jim Shannon

Going up to the second floor, there was better sportswear, coats and dresses, and the ladies' shoe department. Then, on the third floor, we had the infants', girls', and boys' departments.

Courtesy Altoona Mirror

Foundations and lingerie also were on the third floor. So were the sporting goods and toy departments. We also had special departments just for Cub Scouts and Girl Scouts.

Courtesy Frank Barry

On the fourth floor, we had wallpaper, draperies, the photo department, and a display of trains and things like that. And that was where Santa Claus usually was during the holiday season.

Then there was the Twelfth Avenue Building. When you walked in on the ground floor, to the right was the million-dollar china and silverware department. Gable's had the highest quality china and silverware, worth more than a million dollars. Nobody else had anything like it at the time. There also was a bridal registry in that part of the building.

Photo by Philip Balko

And once you got through china and silverware, there was a department full of high-end glass and crystal shipped in from other parts of the country. Then, to the left, we had our stereo department and records and appliances. Behind that were housewares, and to the left of that were lawnmowers and things like that. Plus, there were tables that went down the center aisle. Every department had a table where they could display sale merchandise, so when people walked in, there was nothing to see but sale merchandise.

On the second floor of the Twelfth Avenue building, we had the credit office, bedding department, carpet department, television department, and appliances. The furniture department was on the third floor, with all the beautiful rooms full of furniture. We had offices up on the fourth floor, including the personnel department, the advertising department, the accounting offices, and the president and vice president's offices. The display department was on the backside of that floor, which was the top floor of the Twelfth Avenue building.

We had two restaurants, as well. One was the grill on the right hand side of the Twelfth Avenue arcade. It sat about 70 or 80 people and mainly served grill-style food. You could get milkshakes, soft drinks, coffee, toast, doughnuts, cheeseburgers, soup, hamburgers, grilled cheese sandwiches, French fries, and that was about it. The restaurant downstairs was more full-scale. That was where you could get roast beef sandwiches, meat loaf, fish sandwiches, mashed potatoes with gravy, whatever you'd expect from a more complete menu.

The upstairs restaurant had tables and waitresses, but it also had a counter where people could sit. The downstairs restaurant didn't have a counter. It was all tables and chairs, with basically four chairs to a table, though there also were two setups that held as many as eight people. They had table cloths, linen napkins, and regular silverware in that restaurant.

The fancier restaurant was wallpapered and had pictures on the walls. There were two entrances—one on one side of the downstairs, and one off the ramp in front of the men's furnishings department. There was a cash register in front, with a lady who would tell you if there was a wait. They also had six waitresses there all the time.

That place was in the basement right off the receiving dock. They also had a full-scale shoe repair shop in the basement, which was owned and operated by Frank Lato.

Jamie Powers

Courtesy Matthew Germann

Chapter Twenty-Two

Swan Song

June 18-July 1, 1980

The Chapter 11 announcement had been hard enough to take. When the next bad news hit a few weeks later, it was an absolute bombshell. It was positively apocalyptic.

Other than the decision-makers at L.S. Good, the first to hear the news were a group of Gable's employees...buyers who found out they were losing their jobs on the night of Wednesday, June 18, 1980. Other staff were told Thursday night, and struggled to deal with the shocking information.

"We didn't know what to think," said a sales clerk. "We thought the store was doing so well."

More employees were told when they went to work the next morning. "There was a delay before they opened," said a customer. "But I had no idea this was coming. I thought maybe they were remodeling or something."

All doubt was soon gone from everyone's minds, as the story dominated the front page of the *Altoona Mirror* that day. The headline was one that nobody in town—perhaps not even the competition at the Logan Valley Mall—really wanted to see. And it was a headline that would change the course of history in downtown Altoona forever.

"Gable's Going Out of Business—Final Sale Set."

Truly, it was the end of an era...and the start of a new, almost unimaginable one.

The Work of 96 Years

A week earlier, the Goods had asked the bankruptcy court for permission to liquidate. Judge John Kamiowsky had granted the request, and Sid and Larry Good had set the wheels in motion.

According to David Buxbaum, the consultant hired to liquidate the store, Gable's would close for inventory the week of June 23, then reopen after a few days to start a going-out-of-business sale.

217

Buxbaum expected that sale to last four to six weeks, after which the store would close its doors permanently.

It was as simple—and devastating—as that. The work of 96 years would be completely undone in four to six weeks.

"It came as a shock to me — a real shock," said Altoona Area Chamber of Commerce General Manager Carl E. Maier Jr. "It certainly was a blow. I won't deny that. I had no indication it was coming."

It was a sentiment echoed often as the impact of the news reverberated throughout the area. The state of Gable's had been the subject of much talk around town in recent years, especially as the Logan Valley Mall and Hess's had gotten more traction...but it seemed like no one had foreseen the closing, or expected it so soon.

Or maybe they had all known in their hearts that it was coming, and they just hadn't wanted to admit it to themselves. Maybe the truth had just been too hard to accept.

Until no one could deny it any longer.

Shockwaves and Aftershocks

Gable's was being closed because it was one of L.S. Good's "lesser profitable operations," said Good's attorney, Robert J. Balantzow of Cleveland. "If it were a profitable company, we would definitely want to keep it in business. I'm certain it wasn't profitable."

Not everyone bought into that claim. Some insisted that Gable's had been in the black all along, and L.S. Good was sacrificing it to try to improve its position. After all, Good and Co. as a whole had lost $4.1 million the year before, and another $2.74 million in the first quarter of 1980. According to the bankruptcy documents, Gable's was in the hole for $757,938 of debt owed to 401 creditors...but other companies within L.S. Good shared the total debt burden.

Ultimately, though, none of that mattered. L.S. Good could do what it wanted with Gable's... and what it wanted was to shut the store down. All that was left to navigate was the closing itself and the shockwaves it would send through the region.

Financial hardships, for example, would be immediate for the 250 employees who would lose their jobs when the store closed...and retired employees would suffer too. Letters went out to Gable's retirees, informing them that they would no longer receive gratuity payments—monthly retirement checks provided to those with 40 years or more of service since the company had no pension plan. "It is with great sorrow that we have been advised by our attorneys that we are not permitted to make payments to our retired employees," read the letter from L.S. Good. Gable's not taking care of its loyal retirees? It was hard to imagine.

So was the downtown Altoona commercial landscape without Gable's. Losing downtown's keystone store would leave a giant hole in the business district; the remaining merchants would have to fight to keep their neighborhood viable. According to an editorial in the *Mirror*, "The removal of such a store as Gable's from our downtown is a critical blow to an area we have been trying to redevelop into its proper place in the heart of the city."

"All of us downtown are going to have to promote heavier and spend more money," said Donald Brett, manager of Meyer Jonasson Co. and president of the Downtown Altoona Progress Association. "We'll have to tell people that the downtown is here. We can't roll over and play dead."

Other merchants, like David Gingrich of Ye Olde Hobby Shop, didn't seem worried. "I think it will be okay if we weather it through. Gable's is a big draw, but personally, I think there's more to downtown Altoona."

Still others, like Gable's shopper Paula Miller, had a much less optimistic opinion. "This store has been here since I was a little girl. I really think this will kill downtown," said Miller.

What Next?

As the immediate shock wore off, people began to think in more concrete terms about life after Gable's. The Gable's buildings, in particular, stimulated a lot of speculation. After all, *something* had to be done with them after they emptied out.

The *Mirror* saw an opportunity for another retailer to fill the void. "Gable's, and the downtown, have filled a profound need for many Altoonans," wrote the editor on the *Opinion* page, "and it is to be hoped that means can be found, even perhaps through another merchandising organization, to carry on this fine store."

Could another retailer be found to take Gable's place in downtown Altoona? According to some people, an ideal replacement had already been found, a store that would be a perfect fit for the available space and surrounding environs.

That store was called Gable's.

Every Glimmer of Hope

Why bring in a new retailer if the old one could still be salvaged? That was the thinking among local officials as they beat the bushes for ways to keep Gable's in downtown Altoona.

"We want to examine every glimmer of hope." That's what Altoona Mayor Allan G. Hancock said. And he and his rescue team did just that.

On June 24, 1980, Hancock and City Councilman William Cochran traveled to Wheeling for a Gable's recovery meeting with L.S. Good executives. They came away with a sense that the store's crisis could have been avoided… and reversing the damage would be a complicated proposition.

"I think, judging by their attitude, that it could have been prevented, but it's no longer a decision the Goods are capable of making. It's up to the courts," said Hancock.

According to Hancock, a deal to save Gable's was still possible. "If we can put together a package that is acceptable to the court and to L.S. Good Co., they would stop the sale in mid-sale.

Courtesy Altoona Mirror

"But we have to deal with the mortgage holder, there has to be agreements with the creditors and the performance of it all has to be satisfactory to the courts."

Hancock thought Altoona could still avoid a domino effect that might kill other downtown businesses in Gable's wake, but he couldn't predict the final outcome. "The Goods have been cooperative," he said. "They don't want to leave Altoona. I'm optimistic, but I'm also realistic."

After the Wheeling summit, Hancock and his team devised a three-point plan to save Gable's…or at least downtown Altoona. First, he would hold meetings to determine the full story behind Gable's closing and whether or not a major department store could still be viable in the downtown business district.

Second, the team would put together a rescue package including low-interest loans to help Gable's retain its inventory, special mortgage arrangements negotiated with the Gable's buildings owners, a new parking scheme to encourage shoppers to come downtown, and commitments from local business organizations to ramp up new activity programs to promote downtown Altoona.

The third component of the plan showed that the team was hedging its bets. Hancock and his people weren't going to wait around for the first two points of the plan to fail before considering other measures. In fact, they were already talking to potential replacements for Gable's.

"Yes, we have started to talk to others about replacements," said Hancock. "The process may have gone too far. The key appears to be the court order and its restrictions."

A Hail Mary Pass

When it came to closing Gable's, things were moving fast—and no one could seem to slow them down.

How could the city implement its three-point plan if the going-out-of-business sale started on July 1, just one week after the plan was announced? Once the sale got underway in earnest, how long would it be until there was no inventory or store left to rescue?

As the liquidator stepped on the gas, Gable's doom seemed more and more assured. Then, as July 1 and the sale approached, the city tried a desperate gambit to buy time.

Even as the going-out-of-business signs went up on the store's windows and doors, Altoona City Treasurer Mary Long revoked L.S. Good's license to hold the sale. According to a letter written by Solicitor N. John Casanave and signed by Long, Good had "failed to make written application under oath to the treasurer of the city for your proposed 'Closing Out Sale' and also failed to file the bond required under the aforesaid act." This was a violation of state law P.L. 410, No. 217, wrote Casanave.

City Councilman Leonard Bettwy, director of accounts and finance, didn't describe it as a delaying tactic when he talked to the *Mirror*. The city was just trying to make everything legal, he said. Gable's going-out-of-business sale would be the "biggest sale Altoona has ever had, and certain things must be done to safeguard the public's interest."

The city wanted L.S. Good and Gable's to comply with the regulations called out in the letter, then wait 15 days after receiving a permit to conduct the sale. Maybe, within those 15-plus days, the rescue team would miraculously pull Gable's back from the brink.

Either that, or L.S. Good would refuse to comply, and the sale would proceed as scheduled. Which is exactly what happened.

The city's Hail Mary pass failed to stop the sale. Good sent back a letter that said, basically, that the federal bankruptcy court trumped the state of Pennsylvania's regulations, and anyone who interfered with the judge's order to liquidate the store could be cited for contempt.

Would the city back down? Solicitor Casanave said no. In fact, there would be a hearing in Wheeling to review the court order on Wednesday, July 2. Main Realty Holding Trust, which owned the Gable's buildings, had filed a petition to vacate the order granting authority to close the store. The petition claimed the order should be reversed due to L.S. Good's failure to notify Main Realty of the closing.

Meanwhile, the biggest, saddest sale in Gable's history was underway, as hordes of shoppers carried off the store's contents, knowing full well they would probably never be replaced.

"There Is No More"

The controversy over the license to hold the going-out-of-business sale didn't keep shoppers from swarming Gable's on July 1. People started lining up outside both buildings around 9 a.m. and poured in when the doors opened at 10 a.m.

It was the most crowded the store had been in ages, as shoppers crowded every aisle in the hunt for bargains. "If they'd had a mob like this before, they wouldn't be closing," said one shopper as she waited in line at a register.

The other merchants in town responded by taking advantage of the influx of people, setting up sale tables and racks of goods on the sidewalks outside their establishments. To them, it was just another opportunity to ride Gable's coattails, one last chance to profit from the halo effect of proximity to the once-great department store.

Meanwhile, loudspeakers blared over the noise of the throng inside Gable's. "What you see is what we have," they said. "There is no more."

As distracting as the crowds, bargains, and noise were, they didn't stop some shoppers from pausing amid the bedlam to reminisce and shed a tear. Once the shock of the chaotic scene faded, the melancholy mood of the day reasserted itself among many.

"I just feel like I'm losing an old friend," said Marie Taylor, a shopper.

"Try to keep them here," said her friend, Sarah Roberts.

"We're just numb," said a female sales clerk. "It's mixed emotions. We're angry, but not with Gable's. We're a family here. People are upset with Goods for letting it go this far."

Meanwhile, the merchandise kept flying off the tables, shelves, and racks. The multitude of shoppers, even as they mourned the impending death of the store, continued to take it apart, piece by piece, and haul it away.

The end was in sight…the end of Gable's and more. An old woman on a bench outside called it. "If Gable's closes, we might as well have a ghost town in Altoona."

Courtesy Altoona Mirror

Shoe Repair Businesses Benefit From Hard Times

By JEFF MULHOLLEM
Staff Writer

Not all businesses are negatively affected by a recession.

Some institutions, like shoe repair shops, benefit from the public's efforts to tighten belts and spend more conservatively.

The shoe repair business is tailor-made for hard times. Shoe repairmen are some of the lucky few who are not currently taking an economic beating. Good shoes can be repaired repeatedly, and when the need arises a consumer with a favorite pair of kicks takes a strong interest in someone who can make them good as new.

Shoe repairmen are the businessmen whom people seek when times get bad. Frank Lato is one of these.

Mr. Lato is well known around the Altoona area — at least among those who have had shoes repaired regularly in the past two decades. He took over Gable's shoe repair department in 1968, and his shop in the basement of the downtown department store was a fixture there for 20 years — until it became a victim of the store's closing this summer.

"We were as surprised as everyone else about the closing," Mr. Lato said. "We heard by word of mouth — we were never even given written notice."

Mr. Lato said when he was given only four days warning that Gable's was going to shut its doors, the decision to relocate was thrust upon him.

He expects no changes in service and quality when he opens the doors to his new shop in the Pleasant Valley Shopping Center. Now called "Pleasant Valley Shoe Repair," it is located between the Warehouse Food Market and the Hanover Shoe Store.

"I'm confident our customers will continue to do business with us at our new shop and hopefully find the same prompt service and quality workmanship we provided when we worked downtown," Mr. Lato said.

"When my generation was growing up, people would naturally repair their shoes," he commented. "But in the last 20 years people were not educated to do that. Now that shoes are becoming more and more expensive, people are again learning to save money by having worn shoes fixed."

It has been estimated that there are about 12,000 shoe repair shops operating in the United States. Many of them report they are faced with more business than they can handle. This upswing in business is especially appreciated by shoe repairmen because the current boom follows a slump of about 40 years.

Frank Lato believes many of the skills used in shoe repair are disappearing. He believes truly fine repairmen are expert craftsmen, and he prides himself on his workmanship, and that of his associates.

Men learn skills at the shops and schools before becoming genuine craftsmen, Mr. Lato believes. "The skill of fitting, restoring and repairing shoes correctly is an art," he said. "There are still a few good shops in the community, but none are coming along to take the place of those that will go out of business eventually."

Mr. Lato has been associated with the shoe repair trade since 1946 following

Frank Lato shows his grandson, Kevin how to repair shoes

military service in the South Pacific. Customer satisfaction, he said, is the one thing valued at his shop above all others.

"The art of giving good service is slowly going by the boards," he commented. "Having satisfied customers is our major goal — the one thing we try to achieve most of all."

Mr. Lato has gone to several schools to further his training in shoe repair and restoration service, as well as orthopedic correction. He took over Gable's shoe repair department in 1968, and since then has seen many changes in the craft.

He has two certificates attesting to his extensive knowledge in the field. He studied orthopedic correction at the West Adams Orthopedic Institute in Chicago,

and is proud of being one of the only craftsmen in the area to possess a nationally registered certificate from the Shoe Service Institute of America, which he earned in 1953.

Ashville is the home of the Latos. Mr. Lato and his wife, the former Helen Klem of Ashville, have four children, Frances, Carol, Richard and Christine.

"In the past, at Gable's, we did repairs on all sorts of items like sporting goods, tennis shoes, boots and all types of handbags," Mr. Lato said. "We do luggage, garments with zippers, scissors sharpened, restoration of any valuable item along with shoe repair and orthopedic offerings."

People should shop around to get their items repaired, according to Mr. Lato. He emphasizes in many shops "Can't" seems to be the word of the day.

"If it can possibly be done at all," Mr. Lato said, "we will make every effort to repair items brought in. People shouldn't take only one opinion if they're told something can't be fixed."

Goodyear, the nation's largest rubber maker, is also the largest supplier of soles and heels to shoe repair shops. They report demand for their shoe products has risen sharply in the past year and a half. This is hailed as very good news by Mr. Lato.

Courtesy Altoona Mirror

Courtesy Matthew Germann

Photo by Philip Balko

Altoona Mirror, Wednesday, July 22, 1988

'I Got Old in Here'

For Many Employees, Gable's Store Was Home and Family

By KAY STEPHENS
Staff Writer

"I was real happy to get the job because Gable's was the biggest department store in central Pennsylvania and it was considered a real honor to work there." — **Helen Haller**, accounting, former secretary-treasurer.

"They asked me to work (during the liquidation sale) but I turned them down. I didn't want to watch it." — **Lester Calderwood**, buyer.

"People come in and just give me a kiss. Some ask for my phone number." — **Mary Hoover**, shoe salesman.

"I got out of the service, worked a short time for the railroad and then I found a home." — **Eugene "Red" Hildebrand**, building supervisor.

"When the store closes, it will just be like being lost." — **Tillie Wall**, alterations supervisor.

No one is more affected by the closing of Gable's Department Store than its long-time employees.

"I don't know what I'm going to do afterwards," Miss Haller, 63, said. "I got old in here."

Miss Haller has worked 39 years at Gable's and, according to her mother, her "whole life was that store."

"I used to tell her I was going to go over and make a bed in the store for her," Mrs. Haller said.

Miss Haller admits to working some long hours and taking work home.

She said she grew close to those with whom she worked. "We spent more time in here than we did with our families. We're going to miss each other."

She describes Gable's as "a great place to work."

"It was a family store and we felt we were part of the family. You have to remake your life now."

Lester Calderwood, 73, began working for Gable's in 1928. Starting in men's furnishings, he worked his way up the ladder until he was responsible for buying the stock in his department.

"I traveled to New York, Chicago and down South. I really enjoyed it. Business was my hobby," he said.

"People in Altoona would like. I always stuck to quality and that made my department successful," he said, adding that he fondly remembers his associate in New York labeling him as "one of the last of the old pros left in the business."

Asked why he didn't retire at 65, he replied, "When you have your health and are doing well, why do you want to retire?"

At 58, Mary Hoover would like to find another job. She has worked for Gable's for 41 years.

"I started working in handbags, but was transferred to the women's shoe department," she said, adding that over the years she has declined job offers from other departments.

Selling shoes has changed in the last 41 years, she said.

"Then, you were expected to make a sale by showing the customer different selections, finding one that would please them. Today, you try to give a customer what she asks for."

Mary said she has trained many "shoedogs," a term she uses to refer to herself and other clerks who have remained in the shoe department.

She said she liked her job at Gable's because of the other employees. "This is like a family."

Eugene "Red" Hildebrand began working at Gable's the week before Christmas in 1947. He was assigned the task of gift-wrapping "great, big baskets," but he wasn't discouraged.

At 24, he became the youngest manager of the delivery department, and he worked his way up to be operations manager.

He has trained all the maintenance workers and was responsible for the general operation of the store.

"I know every inch of the building and all the construction work that has gone into it.

"I know all the employees, too," he said, adding that they were the ones who made his job "a pleasure."

Mr. Hildebrand, 57, said he's not ready to retire and wants to stay with the building.

"No one has the knowledge of this building that I do," he said. "I know every inch of it."

Mr. and Mrs. Walter Orkiseski were both employed at Gable's. Mr. Orkiseski, who will be 92 next month, spent 57 years at Gable's as a tailor, retiring only when I.S. Good announced that the store would be closed.

Mrs. Orkiseski was a saleswoman for 18 years. She said she and her husband speak Ukrainian and Polish, in addition to English. "When you can speak their language, they (the customers) trust you," she said.

For the Orkiseskis and other long-time employees, the closing of Gable's could may mean drastic changes in their lives. Many never took annual vacations, and those who had not planned to retire are now being forced to change their lifestyles.

Courtesy Altoona Mirror

Chapter Twenty-Three

Disorder in the Court

July–October 1980

The battle over Gable's going-out-of-business sale continued to rage, even as shoppers continued to pick the store clean.

On July 2, 1980, Mayor Hancock announced that the William F. Gable Co. would be charged a fine of $100 per day as long as the sale continued with a revoked permit. Gable's and L.S. Good responded the next day by asking West Virginia bankruptcy judge John Kamlowsky for an injunction preventing the city from demanding the fines.

Hancock and his team, who were in that very judge's courtroom for a hearing on Good's authority to liquidate, were taken by surprise. They weren't told about the injunction request until City Clerk Constance Hilling called them at the federal courthouse. "I actually had to call them out of court," said Hilling. "I don't think the mayor could believe it. It was hard for him to believe that they were right down there dealing with these people and nobody ever mentioned anything to him."

Kamlowsky postponed the preliminary hearing on the injunction until the following Monday, July 7, and promptly slapped a restraining order on the city in the meantime. The order forbade the city from doing anything that would "frustrate, impair, obstruct and deter" Gable's from conducting the sale.

The city had really taken it on the chin…but then Kamlowsky handed L.S. Good a setback of its own. Kamlowsky issued an order restricting Good from shipping money or goods from the Gable's store. In theory, this would make it less likely that store assets would disappear "in the wind"—though, in reality, the order was probably too little, too late.

After two weeks of liquidation, who could say there were many treasures left to plunder in the Gable's buildings on Eleventh and Twelfth Avenues?

Courtesy Altoona Mirror

All About the Drama

The court battle was becoming more and more moot every day, as bargain shoppers emptied out Gable's department store. Yet the fight also was becoming more and more contentious.

In a series of hearings that often turned heated, the two sides argued in favor of their respective positions: Stop the Goods from liquidating Gable's or let them do as they pleased.

Meanwhile, Mayor Hancock took a shot at saving the store in a more direct way than arguing in court. On Monday, July 7, Hancock joined with other Altoona civic and business leaders to make an offer the Goods couldn't refuse. But guess what? They refused it.

According to Hancock, the Goods wouldn't even negotiate in good faith. Testifying at a July 14 hearing before Judge Kamlowsky, Hancock recounted a July 7 meeting between Altoona city officials and bankers and L.S. Good executives. At that meeting, the Good execs wouldn't answer requests for figures on the value of Gable's operation, said Hancock.

L.S. Good would not provide "the most ordinary business information on every occasion we requested it," according to Nathan Feinstein, attorney for Gable's landlord, Main Realty.

The best the Altoona team could get was a flippant reply from Good's attorney, Howard L. Sokolsky, who said, "You get what's in the store and you pay what it owes."

During the July 14 hearing, Sokolsky fired back, putting the onus on Hancock. According to Sokolsky, Hancock had been unable to secure a definite commitment of financing for the store purchase. Attorney Feinstein countered that claim by insisting, "there are bankers ready now to make the loans."

"Call them as witnesses!" shouted Sokolsky, setting off a round of gavel pounding from Kamlowsky on the bench.

There were plenty of fireworks in the courtroom that day. As Hancock testified, Sokolsky kept interrupting, repeatedly asking that if Gable's loses $100,000 a month, "who would bear the loss were it reopened?"

The Money Funnelers

The $100,000 figure was what L.S. Good claimed Gable's had been losing every month in 1980...Good's justification for shutting down the store when it did.

"We were hemorrhaging, and we had to put the tourniquet on," testified Sid Good. "This thing (Gable's) was losing big money. There was no time for dilly-dallying. The closing was a decision that had to be made."

But Gable's creditors—including the largest, Mid-State Bank & Trust Co.—insisted someone else was to blame for the disappearing money: L.S. Good and Co. The creditors claimed that L.S. Good had systematically funneled assets away from Gable's.

The creditors also claimed that Kamlowsky's order allowing Gable's to shut down and liquidate was illegal because the creditors had been shut out of the decision. They, like Mayor Hancock, wanted the court order to be vacated.

But the determination of victory or defeat in court would have to wait. Kamlowsky put off making his decision again, at least until the next hearing on July 16.

Meanwhile, back in Altoona, Gable's department store got a little emptier with each passing day. The going-out-of-business sale went on as if no one was fighting in federal bankruptcy court to stop it.

As if Gable's had no hope of reopening.

The Elephant in the Room

Main Realty's attorney, Nathan Feinstein, went into the July 16 hearing loaded for bear, determined to prove to Judge Kamlowsky that Gable's should be saved.

When Sid Good took the stand and blamed the store's closing on falling profits due to rising unemployment and competition, Feinstein attacked his claim. Gable's inventory and advertising expenditures had been severely cut back in the past year, said Feinstein, and that was what had weakened the store's standing. Gable's net worth had plummeted from $3.3 million in 1978-1979 and the previous two years to just $235,000 in 1979-1980.

Courtesy Altoona Mirror

Sid insisted the 25 percent reductions in inventory and ad buys had happened *because* of the decline in sales. He stuck to the company line that Gable's troubles had not been caused by L.S. Good, that sales had dropped so much—from $8.8 million to $6.4 million in the past three years—that cuts in stock and advertising had been necessary. Furthermore, said Sid, Gable's had been losing money since L.S. Good bought it in 1967.

Feinstein pressed his case, but Good stuck to his story. Gable's had no one to blame but Gable's itself. L.S. Good had already done everything it could to save it. Good had even "sent out feelers" to try to find a buyer for Gable's before pulling the trigger on the liquidation, "but never got anyone remotely interested."

Now, liquidation was the only possible road for Gable's and its creditors. Its intent was to maximize returns for creditors of L.S. Good and Gable's, according to Attorney Howard Sokolsky, who represented Good.

Besides, what was the use in getting all worked up about the liquidation? Why fight it? Maybe something great would still come out of it—like a new Gable's store in the Altoona area. "It is very possible that once the downtown store is liquidated, we will open a suburban store," said Sokolsky.

Was he for real? Did anyone in the courtroom take him seriously about the new Gable's store?

All that really mattered that day were the judge's rulings, like his renewal of the court order restraining the city of Altoona from "interfering in any way" with the going-out-of-business sale. Sokolsky must have been relieved, as he'd told the judge he was afraid the city would invoke "police and fire powers to hinder the sale." "What's going on in Altoona is absolutely unbelievable," he'd said emphatically.

Judge Kamlowsky also ruled that auditors Ernst and Whinney could be appointed by L.S. Good's creditors to assess the financial status of the firm.

What about the elephant in the room? The decision on whether to stop the going-out-of-business sale at Gable's? Kamlowsky delayed it again, until July 31.

As he banged his gavel to dismiss the court until then, the shoppers back in Altoona kept marching in and out of Gable's, carrying off more and more of its assets with each passing moment.

A Fairy Prince

Not much changed in the weeks that followed. Judge Kamlowsky continued to delay his decision—from July 31 to August 8 and beyond—and Gable's inventory continued to shrink.

By July 31, according to David Buxbaum the liquidator, approximately $800,000 worth of merchandise remained out of the $2 million at the start of the sale. The discounts got deeper from there, dropping to 40, 50, and 60 percent, and the store emptied out even faster.

Meanwhile, as Buxbaum ran the store's last sale, he had a lot to say to the city of Altoona and its merchants, based on his experience in liquidating more than 200 other retailers. "The downtown here has possibilities if they get with it," he told business leaders. "You have to sell a positive attitude here; the attitude just isn't positive enough.

Courtesy Altoona Mirror

"You need more offices downtown, more warm young bodies. Get the young people down here. You have to get them back from the malls. You have to spread the word: downtown is great. Downtown is beautiful."

In an interview in the *Altoona Mirror*, Buxbaum said the city needed to focus on getting better highways, attracting industries, and providing free parking downtown. "I don't think Altoona's dying. I think it's sleeping. You need someone, a fairy prince, to wake it up," he said.

As Buxbaum pontificated to the press, his handiwork—the stripped-down shell of once-mighty Gable's—slumped around him. In the days that followed, it would become even more cadaverous.

"Tomb-Like Darkness"

Tom Gibb, the lead *Mirror* writer on the Gable's beat, described what was left by August 20. "The store is literally being stripped to the walls as shoppers snatch up the leftovers packed onto two floors.

"Amid the obviously-used office furniture and waiting-room chairs on the floor is the ornate chair annually occupied by department store Santas, waiting for the first shopper willing to plunk down $30.

"The once-expansive store is shrinking as store workers move to consolidate the dwindling stock into smaller and smaller areas. What was once brightly-lit store space is now cluttered with empty, unused shelving in tomb-like darkness."

Undecided

The end of Gable's was in sight, and Judge Kamlowsky was still delaying. August 31 was his latest target date for a decision, he announced.

Courtesy Altoona Mirror

At that point, the matter truly became moot. Kamlowsky had delayed so long that the problem went away...for him, anyway. The going-out-of-business sale, which the city of Altoona had been trying to stop, finally ended on August 23.

There were shoppers in the store that day, picking through the last of the merchandise which had been marked down by 70 percent. Not everyone was interested in buying something, though. "A lot of people said they just came in to take a last look," said security officer Lawrence Epple. "I don't blame them. This place has been an institution around here."

"I shopped here as a child," said Kathleen Cophenhauer. "It was just nostalgia. I wanted to be here when it closed."

In the final hours, shoppers were told there would be a surprise in the women's clothing department. When the crowd gathered there, David Buxbaum told them the last of the merchandise would be 90 percent off for the next 45 minutes.

"These people are funny. They're a riot," said Buxbaum as he watched the shoppers sift through the final sale items. "They're just buying anything. They can't pass up 90 percent off. Then, when they get home, they say, 'Hey, what did I buy?'"

Not long after that, the Gable's department store, which once had been so glorious, closed its doors for the last time. All hope for the store was finally gone.

Or was it?

Courtesy Matthew Germann

Courtesy Matthew Germann

As the Editor Sees It

Gable Story Unique

WHAT has been happening in Altoona concerning the William F. Gable Co. department store is unique in the annals of retail merchandising.

Shock waves reached every corner of the county when it was learned the owners were going to close this store, a downtown landmark for most of its 96 years.

City officials led by Mayor Allan Hancock, business leaders and the public joined in meetings to plan how to keep Gable's open.

There are stores, no doubt, that have become integral parts of the community because of long establishment or other reasons, but we never have heard of one for which the entire community became so concerned in efforts to keep it open as has happened here with Gable's.

It ranks as a news story of the first order in business pages, and The New York Times treated it this way in its editions of Tuesday, Aug. 12.

In its business and finance section, the Times published a news report with a three-column head, "Altoona Rallies to Keep Store Open."

The story of Gable's is printed under a three-column news photo from the Altoona Mirror files showing a scene in the Gable store during the going-out-of-business sale.

The Times writer says, "Store executives and city officials received hundreds of telephone calls from customers complaining about the closing. It was 'just a unique experience,' according to David Buxbaum, a professional liquidator from California who was assigned by the court to close the store."

Said The Times, "A number of customers came in and paid off their charge account balances early, plunking down $300 to $500. 'Maybe this will help,' one longtime customer said.

"Multitudes of shoppers, as many as 15,000 a day, poured into the store for the final sale, not only to buy merchandise but also to rebuke Gable's executives about the closing."

The Times final paragraph was this:

"The outpouring of community support for the store did not surprise such longtime residents as Marjorie Helsel, publisher of the Altoona Mirror, who said, "This is a kind of ingrown community and Gable's has been a cornerstone in it for almost a century. If Gable's goes, the community is severely shaken."

The Gable story is not over.

The case still is pending in the court, but efforts continue here to try to do something about it — to fill the gap somehow.

Mayor Hancock says he has several ideas that can help. Efforts continue to find means of keeping the store open, so that it can remain the big sparkplug for business in the downtown that it has for so many years.

Countless thousands of Blair Countians through the years have made Gable's a meeting place — "I'll meet you at Gable's" — and the community is going to try to keep it that way.

Courtesy Altoona Mirror

Courtesy David Seidel

Courtesy Frank Barry

Chapter Twenty-Four

Resurrected or Disrespected?

September-October 1980

If it happened, it would be the most amazing comeback since Elvis. And it was starting to look more and more likely that it *would* happen.

Officials had been talking about the possibility for weeks, but it was only now, in September 1980, that it was starting to look like it might become a reality. Only after the going-out-of-business sale ended, and the store locked its doors, did a new solution begin to take shape.

Only then did it start to seem that Gable's department store might actually reopen for business.

Born Again Gable's?

"Each agreement has to get in line and stay in line for anything to happen. But I believe there is an excellent, realistic chance for everything to come together." That's what Attorney Nathan Feinstein, representing Main Realty Holding Trust of Great Neck, Long Island, said on Sept. 9, 1980, about the possible reopening.

Main Realty's head, Samuel Leigh, was so optimistic, he thought the reopening might happen within a week or two.

Pact 'Near' On Gable's

By TOM GIBB
Staff Writer

The owner of the former Gable's Department Store buildings said today he thinks an agreement for the opening of a downsized Gable's can be reached within the next week or two.

Gable's, part of the financially troubled L.S. Good & Co., closed Aug. 23, then announced the next day it may reopen. That reopening hinges on an agreement between the Good Co. and building owner Main Realty Holding Trust of Great Neck, Long Island, N.Y. for Gable's to pull out of most of the store's former 12th Avenue building and consolidate in the more than 100,000 square feet of space in the 11th Avenue building.

"I think so," Samuel Leigh, head of Main Realty, said this morning when asked if the department store might reopen in the next week or two.

But both Mr. Leigh and his attorney, Nathan Feinstein of Philadelphia, appeared reluctant this morning to talk about the specific arrangements that have to be made before the store can reopen.

The two top officials at L.S. Good were not available for comment this morning.

Attorney Feinstein forecast 12 days ago that the agreement for the store reopening could be signed within a week. Today, he was not making any predictions, but he said he was still optimistic.

"Each agreement has to get in line and stay in line for anything to happen," he said. "But I believe there is an excellent, realistic chance for everything to come together."

The arrangements, he added, are being taken up in "continuing discussions."

Those involved with the negotiations have so far been reluctant to say what agreements must be reached.

"I don't think there is any value in those details showing up in the newspaper," Mr. Leigh said.

One item that apparently has to fall into line revolves around L.S. Good securing a government loan for the purchase of stock to reopen.

"We understand that's likely," Attorney Feinstein said this morning, "but that's just one cog in the wheel."

The reopening of the store, Mayor Allan G. Hancock said two weeks ago, would probably come in late October or early November.

Added one source, "I know that, if they open, they'd like to open before the Christmas shopping season."

Courtesy Altoona Mirror

229

But the deal depended on a lot of moving parts, like a government loan enabling L.S. Good to buy new merchandise to replace what had been sold in the going-out-of-business sale. There also would have to be an agreement between Good and Main Realty, stipulating that Gable's would pull out of its Twelfth Avenue building and consolidate operations in the 100,000-square-foot store on Eleventh Avenue.

Did it seem like a long shot, especially after the recent courtroom wars between the parties involved? You would think so, but people sounded upbeat. Feinstein said it was likely that the government loan would come through. Another source said that L.S. Good would like to reopen Gable's before the Christmas shopping season.

Was it possible? Gable's was overdue for a miracle, but would this be it?

Maybe, just maybe, the Daylight Store would see the light of day again.

On Second Thought

Was there such a thing as good news about Gable's anymore? Did every glimmer of hope have to be followed by crushing disappointment?

By Sept. 13, the headline on the front page of the *Mirror* read, "Gable Store Hopes Fade, Lawyer Says." Things only went downhill from there in the story that followed.

According to Robert Sable, a Pittsburgh lawyer for Gable's creditor Mid-State Bank & Trust Co., the chances of the store reopening were nowhere as good as Altoona area residents had been led to believe. "There is no commitment by anyone right now as far as I know," said Sable. "As time goes on, things look worse and worse. There's a seasonal thing to this, and as time goes on, they get further into the Christmas buying season."

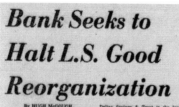

It didn't help that L.S. Good was tied up in another legal firefight. This time, Wheeling Dollars Savings & Trust Co.—Good's largest unsecured creditor—was trying to push Good from Chapter 11 into Chapter 7 bankruptcy. Unlike Chapter 11, which granted protections as a business reorganized, Chapter 7 would force L.S. Good to stop whatever reorganization it was conducting and immediately distribute its remaining assets to its creditors. According to Wheeling Dollars, L.S. Good was fading so fast, it wasn't likely the company could be saved by any amount of reorganization.

Since the firm filed for Chapter 11, said the bank, "there has been a continuing loss to and diminution of the estate, and the prospects are that such loss and diminution will continue. It has become obvious that there is no reasonable likelihood of rehabilitation of the debtor or his business."

In other words, L.S. Good was going down...sooner than later, if forced into Chapter 7. And that meant it might not even be in business in the near future, let alone about to reopen Gable's.

Courtesy Altoona Mirror

Over and Done With

Attorney Sable had hit the nail on the head. By late October 1980, there was still no deal in sight to reopen the store. Whatever hope had been driving the resurrection efforts was in short supply now.

"Gable's: No Reopening in '80," read the front-page *Mirror* headline on Oct. 28. According to the article, city officials and businessmen finally realized there would be no Gable's rebirth in time for Christmas, or anytime in 1980.

"Logic would tell you that nobody could open that store before Christmas," said Edward Giller, chairman of the new Central City Development Committee. "Even if the original L.S. Good were to reopen the store, I don't see how any reopening would be possible before Christmas. It probably couldn't open until spring, at the earliest."

Main Realty, the store's landlord, was focused on finding a new retail tenant, and so was Altoona Enterprises. With L.S. Good still bogged down in court with its latest legal travails, it seemed salvation for downtown Altoona would have to come from another source.

That source wouldn't be Value City, though. Schottenstein-Value City Inc. was interested in buying other stores in the L.S. Good collection, but wanted nothing to do with "the Gable situation."

It was starting to seem like Value City wasn't alone in that. Rumors circulated, people had ideas and chased down leads, but no one cooked up the miracle that everyone in Altoona had been waiting for. No one pushed through the right plan to bring back Gable's, and no one found a replacement to fill the store's vacant space. Multiple parties had been approached as a possible replacement for Gable's—including Gimble's of New York City; Bon Ton of York, Pa.; and Johnstown-based Glosser Bros. and Penn Traffic—but none of them had been willing to commit to setting up operations in the store. When it came to solutions, the problem-solvers kept running into brick walls like the one surrounding the closed-for-business Gable's buildings.

Gable's was just...over. There would be more brainstorms to try to save it, more false leads from parties near and far, and more gossip on the grapevine—but no more Gable's.

Photo by Red Hildebrand

Courtesy Matthew Germann

Chapter Twenty-Five

Powerless

November 1980

On Nov. 28, 1980, the day after Thanksgiving—the day that used to be called $100,000 day at Gable's department store—President Bob Powers and his son, Jamie, went up to the corner office one last time.

Bob gathered up some papers, put them in his briefcase, and closed it. He and Jamie looked around the place, all too aware that they wouldn't be coming back. All too aware that the proud line of businessmen who had sat at the big desk was ending with them.

Then, they switched off the lights and left. Their footsteps echoed through the empty floors of the store, once so full of life and spirit—now quiet and dark and dead.

Bob and Jamie made their way to the last door leading out of the store, the door to the second-floor parking deck—the only door for which they still had a key. Hearts pounding and eyes welling up, they walked through it one last time.

"It was pretty emotional," remembers Jamie. "It was a dark moment, but at least we could help each other through it."

The door fell shut behind them. Hand in hand, they plugged the key in the lock, then turned it. The deadbolt slid home with a *clack*, and that was that. Whatever the future held, father and son knew one thing for certain.

They were never coming back to Gable's department store again.

What About Bob?

During the previous months, as the court battle raged and the going-out-of-business sale emptied out the store, Bob Powers hadn't been overly visible. He hadn't been quoted in the copious news coverage, and he hadn't been prominent in the efforts to rescue the company. People must have wondered where the president of Gable's was during its greatest hour of need.

The answer was, Bob was on the road. "For many months, Dad was constantly going back and forth to L.S. Good corporate headquarters in Wheeling," recalls Jamie. "He was working on the mountain of paperwork and special arrangements it took to move Gable's through the Chapter 11 bankruptcy and liquidation process."

It was all he could do, given the circumstances. Though he was president of William F. Gable and Co., that firm was owned by the L.S. Good conglomerate. Sid and Larry Good were his bosses, plain and simple. What autonomy Bob and Gable's might have had earlier went up in smoke when L.S. Good went into Chapter 11.

Which isn't to say he didn't wish he could do more to save the grand old store. It's safe to say he would have done just about anything to rescue it from extinction. He would have paid just about any price to preserve his family's legacy.

But his hands were tied. His responsibilities were clear: To follow his bosses' orders and conduct Chapter 11 activities until completion. To help dismantle the institution that had served as the commercial hub of Altoona for nearly a century...that had supplied the needs of untold thousands of customers over so many decades...that had brought so much joy and magic to so many hearts for so long.

To tear down what his legendary grandfather had built with his own hands, genius, and determination.

Just imagine. Take a moment and *imagine* what that must have been like. Put yourself in Bob's shoes and ask what it was like to live through that.

The word *nightmare* comes to mind, doesn't it?

One More Day

Christmas wasn't easy that year, for anyone. It was Altoona's first Christmas without Gable's...Bob and Jamie's too.

The Logan Valley Mall was plenty busy, but Gable's was quiet and still. There were no holiday window displays, no carolers on the stairs, no photos or breakfast with Santa. For the first time in almost a century, no rivers of

Courtesy David Seidel

shoppers streamed into and out of the store, carrying shopping bags emblazoned with Gable's familiar colors and logo. For the first time that anyone alive in Altoona could remember, there would be no festive decorations or Christmas sales or seasonal music. There would be no Dave Little whooping "Merry Christmas!" and slapping you on the back or shaking your hand when you walked in the door.

Shoppers still straggled downtown to hunt for gifts at the Young Men's Shop, Meyer Jonasson, Monarch's, Ye Olde Hobby Shoppe, or Shirley's Shoes. They wandered past Gable's buildings on their way to other merchants, for the first time not able to step inside at Christmas time. Did they feel sad as they stared at the abandoned store, as they realized they would never experience Christmas at Gable's again? Did they regret the loss of something treasured, the true value of which they might not have understood until that moment? Did they wish they had done more—been more faithful, supportive, outspoken, persistent—to try to save it? Did they wonder if any other store or mall or attraction could ever replace Gable's in their lives?

Did they wish for one more day—just *one more day*—to experience that familiar and wonderful place? *Just one more day* to bask in the tradition, community, and comfort it had always brought them?

What do *you* think?

"Friends Loved and Never Lost"

It is hard to describe the closing of Gable's in any way that does justice to its impact on the people whose lives it touched. Someone once did, though, in a letter to the editor of the *Altoona Mirror*, written in the throes of the store's end times.

The letter writer, sales clerk Barbara Cogan, captured the spirit of the store and the hardship of its collapse with an understanding only possible for someone who has lived and loved the Gable's life.

"One thing that never changed was the family of workers," wrote Barbara. "Though faces changed through the years, the policy begun by George Gable of courtesy and service never wavered. That family of clerks adopted many customers into their family bond. And that bond grew. Customers remembered clerks at Christmas and holidays and prayed for our families in times of sickness.

"As our counters were headquarters for ladies waiting for buses or calling for taxi service, our friendships grew. We knew each other's problems, illnesses, grandchildren and loved ones. Just about everything was out in the open because the people were not only customers but friends. We worked together, laughed together and cried together.

"Today, the customers call us from nursing homes and private homes alike, crying and pondering who will care for them. To many, we were all the family they had. Who else would take special pride in choosing a perfect little item for a stranger? Who else would talk to one during a busy day, knowing they called only to hear a friendly voice on the telephone? Whoever tries to fill this void for Gable's will have a monumental task!

"Reality is setting in already, knowing that we seldom miss something or someone till they're gone. The fast traffic of our malls and the small coins we saved by parking free have told the tale. Those small coins were a big price to pay for the loss all of Altoona is feeling already.

"After the bitterness passes and the several hundred self-supporting people straighten out their lives, we will ponder the good times we had. We'll be grateful for the time we had together. Whether it was my mere four years or a friend's score and ten, we will realize it was but a fleeting memory.

"Yes, the doors will soon close behind us for the last time. But those departments hold dear memories. The mannequins left behind could tell great stories for years to come. Memories no closed door will ever erase or blot out of our lives. Memories of many friends loved and never lost."

Courtesy David Seidel

Gable's VIP

EUGENE "RED" HILDEBRAND
BUILDING SUPERINTENDENT
47 YEARS SERVICE 1945-1992

Red Hildebrand walked the empty floors of the Gable's buildings, his only companion a German shepherd named Heidi.

Peering into the eerie shadows, Red remembered the well-lit racks of merchandise that had once filled the rooms. He remembered the happy, busy crowds of shoppers that had swarmed through the space, beaming and chattering as they searched for bargains.

Ever since the closing in 1980, all of that had been gone—all the merchandise, all the shoppers, all the life. All the employees were gone too, except for Red. All he had to keep him company was his faithful dog...and the ghosts of the past.

Suddenly, Heidi stopped and barked at a shadow. Heart racing, Red swung up his flashlight for a look. After all, it was his job to keep an eye on the place.

It was his job as the very last employee of William F. Gable and Co.

Courtesy Altoona Mirror

Last of the Living Legends

Hired in 1945 after serving in the tank corps in World War II, Red—a Bellwood native—had started in the gift shop at Gable's, then became delivery manager at the age of 22. Later, he also became supply manager. From 1959 to 1967, he served as George Gable's chauffeur.

But he reached the apex of his career in 1962, when he became "superintendent of the whole damn place," as he put it. It was a job he held until long after the store's closing. Main Realty Holding Co., owners of the buildings when Gable's folded, kept him on to watch over and maintain the property and share his intimate knowledge of all its nooks and crannies with new tenants and interested parties.

Courtesy Helen Hildebrand

Many times, in the years after the closing, Red and Heidi patrolled late at night through the deserted store. "I thought it was a scary place, especially the basement," says his wife, Helen. "But it didn't seem to bother him. I think it helped that he had Heidi with him, though I doubt she would have bitten anybody. It also helped that Red knew every inch of that store inside and out. It was like a second home to him."

A Marriage Made in Gable's

In earlier days, Red—who got his nickname because of his bright red hair— had been a standout among the hundreds of employees on staff at Gable's, with a reputation as a standup guy. "He was kind to everybody," recalls Helen, who also worked at the store. "He was never mean to anybody, and he would do anything for anyone if he could. I never heard anybody ever say a bad word about him."

Helen knew Red better than anybody. After all, she ended up marrying him.

Courtesy Helen Hildebrand

They met on the job in 1954 and hit it off right away. "I was working in the foundations department at the time, and he was in delivery. He would pick up packages in my department, and that's how we got to know each other."

Red and Helen got married on July 24, 1957, and it was a marriage made in Gable's. They had two sons, Lynn and Leslie, who inherited their father's and mother's love for the store. At one point, when the boys were teens, the whole family had jobs at Gable's at the same time.

Courtesy Helen Hildebrand

Pet Shop Pigeon

Working at Gable's was a family affair for Red, and not just because of his wife and kids. He considered *all* his co-workers to be family, and they felt the same way about him.

One of his favorite ways of bonding with fellow employees was playing practical jokes. Once, for example, he found a wild pigeon in the alley and put it in the pet department. "He put it in a bird cage like a parrot," says Helen. "When the department manager got there the next morning, he laughed and said he knew right away who must have done that. It had to be Red Hildebrand."

Red wasn't above acting silly to get a laugh—or *dressing* silly. During the annual Women's Day at Gable's, when female employees switched places with store executives, he prided himself on donning funny outfits. "Once, he dressed up like a cheerleader, complete with skirt and pompoms," says Helen.

With his sense of humor and friendliness, Red was well-liked around Gable's...and beyond. According to Helen, many people from around Altoona got to know and like him at the store, and recognized and spoke well of him elsewhere.

Last Round

When Gable's went out of business in 1980, Red's life on the job became much lonelier. His fellow employees were gone, leaving him the sole keeper of the store buildings, which owner Main Realty converted to office space.

When local developer Maurice Lawruk bought the properties, Red survived that changeover too. Lawruk kept him on just like Main Realty had, tapping his knowledge of the buildings' intricacies, history, and secrets.

It was a role he relished, one he wouldn't give up voluntarily—even when colon cancer struck. After surgery and chemo, he went right back to work with Heidi at his side, happy to return to his beat.

He would have kept at it forever, but he relapsed in a big way. He finally retired in 1992 and died on Feb. 20 of that same year, seven days short of his 69th birthday.

Helen says he never really suffered or experienced great pain when he died...and he was happy with the life he'd led. "Red had a good life. He enjoyed everything about life—work, travel, family, friends. And he was loved.

"To this day, sometimes people I don't know will ask me if Red Hildebrand was my husband. When I say yes, they say, 'oh, I remember him, he was quite a guy.'"

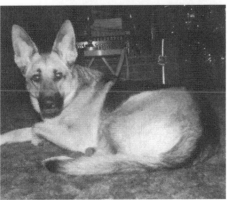

Footsteps

There are still parts of the Gable's buildings that are full of shadows. There are places where you can see remnants of the old store—but only if you shine a flashlight on them.

If you go in there late at night, might you hear the soft tread of a German shepherd's paws in the darkness? The footsteps of a man by her side, keeping watch in the night?

If so, you'll know you're safe, and so is Gable's. You'll know exactly who's protecting you, still hard at work after all this time.

All Courtesy Helen Hildebrand

Gable's Stirring Back to Life While Central Trust Struggles

By TOM GIBB
Staff Writer

This is a tale of two buildings — one going through a rebirth, the other emptying and looking at an uncertain future.

One is the Gable's building, the one-time downtown anchor that lay empty at the start of the year, without prospects of an immediate reopening. Today, it is Gable's Office Building, with two tenants and three more waiting to move in.

The other is the Central Trust Building, quickly emptying as it prepares to close and as tenants look for other spots. Jack Rawlings, son of the building's owner, predicted today the building would not be vacant for an extended period but said the building's future has yet to be firmed up.

The Gable's structure first attracted the Kidder Peabody & Co. investment firm, which moved onto the ground floor of the building's 12th Avenue side last month.

Last week, local ophthalmologist G.T. Fabinyi followed. And over the next month, the ranks of tenants are scheduled to grow to include ophthalmologist Ralph F. Himes Jr., Standard Register Co. and Bankers Life of Des Moines, Mayor Allan G. Hancock's insurance office.

For the past few months, Altoona Area School District has bandied about the idea of moving its tax and administration offices to Gable's.

"It's an excellent location," Dr. Fabinyi said. "This could be the last chance to cultivate the downtown, and from my own, professional point of view, it's a good location."

Dr. Himes said Monday he expects to move into the building Nov. 1. Jill Hannah, private secretary to Mr. Hancock, said this morning the insurance offices are shooting for a Dec. 1 move-in. Standard Register officials were not available for comment.

Three of the five tenants at Gable's came from Central Trust.

Kidder Peabody moved in order to expand its operations, company office manager Christopher Gable said in August. The departure came after other tenants had gone.

For instance, the law firm of Jubelirer, Carothers, Krier, Halpern & Smith left last summer for quarters on West Plank Road.

But Dr. Fabinyi and Dr. Himes — and the rest of the dozen remaining tenants at Central Trust — are leaving because the building is scheduled to close at the end of October.

John Rawlings, who, with his wife, Marjorie, owns the building, said in August that the building's percentage of vacancies made it cheaper to let it sit vacant.

"We do have prospective tenants to use the building," Mr. Rawlings' son and real estate partner, Jack, said this morning. He declined to indentify potential occupants but said, "It could be converted to any number of uses."

Asked if he foresees extended vacancy at the building, Mr. Rawlings replied, "Not over a period of years."

"It's too bad," attorney Harold Miller, who plans to move next door to Central Counties Bank, said Monday. "I've been here since I got out of the service in '45, and I was always happy here. Now everybody's going, and I've got to go somewhere."

Among the other tentants:

• Altoona Symphony will move to the ground floor of IDA Tower within the next few weeks.

• Beauty salon owner Ann Korol will also move to the ground floor at IDA.

• Dr. Joseph Fried, a dentist, said he will move to Executive House 1, in the Cricket Field Plaza, in two to three weeks.

• Gieg & Gieg law offices will move their offices into a former house at 4th Avenue and North Logan Boulevard.

• Dr. Harvey Hill, a dentist, said his moving plans are not complete.

• Dr. David Mauro, an optometrist, will move to the Walton & Walton law office building under construction at 410-18 N. Logan Blvd.

• Attorney Neil Murchison is in the process of moving to the Black & Yon Building.

• Walton & Walton will move to their North Logan Boulevard office when it is completed sometime around the end of November.

Ex-L.S. Good Chief Files For Personal Bankruptcy

WHEELING, W.Va. — The former chairman of the William F. Gable Co.'s parent firm has filed for personal bankruptcy, listing debts of more than $2 million — including a reported $350,000 in gambling debts.

Sidney S. Good Jr., who now lists a Fort Lauderdale, Fla., address, was chairman of L.S. Good & Co. when Gable's was closed in the summer of 1980.

L.S. Good originally sought protection from creditors under Chapter 11 of the federal bankruptcy codes. Since, all the subsidiaries but Good Credit Co. have been placed under straight bankruptcy.

Bankruptcy court records show that Mr. Good owes $1.35 million to a bank and a loan company in Binghamton, N.Y.

His gambling debts, reportedly run up in 1978, were spread across a number of casinos.

Records show $150,000 plus interest due to Caesars Palace Hotel in Las Vegas, $109,000 to the Sands Hotel in Las Vegas, $65,542 to Loews Monte Carlo, $39,475 to Desert Inn and Country Club in Las Vegas, $35,190 to San Juan Hotel, Puerto Rico, and $20,000 plus interest to the Sahara Hotel, Las Vegas.

Chapter Twenty-Six

Anniversary Without a Store

May 19, 1984

Glasses raised, the crowd of more than 150 former Gable's employees toasted the store's 100th anniversary—even though the store no longer existed.

It was May 19, 1984, and Gable's department store had been gone four years. These employees weren't going to let the 100th birthday go by without a party, though. Didn't Gable's deserve it after making it all the way to 96 years before giving up the ghost? And didn't the faithful workers who'd carried it that far deserve a celebration too?

Beverly Kay Slutzker thought so. After working as a buyer at Gable's for 22 years, she'd come up with the idea for the get-together and recruited Mary Rose Keen, a division merchandise manager and fellow buyer, to help.

Beverly and Mary Rose arranged to hold the event at the Penn Alto Hotel on May 19 at 7 p.m. All Gable's employees and spouses would be invited, but finding them would be another matter.

After all, they'd gone from spending every workday together to scattering to the four winds, only seeing each other occasionally at church, the grocery store, the mall, the bank, etc. How could they possibly come back together after all that time?

Gable's Nation Responds

As it turned out, a newspaper ad did the trick. The ad, which ran in the March 24th edition of the *Altoona Mirror*, wasn't even a big one, but it generated plenty of interest.

"ATTENTION: Gable's 100th Anniversary Reunion 1884-1984." How's that for an attention-getting headline?

"A Party is Being Planned for ALL Gable Employees and Wives and Husbands of Gable Employees," it continued. "PENN ALTO HOTEL — LOGAN ROOM. Excellent full course buffet dinner and dance. SATURDAY, MAY 19th at 7:00."

According to the text of the ad, tickets cost $12.50 per person or $25 per couple, and the event was "planned on response to reservations." All money would be refunded "if there isn't a good response."

But refunds were never an issue. Between the ad and word of mouth, the right people found out about the party and ordered tickets by the deadline of April 14.

The people of Gable's were going to reunite. The hundredth-anniversary-without-a-store would happen no matter what.

Who's Who of Gable's

On the night of May 19, one familiar face after another walked into the Logan Room. Each new guest brought a round of enthusiastic greetings and hugs, as if they hadn't seen each other in 40 years instead of four.

It was a real Who's Who of Gable's, from President Bob Powers to Tillie Wolf to Jim Shannon. Jamie Powers was there too, and Virginia Norton-Gordon, a granddaughter of William F. Gable.

There were guests who'd worked at Gable's forever and guests who'd only worked there a short time. They all joined together in an outpouring of love for each other and the store.

Interviewed by the *Mirror,* Jean Reale, who'd worked in the cosmetics department in the mid-60s, said it was a thrill to be there. "I've seen some old familiar faces I haven't seen in 20 years."

"It's great. It's like seeing family," said Jean Beatty, who worked at Gable's from 1944 until the closing in 1980. "I'd give anything to get Gable's back."

"I wouldn't have missed it for anything," said Cindy Kensinger-Clapper. "We were all really close at Gable's. Everybody knew everybody else's troubles. You didn't make the highest wages, but the people and atmosphere were great."

Restaurant waitress Amy Kasianowitz was there. So was Vince Weld, a 27-year carpenter and maintenance man at the store. More than 150 people showed up, all told, and every one of them had Gable's in common.

Gable's and each other.

The Last Guests

In the end, it all flew by too fast. People laughed and chatted all the way through dinner, then did the same while dancing to the music of the Hallmarks. They made toasts, told stories, bought each other drinks at the cash bar…even sang a song together called "Gable's" by Rita Elder.

For those few, happy hours, it was as if the store had never closed at all. There in the Penn-Alto, where so many Gable's occasions had been celebrated in the past, it was easy to imagine, at least for a while, that the store still existed, and this was just another company-sponsored event.

But as easy as it was to pretend, as abundant as the joy was in that room, there was still a bittersweet flavor underlying it all. The store was gone, and everyone knew it wasn't coming back.

As the evening wound down, the guests hugged and said goodbye. Many had tears in their eyes. Some didn't want to let go of each other or leave. But, eventually, the room emptied out…except for a few stragglers, no doubt.

So who were the last guests at the party? Who hung back as everyone else went their separate ways?

Imagine those last two or three people, filling their glasses one last time. Melancholy smiles on their faces as they looked around, remembering. Then the glasses clinking together, the only sound in the Logan Room.

To Gable's. That's what they would have said, that one last time, whoever they were.

To Gable's. We'll leave them like that, glasses raised, in that magical moment… drinks not yet drunk, party not yet over, friends not yet departed. Gable's gone, but still fresh in their minds.

AN EVENING TO REMEMBER

SATURDAY MAY 19, 1984

All Courtesy Jim Shannon

Engraving from Photograph taken in Gable & Co.'s Photographic Studio

Our Men's and Boys' Clothing Section

Brief Facts About The People's Store

There are forty-five or more Separate Departments, each a complete store in itself.

From 375 to 500 people are employed, according to the requirements of the season.

The latest model in Cable Cash Carriers, operated by electricity, is installed to transfer money to the cashiers and quickly return change to the customers. Ninety stations are in operation.

Ten Delivery Wagons are required to transfer the customers' purchases to their homes in Altoona and surrounding towns.

A modern system of steam heat keeps the entire building comfortable on the coldest day of mid-winter, while the many windows and doors allow a free circulation of air to keep the summer heat to a minimum.

It is located on Eleventh avenue, just one and one-half blocks from the P. R. R. Passenger Station, and trolley lines from all parts of the city and suburbs pass its doors.

The One Price System that enables everyone to buy at the same price, is strictly enforced.

Its prices are the "Lowest East or West of the Alleghanies"—one reason why the store has grown so rapidly in the 30 years of its existence.

It is a homelike store and visitors are always welcome, regardless of whether they come to buy or simply to see the goods.

It is protected from fire by a Modern Overhead Sprinkler System that renders the entire building practically fireproof.

Is equipped with a first-class modern electric elevator.

Buying for cash and selling for cash, has, in a large measure, contributed to the wonderful success of this "Store of the People" since its inauguration, thirty years ago.

Our New Photographic Studio

It is the largest between New York and Chicago. During the daytime daylight is used to make the sittings—the sky-light being 18x11 ft., and is the largest in the city. At night tungsten and nitrogen electric lights are used—thus doing away with the undesirable flash. The dark rooms and finishing rooms are equipped with the very latest photographic apparatus; large slate sinks and tanks are used instead of the ordinary wooden ones, and the floors are all of rubber cement. The Studio equipment includes three of the largest and latest model portrait cameras, which make three sittings possible at one time.

The Commercial Photographic Department is equipped and ready to make pictures at a moment's notice—the equipment includes View, Banquet, Graflex and Cirkut cameras, and the latest smokeless flash light apparatus, so that pictures can be made "any size, any place, any time."

Memory Department

I remember going through Gable's as a kid. It was a complete department store, the big store in town. They had just about everything you wanted. The toy department was my favorite, of course. I especially loved the electric trains.

Gable's was the center of the city back then. All the street cars ended up there at Eleventh Avenue, and most of the movie theaters were there. If Gable's was closed, downtown was closed. People would always say "I'll meet you at Gables."

George Sheedy

Gable's was open Mondays 10 to 9, Tuesdays 10 to 5, Wednesdays 10 to 5, Thursdays 10 to 9, and Saturdays 10 to 5. We were closed Sundays, except for a Christmas shopping season or two toward the end. I don't remember ever being open on Sundays again after that.

We had incredible employees. They were like family to us. We didn't pay a lot, but we had steadfast people who went the extra mile to make sure we did everything right. And they were very, very honest. We had very little internal theft—less than 1 percent shortages, which is unusual in retail.

Everyone worked together to present a friendly, professional image for the store. In the men's furnishings department, employees wore

Photo by Gelon V. Smith

slacks, a shirt, and a tie every day. In the suit department, they wore suits every day. Women wore nice, dressy slacks and tops, and some of them wore blazers or dresses. Though they didn't make a lot of money, employees were able to dress well because they all had 15 to 20 percent discounts, based on time served. And they had the first pick of all the sale stuff.

We treated our employees like family, and they treated us the same way. For example, my dad (President Bob Powers) had white or pink carnations delivered to the store every day. He would go through the store and hand out those flowers to any employee having a birthday that day.

245

If the employee missed out because his or her birthday fell on a Sunday, when we were closed, Dad would deliver that person a flower on Saturday or Monday.

At Thanksgiving, there was a bonus of $25 so everyone could get turkeys. At Christmas, everyone got $50 to help buy a turkey and presents. There were Christmas parties too.

We also had a Quarter Century Club for employees who'd been at Gable's for 25 years or more. We had an annual dinner to honor them.

It was a special place, that's for sure. Gable's might be gone, but it will never be forgotten.

Jamie Powers

Photo by Gelon V. Smith

I think Gable's was special to everybody. It was a great old store.

They just had everything. For example, they had a car care center under the store where you could get basic tire service, grease jobs, car washes, waxes, that sort of thing. They even had a miniature golf course in the store briefly when they built the new arcade.

At one time, the Logan Valley street car company actually designated a stop at the arcade. That was one of their advertised stops. Gable's would sponsor free rides to the store on certain shopping days.

Gable's belongs to an era that's long gone and you'll never see it back. It's something worth remembering. It's a whole different culture and way of life that people aren't familiar with.

George Rowles

Gable's was a wonderful store. I still have a lot of jewelry and other things that I bought there.

It was one-stop shopping. You could buy kitchen, housewares, and furniture items at Gable's. You could buy better dresses, coats, and other clothing upstairs, but they also had lower-priced merchandise in the bargain basement. You could get your shoes repaired at Gable's too, or buy records or eat at the nice restaurant in the arcade.

Gable's was almost always giving something away, which was fun. For example, sometimes they would hand out flowers. My girlfriends and I would go in one door and get a rose or whatever flower it was, and then we'd go around and walk in another door and get another flower. By the time we were done, we'd have a nice bouquet for my mother.

My favorite thing was going to the store's lending library, which was in the mezzanine. I think it cost ten cents to borrow a book for seven days.

Marlene Stone

Pictured Here Is Gable's New
Lending Library
On the 14th Street Balcony

New Books When New . . . Good Books Always

A quiet corner in which to browse, reviewing your old favorites and becoming acquainted with the very latest and best literature. Here you will find the new Books "when new" and not weeks later. Our gracious new Librarian will gladly help you in your selection. She will give you a brief resume of any Book in which you might be interested and will recommend the Books she thinks you will enjoy most. They will be delivered to your home if you wish.

3c a Day!   **No Deposit Required!**

Book Review Broadcast
Every Tuesday and Thursday, 3 P. M.

Every Tuesday and Thursday at 3 p. m. the Librarian will give several Book Reviews on the latest and most widely read Books. Tune in on this broadcast. It will help you in your selection.

GABLE'S
14th STREET BALCONY—11th AVENUE

Courtesy Altoona Mirror

At one time, I think Gables employed five hundred people. I remember they always had a maid to take care of the restrooms. There was a man named Alex who used to clean and polish the brass. He was so sweet. There was an African-American man named Sam Pattillo, a real nice man who took care of a lot of stuff for Mr. Gable. He was such a gentlemen and so nice. There were so many nice people who worked at the store.

Helen Hildebrand

My dad worked at Gable's from 1926 to 1970 and did a little bit of everything. He fired the furnace and boilers, was a floor walker, a security guard, and ran errands for George. He was George Gable's right-hand man and got to know him real well.

I also worked at Gable's for a short time during high school, before serving in the Army in World War II. My mother worked there too, as a matron in the late 40s.

Earl Pattillo

Gable's used to have heated sidewalks to melt the snow. That's all but dead now, after the remodeling done since the store closed.

There were wires all through the pavement, leading to an electrical source in the basement. Some of the sidewalks also were threaded with pipes that connected to the boiler. They ran hot water from the boiler through those pipes and heated the walks to melt the snow.

It was done to take care of the customers, so they wouldn't slip on the ice.

Morey Lawruk Sr.

Courtesy David Seidel

I would say that every citizen of Altoona went in and out of Gables multiple times during the week. For those living in the rural areas out around Altoona, it was mostly a weekend experience.

Gables was *the* department store. This was before "the malling of America." To give you an idea, most department stores in any mall today probably have close to a hundred employees. A lot are part-time, and the total number increases near Christmastime. Gables Department Store, through the year, probably had close to three hundred employees. They were basically part-time, except for department heads and that sort of thing. A lot of them were more mature employees instead of younger ones, and it was like a family. When you got into the holiday season, Gable's probably had close to 500 employees in the buildings, all servicing everybody's needs.

It was a focal point for the community. Their toy department at Christmastime was phenomenal. I can liken it somewhat to the department store in the movie *A Christmas Story*. I was always fascinated by the Lionel train exhibits. Unfortunately, in all the things that we've collected about Gable's, the one missing element seems to be photographs of the toy department at Christmas. I would love to see those sometime, but it's just one of those things.

At home today, we still have a number of items from Gables, including our dining room table. I still have clothing with the Gable's label inside. It's well-made stuff, and timeless in a way, though I don't wear it much today. I'll never get rid of it, though.

I bought my dining room table in Gable's Arcade. The entrance to Gable's Twelfth Avenue building led in to a level hallway that we called the Arcade. That's where they showcased or featured particular products for a particular week or a particular day, or clearance merchandise.

Gable's was the focus and the anchor. It drew everybody else into downtown. They also were noted for the volume of their newspaper advertising. They ran full-page ads weekly. I'm sure Gable's was the economic driver for the *Altoona Mirror* and the *Altoona Tribune* (which ceased publication in 1957).

David Seidel

Time brought many changes to Gable's, as time should. But some of the changes were not advancements. The quality of merchandise, it seems, has deteriorated; there has been too much of a bargain basement atmosphere in the whole store; some of the decorations are gaudy and in poor taste. Of late, there has been sort of a carnival atmosphere...but Gable's still was preferable to the shops at the mall, where cheap merchandise, ugly displays, self-help buying and sometimes disgruntled clerks are the order of the day.

I went to Gable's last Saturday to pick up a few items that I have been able to buy there for years, and I am sorry that I went. It was like seeing the body of a loved one dismembered, worn, battered, wasted. The best merchandise was gone, sent to other stores. There was so little left that I can't help wondering what is left to be sold at that closeout sale beginning on July 1. I for one shall not attend. It might be better if the Good Company would pack it all and take it away. That way, no one would see the final demise of an Altoona institution.

Farewell to the William F. Gable Company.

Author Unknown, 1980

Chapter Twenty-Seven

Going Back to Gable's

2016

Photo by Philip Balko

It's been decades since the Gable's department store closed its doors forever. Wouldn't it be great to see what the place looks like inside after all these years?

If you had the chance to revisit the store, you couldn't find more perfect tour guides than Jamie Powers, Morey Lawruk Sr., and Morey Lawruk, Jr. Morey Sr. and Morey Jr. own the buildings and know them like the backs of their hands after all the renovations they've done to them. Jamie, son of Gable's President Bob Powers and great-grandson of William F. Gable, brings Gable family expertise and a strong historical perspective. He worked at Gable's for years, heard all the stories, and was there with his dad to lock the doors on the day the company went out of business.

Nobody knows the Gable's buildings better than these three guys. That's why we picked them to take you on a tour in the pages that follow, exploring the old buildings from end to end and top to bottom, seeing what's new within those historic walls...and hunting buried treasures from the store's fabled past.

On your own, you could never see everything that Morey Sr., Morey Jr., and Jamie are about to show you. You wouldn't have access to all the floors, and you wouldn't have keys to all the doors. Even if you did, the place has changed so much that you wouldn't necessarily know what used to be where...and you wouldn't have any idea where to find the hidden treasures left over from the old days.

Lucky for you, Morey Sr., Morey Jr., and Jamie found the time in their busy schedules to take you around. So get ready to go where few Gable's fanatics have gone since the closing of the store. Get ready to see things you've wondered about since the old days. And keep your eyes peeled for surprises, because you just never know what you might glimpse in the shadows in big old buildings like these with such a rich history.

Horses Slept Here

Your first stop is the garage at the rear of the Twelfth Avenue building. This is where Gable's delivery trucks parked, loaded, and unloaded. Before the trucks came along, horses and carts were kept in this space.

Large merchandise came down the freight elevator in the rear left corner of the garage. Smaller items arrived elsewhere.

Walk through the doorway to the right, and you'll find a big, adjacent room that was once lined with horses' stalls. In later years, it was converted to Gable's appliance and furniture warehouse...but it doesn't look so good these days. According to Jamie, after Gable's closed for good, vandals broke in and ripped the place apart. They ransacked whatever areas they could access, stealing everything of value that they could carry.

Next, follow Jamie and the Lawruks through a doorway to the left, which leads you to what was once the delivery room. This is where the smaller items arrived, sliding down a spiral ductwork chute from the upper floors of the store. It was then sorted into bins along the wall according to destination. "We had bins for Bedford, Huntingdon, Hollidaysburg Dubois, Clearfield, and other locations.

"We had three different bins just for Altoona," says Jamie. "Once the items were sorted, we would get them ready for delivery by truck or shipping by the Postal Service."

Today, the chute is gone, and the delivery room is used as storage by the Lawruks. Between the two buildings, Morey Jr. estimates that 90 percent of the total space is currently used for storage. That's a lot of space, considering the total area of the buildings is approximately 265,000 square feet over nine floors. "That's larger than any department store that's out there today, by far," says Jamie. According to Morey Sr., current tenant M&T bank once occupied 80 percent of the total space, then reduced their footprint.

"M&T used to occupy six floors between the two buildings," he says. "One of the reasons my dad and his partners bought the buildings was to provide the space M&T wanted to rent. They started off with two floors and kept expanding…then eventually cut back to what they have now."

No More Rats

Leaving the delivery room, you step through a doorway into a dark passage. Look to your left, and you see the corridor leading under the street that connects the Twelfth Avenue and Eleventh Avenue buildings. Look to your left, and you see steps leading up to what was once the supply department. You also see the top of a ramp in that direction, descending into darkness.

Guided by flashlight beams, you follow Jamie and the Lawruks down the ramp into the basement. Do you hear the sounds of tiny creatures skittering in the shadows around you? Or are those the sounds of something…supernatural?

It's probably just your imagination. Morey Jr. has spent lots of time in the Gable's buildings and never seen a trace of vermin *or* ghost. Jamie says that rats occasionally came up from the sewers back in the day and ran through the walls, but their entry point was eventually found and blocked off.

251

Photos by Philip Balko

Electric Slide

Up ahead, the original boiler for the Gable's store is still in place...all 15 tons of it. Brought down and installed in sections, it was used until the 1950s or 60s, then replaced.

The hot water pipes leading from the boiler were originally covered with asbestos. Morey Sr. says it had to be removed by a special asbestos abatement company in the 1980s. "That was all the asbestos we found in the building," says Morey Sr. "Whatever was wrapped around those pipes in the boiler room."

Past the old boiler, you step through a doorway on your right and find yourself in the old coal room. Back when Gable's was coal-heated, and before the alley outside was covered, coal was delivered through a chute near the ceiling. Employees would haul it out and feed it into the boiler to heat the store.

Leaving the coal room, Jamie and the Lawruks unlock a door, and you follow them through it. In a high-ceilinged room, you see the electrical panels for the whole store mounted on the wall.

The main panel is labeled "DANGER 2300 VOLTS."

You can hear the power humming through the panels, which are still in operation. The draw from the buildings above is different these days, though, as the inefficient old Typhoon electrical heaters were removed long ago. "Getting rid of the Typhoon units cut our energy bills by more than half," says Morey Sr.

Who Wants A Bobwhite?

Next, you walk down a short corridor under the alley between buildings, crossing from the Twelfth Avenue structure to the one on Eleventh. Morey Jr. opens a door, and you enter the famous Bargain Basement of the Eleventh Avenue building.

"The slogan was, 'Gable's Basement, Never Knowingly Undersold,'" says Jamie.

Though all the furnishings were cleared out ages ago, you still see traces of the original Bargain Basement—a floor covering here, a wall covering there. Otherwise, it's a big, empty room...though Jamie remembers exactly what once occupied it.

On the far left, he points to where the men's restroom and shoe department were once located. Menswear was straight ahead, and women's wear was beyond it at the far end of the room. Boys' clothing was on the right side of the room. The basement buyers had offices in the right rear corner.

Photos by Philip Balko

The shell of the old basement restaurant remains on the near right, with bits of original carpeting clinging to support beams. The old tin ceiling is visible where the drop ceiling collapsed, though the paint is worn away in places. One wall is still covered with an unbroken length of wallpaper from the pre-closing era. If you stare at it long enough, you can almost imagine you're back in 1975, ordering a bobwhite from the waitress.

"We could seat 80 people in here," recalls Jamie. "We had more than 250 employees here at Gable's, and plenty of them would eat here. So would shoppers and business people. There weren't that many restaurants in downtown Altoona back then."

Outside the restaurant, in front of walls papered with alternating dark and light blue strips, is a bare spot cut in the old brown linoleum. Take a close look and think back. Do you remember what used to be there?

"That's where they had a hobby horse the kids could ride for ten cents," says Jamie. "Little kids used to get the biggest kick out of that thing."

3-5 Year Carpet

Back in the main area of the basement, there are craters where the floor was damaged and broken away. Jamie explains that they always had trouble with the floor down there because of water infiltration.

"The floor would buckle. It was always uneven. We had to patch the floor and replace the carpet every three to five years."

According to Morey Sr., the problem was with the wood sleepers used under the terrazzo flooring. Moisture rotted the wood, causing it to warp and break up the terrazzo. Laying several inches of concrete down there could have fixed the problem, says Morey Sr.

"No one thought of that at the time," says Jamie. "It's too bad, because Gable's owned a contracting firm, so we could have fixed it at cost."

Let's Do the Time Warp

Crossing the Bargain Basement, you see an original stairway, the main access from the first floor. It's been closed off from the floors above since the mid-80s, when Mid-State Bank (later acquired by M&T Bank) moved into the place.

The brass handrails are gone from the stairway, stolen by unknown parties who had access to the basement during the past two years. All that's left are holes where the rails were taken out of the walls.

"Those rails were worth some serious cash. They were the real deal," says Jaime.

"We've caught a couple people who've stolen things from the building, but not all of them," says Morey Sr. "We've caught some on security cameras, but others got away with it."

The stairs themselves are covered with bits of debris, but the paint on the walls—applied in the 50s or 60s—is still solid. If you squint a little, you can almost imagine you're back in the old days.

Take a deep breath as you gaze at this little forgotten corner of the past. It almost makes you wonder: If you walked up those steps and wished hard enough, might you somehow emerge in the glory days of Gable's, with the store humming and twinkling all around you?

Photos by Philip Balko

Siren Song of Gable's

In another part of the basement, you find a second stairway, better preserved than the first. This one still has intact brass railings, and it looks familiar. Thick panes of textured, decorative glass are mounted along the rails, each bearing frosted stripes that alternate with unfrosted ones.

Though the remains of a broken pane are scattered on the landing, it's easier to imagine that this stairway might lead you up to old Gable's in its heyday. The treads on the steps are cleaner, and there's some shine on the handrails. The paper on the adjacent wall—silver foil diamonds in a yellow latticework—looks as fresh as the day it was put up.

It's tempting, isn't it? Who's to say magic never happens? Maybe, when the others turn their backs, you could just put your foot on the first step and close your eyes. Then the second step, and the third. Maybe you'll even hear the hubbub of shoppers and the music on the P.A. system as you get closer.

Or, as turns out to be the case, Morey Jr. might snap you out of your daydream by shouting for you to catch up with the rest of the group. After all, you still have the rest of the store to get through.

Elvis Has Left the Building

Leaving the basement, you follow Jamie and the Lawruks into an elevator and ride it to the third floor of the Eleventh Avenue building. You step out into darkness, again lit only by the beams of flashlights.

As the Lawruks switch on a few scattered lights, you notice the gold foil wallpaper on and around the elevator doors behind you. The paper, with its elaborate scrolled designs reminiscent of French *fleurs-de-lis,* has hung there since the 1960s, according to Jamie and Morey Sr.

Turning, you see a vast space open up around you—the sales floor that was once divided into departments and crowded with tables, racks, shelves, mannequins, registers, employees, and shoppers.

Photo by Robert Jeschonek

Striking colors pop up, catching your eye in the drab, shadowy gulf: a bright yellow display stand, now empty, in the middle of the floor; a wall striped with red, white, and blue that haven't faded in the slightest after all these years.

As in the Bargain Basement, Jamie remembers everything that was here in the old days. "Sporting goods was here. So were the infants', girls', and boys' departments. We had the Cub Scout and Girl Scout departments here, too." He gestures at the sales floor sprawling before him...then turns and points at a nearby doorway. "And that was the pet department over there."

You step through the doorway into a big, high-ceilinged room. Here, you see bright yellow walls and rows of windows that once had many kinds of animals behind them. "We had hamsters, gerbils, dogs, and cats," recalls Jamie.

"Plus more exotic pets like monkeys and chimpanzees. We also had a mynah bird named Elvis that would talk."

Photos by Philip Balko

The original entry to the room was walled off years ago, before the Lawruks took over, but you can still see where the doorway was located. The word "Pets" was once painted on the wall above it, but it's long-gone now.

"Our pet department brought in $200,000 a year. It was a leased department, rented and operated by an outside vendor. We finally closed it in the late 60s," says Jamie.

Where the Hair Used to Hang Out

Next, you follow your guides across the third floor to the beauty shop area. Outside the shop, you see some familiar artwork on the wall—a mural of a Parisian street scene. It's another remnant of the beloved old store, unchanged from the heyday of Gable's.

Turning, you see more of the exposed tin ceiling where the drop ceiling fell down. Morey Sr. points out a pillar he added years ago to shore up a computer room installed on the floor above by M&T bank. The pillar rests atop what was once an exterior wall of a building annexed by Gable and Co. back in the day. You can see the base of the pillar and the top of the wall through a hole in the floor.

Prompted by Jamie and the Lawruks, you enter the former beauty shop. This part of the building is well-preserved; you can clearly see the outlines of the original layout. Along one side of the room, you see a long row of shelves that once served as the backdrop of the shop's styling stations. The chairs and equipment are long gone, but it's easy to see where the stations were originally set up.

The other side of the room is lined with bays, still framed by low walls, where the stylists washed customers' hair. The sinks are gone, but you recognize the floral pattern wallpaper where they were once mounted...another blast from the past.

Photo by Robert Jeschonek

You recognize the sign painted high on the back wall of the shop, too—the word "UNI" with the symbols for male and female superimposed over a rainbow. It reminds you that men, as well as women, could have their hair done here in later years.

After the beauty shop, Morey Sr. and Morey Jr. walk you over to a section of interior wall that's been torn away. Here, you can see an original window, open wide to reveal the inner surface of the brick wall surrounding the building.

Photos by Philip Balko

"They used metal studs to frame it, then anchored the brick to the studs," explains Morey Sr. "The windows are opaque because they're caked with mortar dust, but if they weren't, and the wall was gone, you'd be looking out at Eleventh Avenue right here."

Photo by Robert Jeschonek

Arcade Lobbyists

Now that you've explored the third floor thoroughly, your guides lead you to an elevator, which you ride down to the second floor. There, you follow a walkway to the lobby of the Twelfth Avenue building, which used to be Gable's Arcade. These days, it's lined with beautiful marble walls, glass, and solid wood doors, looking like the lobby of an office building in a big city.

Jamie, of course, remembers what occupied the space in the old days. "Right here, the Arcade tables were lined up." He gestures to indicate the middle section of the lobby and an intersecting hallway. "The tables were full of specials from every single department."

Next, he points at the far wall. "Way over here, at one time, was the Arcade Grill, which closed down in the mid-60s."

Ladies' sportswear and dresses also were sold in the Arcade, according to Jamie. "And over here was our million-dollar china and silverware department. It was the largest in the state of Pennsylvania at the time." He points toward the front area of the lobby, now occupied by the offices of a company called Vector.

"Our record department, which was closed in the early 60s, was over here." Jamie points at the other side of the front lobby area, which is occupied by the local office of the Department of the Treasury and the district office of State Representative John McGinnis (and once housed the business office of Bell Telephone). "We also had lawnmowers and outdoor equipment here." He gestures at the near side of the lobby, where the elevator is located. "Later, this all became a housewares department. All the way down here was housewares."

Other tenants on the first floor include Affordable Energy, Adelphoi MST, Express Employment, and Keystone Connect.

Radio Days

From the lobby, you ride the elevator to the second floor. When the doors open, Jamie says you're stepping into what was once the carpet department and credit office. The appliance and television departments also were located on the second floor, he says.

But there's no trace of the old departments or their layout. "This is one of the most changed floors in the Gable's buildings," says Morey Sr. "It's all divided up into offices."

The offices here include AppCove, Inc., Adiaon/Catalyst, the Center for Community Action, and Johnson Associates.

There isn't much to see here or on the third floor, which also is occupied by offices. Tenants on the third floor include Evolution Counseling, Novotech Construction, and Adelphoi Foster Care.

Skipping the third floor, you all take the elevator up to the fourth floor. This level hasn't been modernized as others have, so the bones of the old Gable's are more visible.

Turning a sharp right from the elevator, Jamie leads you through a doorway into what was once the display department. "This is where we kept all the display stuff for the whole store," he says, spreading his arms wide to take in the whole huge room. "All the props and decorations for all the windows and departments."

Along the back wall of the room, you see original windows that haven't been covered by dry wall. If only the exterior brick wall wasn't there, you could see the view that the display crew saw many years ago.

261

Photos by Philip Balko

Along the front wall, Morey Sr. and Morey Jr. open a heavy wood door and shine flashlights into what was once the studio of WFBG radio. "The door was thick as part of the soundproofing," explains Morey Sr. "It used to have a window, so people could look in and see the broadcasts in progress."

At one time, the walls were lined with windows too, but they've been boarded up. The old studio is full of debris from past remodeling efforts, a far cry from its heyday as the nerve center of WFBG-AM.

Close your eyes. Can you hear faint echoes of the old announcers reading the news, or conducting a quiz show? Can you hear the distant strains of Gable's Golden Trio as they play the classics during their daily show?

Almost…almost…

Original Originals

Your next stop provides another glimpse of the distant past of Gable's—the *original* original Gable's. Turning a corner from the studio, you see a descending staircase hewn from solid mahogany…and Jamie tells you it's an artifact of the earliest days of the store.

"Those are the original railings that were all through the store at one time," he says. "Back before they remodeled and installed the brass and glass."

There's even a light switch set into a post at the top of the stairs. Nothing happens when you flick it, but it once activated lights that illuminated the path downstairs. That path leads nowhere now, as the second flight down ends in a dividing wall ahead and a suspended ceiling below. But the stairs themselves were built to last and are in excellent shape—worn from use, but not bowed in the middle as stairs sometimes get from repeated use.

Lean over the railing at the top, and you can imagine gazing down the deep stairwell in the old days, before the steps were blocked off. But don't lean *too* far; building codes were different back then, and the railing is only waist-high.

Looking up, you see another old window, covered like so many others. It faces the parking garage on the

Thirteenth Street side of the building.

Safe from Prying Eyes
Moving on from the antique stairway, Jamie and the Lawruks lead you to the main open area of the fourth floor. This space was once occupied by the store offices; it's here that the office work was done every day to keep the store operating smoothly.

To the right, according to Jamie, was the advertising department. Alongside that was the buyers' conference room, where the 50 or so buyers who worked for Gable's attended weekly sales

meetings conducted every Friday morning by the company president.

The accounting office was located on the opposite side of that half of the floor, says Jamie. A payroll safe was mounted in the wall there, and only three people had the combination—the president, vice-president, and secretary-treasurer of the company. No one's sure what happened to that safe, though

Photo by Robert Jeschonek

the wall where Jamie says it was located is now hidden in a partitioned space that might be big enough to conceal it. It's possible, when remodeling was done years ago to accommodate the Census Bureau, the safe was too heavy to move and was tucked away behind wall board instead.

Photos by Philip Balko

Four Doors Down

On the far side of the fourth floor, four doorways beckon. From left to right, Jaime identifies the occupant of each one: the secretary-treasurer, the secretary, the vice president or general manager, and the president. "That was my dad's office," says Jaime, and then he leads you around the corner to another doorway. "This was a small side office where my dad had meetings." Entering the small office, he shows you another room branching off to the side. "And this was the conference office."

The conference office is a big room with light brown wood grain paneling and three windows, blocked by the exterior brick wall. Pale green curtains hang between them, ancient and faded. On another wall, there's a recessed white alcove with inset fluorescent bulbs above it, lighting the board from behind the overhang of paneling.

"This room looks exactly the same as I remember it, right down to the curtains, except the

furnishings are gone," says Jamie. "There was a beautiful mahogany table in the middle with twelve chairs around it. Framed pictures of the store hung on one wall. On the opposite wall, right here, he had a board you could write on." Jamie gestures at the white alcove with the fluorescent lighting. "There also was a screen you could pull down to project videos on."

Mr. Gable (or Powers) Will See You Now

Next, Jamie leads you through a doorway into the legendary corner office once occupied by his father... and Robert Gable, George Gable, and W. Stanley Truby before him.

"Wow." Jamie walks slowly around the perimeter of the room. "I haven't been here since Nov. 28, 1980, when Dad and I locked up the store for the last time."

The paneling in this room is rich mahogany, like the railings in that one ancient stairway you saw. Big windows follow the curve of the room, also trimmed with mahogany. This office must have been a bright, elegant space back before L.S. Good closed it off from outside with brick and limestone. Of course, all that sunlight had a drawback; it heated up the room, especially when hitting it directly. That's why there was an air conditioning unit in one window, according to Jamie.

"Dad's desk was right here. It was a big mahogany desk with a high-backed chair." Jamie indicates a space near the windows, on the left side of the room. "He had a small side desk over here, where he kept books and things." He points to the right of where the main desk would have been located.

The view from the windows must have been amazing…but the view in the other direction was inspirational. Jamie says a huge, beautifully framed portrait of William F. Gable hung on the wall facing the president's desk, reminding him always of the legacy he had to honor.

Now, there's just a big white square on the wall where that portrait once hung. The same goes for a space on another wall where a big picture of the store was once displayed. Both were stolen in the chaotic days of the liquidation back in 1980.

"Dad put them in the small meeting room over here and locked the doors," explains Jaime. "When I came in to get them, they were gone. Later, in 1997, I tracked the William F. Gable portrait down in the collection of a local antique dealer and bought it back for $1200. I never did find the other piece that hung here, though."

As you and your guides get ready to leave, Jamie lingers in the office. Smiling to himself, he runs his hand over the mahogany wall. "I spent a lot of time in here with my dad," he says softly, nodding. "I have a lot of good memories of this place."

Photos by Philip Balko

In a basement storage area, you see four old shopping bag dispensers, once used to sell large shopping bags to customers for 15 cents apiece.

You follow your guides to another part of the basement, where natural light still floods in from windows that were never bricked over. According to Morey Sr., this area, situated under the parking garage, once housed the cabinetry and electrical shops and the maintenance department.

Red Sat Here

After the president's office, Jamie has to go, so the Lawruks continue the tour without him. They take you down to the basement of the Twelfth Avenue building, where you see a wall painted with the words "Biser Motors" and "White Trucks." "That was once an outside wall," explains Morey Sr. "That part of the building used to be Biser Motors. They sold White trucks, which were made in Altoona."

On the better-lit side of the room, you see the framework of what was once an office area. All that's left of one wall are the old studs, but a door still hangs in the doorway. The name "RED" and the years 1971, 1972, and 1974 have been spray-painted on the pale green surface of the door, with good reason.

"This used to be Red Hildebrand's office," says Morey Sr. "He worked here forever, watching over this place."

Photo by Robert Jeschonek

Next, you pass through a brick archway into another big room. Once part of the cabinetry, electrical, and maintenance area, it's filled with a forest of stout steel support columns that help to hold up the parking garage.

The End Is Not the End

Finally, your guides lead you through the maze of basement passages back to the delivery truck garage and outside. You've seen everything you can in the old Gable's buildings. The rest of the space, occupied by the offices of M&T bank and other tenants, is off-limits.

Fittingly, it is here that your tour ends, in the alley between the Eleventh and Twelfth Avenue buildings. You shake hands with Morey Sr. and Morey Jr. and wave goodbye as you stroll down the alley.

As you walk, you can't help gazing up at the brick walls towering on either side, can you? You can't help thinking about how busy they once were, teeming with life and commerce. You feel sad because all that's gone forever now, and the world continues to move on without it.

But then you feel better because at least you got to know the place when it was special. At least you got to experience it when it was still wild and bright and burning like the sun. And you know that all you need to do to recapture that magic is close your eyes and let your mind drift back to the time of wonders and giants, the golden age that lives forever in your gauzy, glittering memories.

Either that, or read about it in this book, which might just bring it to life for generations to come as well.

267

Photos by Philip Balko

Chapter Twenty-Eight

What the Trees Are Saying

Gable's is back.

How long have we waited to read or hear those words? How long have we wished in our hearts for them to be true? For the glorious old department store we remember to come back to life, better than ever?

Since we lost the store, our longing for it has only intensified. Looking back, we know the good thing we had. We realize we should have held on to it more tightly.

The best parts of it are things we could use more of now, things that seem to be in short supply everywhere we turn:

At Gable's, customers and employees alike were treated with kindness and civility, like family. Everyone got along.

Photo by Philip Balko

At Gable's, customer satisfaction was front and center. Business was about more than wringing every penny out of every transaction, cutting corners at every turn, and getting away with inferior merchandise or poor service.

At Gable's, ample staff was provided to meet customers' needs. The store wasn't so short-handed that employees couldn't take time to get to know shoppers and their preferences, encouraging repeat business.

At Gable's, yesterday was as important as today and tomorrow. Traditions were the backbone of the store, and people treasured them. Longtime employees were honored in the Quarter Century Club, and longtime customers were honored at the Anniversary Sales.

Like the trees planted by William F. Gable long ago, these ideas continue to grow and spread. There's a deeper longing for them than ever as our society, in many ways, becomes colder and more distant and quarrelsome, and we can't shake the feeling that we're *missing* something that we got right before.

And we could get it right again, if we really try.

Gable's is back.

Wouldn't it be wonderful if that was the headline today? If, miraculously, someone brought the store back to life, reminding us of the wonderful qualities it possessed in its heyday?

But what if we didn't need to bring it back at all? What if we didn't need to restore it, because…

Gable's never left.

Just look at all the people who remember it and share their memories in this book. Just look

at all the members of the Gable's family who came to the reunion to celebrate the joys of the store and the people who made it great.

Photos by Philip Balko

270

Photo by Philip Balko

Just look at the historians and collectors who have preserved so many photos and artifacts from the store, enough to fill the pages of this book and then some. Just look at the devoted social media communities that have sprung up to keep the truth of the store, its founder, and its guiding lights alive.

Just look at all of you, who in so many ways, every day of your lives, practice the lessons you learned at Gable's. Every time you treat a neighbor or stranger like family, you're keeping the Gable's way alive. Every time you go the extra mile on the job to help a customer or client, to make sure they're satisfied, you're channeling the Gable's philosophy. Every time you honor traditions or your elders, every time you acknowledge the importance of the past, you're on the path of Gable's.

Knowing that, we can work even harder to make Gable's an important part of our lives. To counteract the negativity that too often undermines our shared heritage of a civil society in which fairness, hard work, and mutual respect intertwine for the benefit of all.

It's what William F. Gable would want, isn't it?

Wouldn't he approve, if we continue in that positive direction? What if, late at night, the brick façade parted and the mortar dust cleared from the windows of the corner office on the fourth

Photo by Philip Balko

floor of the Twelfth Avenue building? What if, hands folded at his back, he looked out from the glass and took in the city around him, and all the county too? What if, eyes narrowed, he was able to see the map of our goodwill, take the measure of Gable's influence on our thoughts and words and deeds?

Would he find us wanting? Would he be disappointed? Would it make him wish he could walk among us again and do more?

Or perhaps, there would be no cause for regret after all...

See that sales clerk, taking extra time and effort to get an order just right for a customer? See that man, holding the door for an elderly woman? See those kids, doing yard work for a shut-in without asking for any reward?

The trees—silver maples and catalpas, elms and white ashes, mulberries and walnuts, all planted by William—wave their boughs, leaves fluttering and whispering in the breeze. Listen, are they trying to tell you something?

He never left, either.

William F. Gable is still here.

Courtesy Altoona Mirror

Miss Pennsylvania
Goes Shopping at
Gable's

Miss Mary Behe, oldest active employe of the William F. Gable company store and the subject of "This Is Your Life" sketch at the annual employes' dinner Saturday evening at the Penn-Alto hotel, is shown looking over the program for the evening with George F. Gable (left), president, and Stanley W. Truby, vice president.

Courtesy Altoona Mirror

Courtesy Anne Dixon

Courtesy Altoona Mirror

Courtesy Georgia Parsons

Chapter Twenty-Nine

A Tribute to William F. Gable

By Samuel A. Hamilton

FIRST CUSTOMER

SAMUEL A. HAMILTON

When I pass over the bridge connecting the Eleventh and Twelfth avenue buildings of the William F. Gable Company, above which hangs the medallion portrait of the founder; and, as I give my salute, my mind reverts to the famous lines of Longfellow:

"The lives of great men oft remind us,
We can make our lives sublime,
And departing, leave behind us,

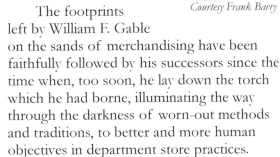

Courtesy Frank Barry

Footprints on the sands of time."

The footprints left by William F. Gable on the sands of merchandising have been faithfully followed by his successors since the time when, too soon, he lay down the torch which he had borne, illuminating the way through the darkness of worn-out methods and traditions, to better and more human objectives in department store practices.

It has oft been said that the memories of even the greatest of men mellow, and soften, and fade out with the lapse of time; first into tradition, and then into legend.

Courtesy David Seidel

273

THE BIG STORE, WILLIAM F. GABLE & CO., ALTOONA, PA.

Courtesy Georgia Parsons

But, the memory of William F. Gable will remain an ever constant guide in the minds and hearts of those who have taken up the burden of carrying out the many objectives he had in mind while in the zenith of his powers.

The memory of William F. Gable will never become traditional or legendary, because he builded too well! On the foundations he built from the beginning of the Gable's stores, his successors are now erecting the superstructure of the greater Gable's, thus bringing to fruition the things which he had planned; and those who are carrying on his work will have his memory, not as a tradition or a legend, but as a guiding star, leading them to the fulfillment of his vast ideals, until the time when they too, shall follow him into the dim, long, silent night of the Great Beyond.

You are always Welcome in this Store, and we thank you for being with us to-day.

Altoona, Pa.
March 1st 1918.

William F. Gable

Courtesy William Burket

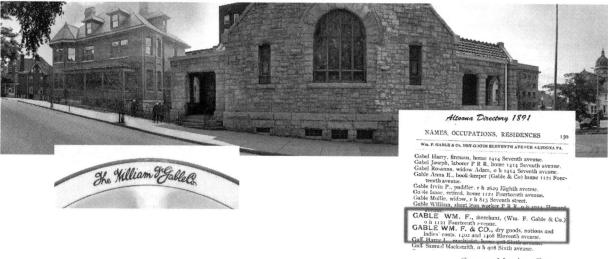

The William F. Gable Co.

Courtesy Matthew Germann

Acknowledgements

They say it takes a village to raise a child. Sometimes, it takes a village to raise a book, too...especially a book like this one.

Telling the whole story of Gable's department store would not have been possible without the village of eyewitnesses, collectors, historians, and preservationists who stepped forward to help bring it to life. Generously and graciously, they provided photos, clippings, artifacts, keepsakes, and guidance. They agreed to interviews to capture oral histories related to the store. Beyond all that, they provided support, encouragement, and hospitality, all in the expectation of one reward and one reward only: to see this book become a reality.

Many of them had wanted a book like this for a long time. They'd been waiting for it to happen, had saved up their photos and stories and souvenirs in the hope that they, like you, could someday hold a copy in their hands. Without them, this book wouldn't be here right now.

So let's raise our glasses to all of them, from the individuals who were personally interviewed to those who attended the Gable's reunion, to the faithful Gable's Facebook followers who provided recollections for the Memory Department chapters.

We also owe a special toast to those who went above and beyond in enriching this book, including: David Seidel, lover of history and keeper of an extraordinary online gallery of Gable's photos; Jeffery Holland, another historian and collector who contributed an enormous and well-documented photo archive; Matthew Germann, who also supplied an incredible collection of images and artifacts, plus personal guided tours of historic Gable's sites; Frank Barry, whose collection of Gable's treasures is matched only by his generosity of spirit; Morey Lawruk Sr. and Morey Lawruk Jr., who provided a tour of the modern Gable's buildings, which they and their partners own; and Jamie Powers, Virginia Parsons Brantner, and Georgia Parsons, grandchildren of William F. Gable, whose memories, insights, and keepsakes opened a window on the personal history of the Gable family and its relationship to the store and all of Blair County.

We also must give a round of applause to the local organizations that gave us a helping hand, including the Blair County Historical Society and the Blair County Genealogical Society. These two groups provided access to records, images, and artifacts unavailable from any other source. They do great work and deserve your support.

Then there's the *Altoona Mirror* newspaper, which rates its own special category of gratitude. The *Mirror* opened its on-site archives for this book and made it possible to publish little-seen images of Gable's through the years. The *Mirror's* online archives also provided rare images, plus invaluable information and eyewitness accounts that enabled us to reconstruct the Gable's story in full. The work of *Mirror* reporters like the late, great Tom Gibb (who led the coverage of the store's later days) offered a detailed account of Gable's history. We would be remiss if we didn't also salute the many unnamed reporters and editors who recorded the store's epic life down through the decades in countless editions of the *Mirror* and the *Altoona Tribune*. Hats off to the unknown journalists who helped make this book a dream come true for all of us in Gable's Nation.

Now that we've applauded, raised our glasses, and taken off our hats for the book's many guiding lights, let's give three cheers for the members of the book's production team, whose outstanding services made it shine so brightly: Philip Balko, photographer and photo editor beyond compare; Ben Baldwin, mega-talented cover artist and graphic designer; George Rowles, researcher and fact-checker; Ruth Rice, copy editor and proofreader; and Linda Hudkins, first reader, who deserves an *extra* cheer for inspiring this book in the first place.

Speaking of early supporters, Russ Stone gets a shout-out for helping to pave the way for this project. Russ, a lifelong fan of the Gable family and their store, created a Facebook group a while back for those who shared his appreciation of all things Gable. By opening the group to the author, Russ opened doors to people and resources that proved vital to the groundwork for this book.

When it comes to vital people, my wife, Wendy, takes the cake, as always. Words cannot express my full gratitude for her endless support, love, and understanding. Her contributions and sacrifices during the creation of this book are too many to count. Without her, there would be no book.

The same goes for all the shoppers, employees, and executives who made the Gable's department store such a success for so many years. Together, they (and *you*, if you're one of them) created something special with a lasting impact that will never die as long as we keep the story alive.

Finally, let's offer a standing ovation to the man who started it all—the founder, William F. Gable. His vision and reach changed Altoona...and, in some ways, the world. Perhaps most importantly of all, he showed us what can be accomplished when love and kindness go hand-in-hand with business. We can succeed without stepping on the people around us; that's just one of the things he taught us.

Books are wonderful; he taught us that, too. Would he be proud to be the star of *this* book, carrying his story forward so long after his untimely departure from this life? Would he love to be immortalized in these pages, read by you, and shared with future generations?

What do *you* think?

September 25, 2016, Johnstown, Pennsylvania

Courtesy Frank Barry

About the Creators

Robert

Author and editor Robert Jeschonek grew up in Johnstown, Pennsylvania, lived for years in Altoona, and has made it his mission to keep the rich history and culture of the region alive in his writing. His books and stories include *Long Live Glosser's*, *Christmas at Glosser's*, *Easter at Glosser's*, *Halloween at Glosser's*, *Death by Polka*, *Fear of Rain*, and *Penn Traffic Forever*, all set in and around Johnstown and Cambria County. He's written a lot of other cool stuff, too, including *Star Trek* and *Doctor Who* fiction and *Batman* comics. His young adult fantasy novel, *My Favorite Band Does Not Exist*, won a Forward National Literature Award and was named a top ten first novel for youth by *Booklist* magazine. His work has been published around the world in over a hundred books, e-books, and audio books. You can find out more about them at www.piepresspublishing.com and www.thefictioneer.com or by looking up his name on Facebook, Twitter, or Google. As you'll see, he's kind of crazy... in a *good* way.

Philip

Philip Balko is an internationally published and award-winning portrait and wedding photographer. When not engaged in providing personalized custom-designed photographic art for his individual and commercial clients, Phil can be found wandering local hills, valleys, and towns, recording the daily life and natural beauty of the Allegheny Highlands. Phil's commissioned work can be found at www.philipbalko.com and his landscapes and lightscapes can be viewed at www.laurelight.com.

Ben

Cover artist and graphic designer Ben Baldwin is a self-taught freelance artist from the UK who works with a combination of traditional media, photography, and digital art programs. He has been shortlisted for the British Fantasy Award for Best Artist for the last six years and has also been shortlisted for the British Science Fiction Association Award for Best Artist. In 2013, he won "Best Artist of the Year" in the annual This Is Horror Awards. You can find out more about Ben and his work at www.benbaldwin.co.uk and https://www.facebook.com/pages/Ben-Baldwin/343132594365

Bibliography

Gable & Co.'s 30th Anniversary Souvenir. A Brief History of Altoona and the People's Store. William F. Gable and Co., 1914.

Frees, H. Luther. *The Tale of a Friendship*. Stratford Press, 1917.

"Robert B. Gable Heads Store Firm." *Altoona Mirror*, February 1, 1922.

"Gable Company to Build on 12th Avenue." *Altoona Mirror*, May 15, 1922.

"Formal Opening and Reception in Gable's Arcade Annex and New Main Store Shops." Advertisement. *Altoona Mirror*, November 20, 1923.

Gable's Golden Anniversary. Altoona Mirror and *Altoona Tribune*, 1934

"Expansion Marks Entire 50 Years." *Altoona Mirror*, February 28, 1934.

"Changes Made to Improve Service." *Altoona Mirror*, February 28, 1934.

"Gable Store Has Grown 300 Fold." *Altoona Mirror*, February 28, 1934.

"Gable Brothers Manage Company." *Altoona Mirror*, January 16, 1931.

"Robert B. Gable Heads New Store." *Altoona Mirror*, April 14, 1932.

"Expansion Marks Gable's 52 Years." *Altoona Mirror*, February 28, 1936.

"Gable Store Is Ever Enlarging." *Altoona Mirror*, February 28, 1936.

"Marked Changes Noted at Gable's." *Altoona Mirror*, March 27, 1936.

"Personality Is Shown in Memoir." *Altoona Mirror*, March 27, 1936.

"Gable's First to Hold Anniversary." *Altoona Mirror*, March 27, 1936.

"'Thrifty' Store Popular Center." *Altoona Mirror*, March 27, 1936.

"Gable's Purchase Fine Mannequins." *Altoona Mirror*, March 27, 1936.

"Writes History of Gable Store." *Altoona Mirror*, February 26, 1937.

Hamilton, Samuel A. "A Tribute to William F. Gable." *Altoona Mirror,* February 26, 1937.

"Anniversary." *Altoona Mirror,* February 26, 1937.

"Notable Tribute Paid J.G. Anspach." *Altoona Mirror,* March 24, 1937.

"New Rights for Gable Customers." *Altoona Mirror,* October 16, 1937.

WFBG: The Gable Broadcasting Company: Radio Personalities. Gable's Publishing, 1939.

"Future Growth Visualized by Gable's Founder." *Altoona Mirror,* February 28, 1939.

"Improvements Are Up-To-Minute in Gable's Stores." *Altoona Mirror,* February 28, 1939.

"Gable Firm Head Is Host to Press on Anniversary." *Altoona Mirror,* March 2, 1939.

"Gable Store Founder Was Real Citizen." *Altoona Mirror,* March 7, 1939.

"Gable's Will Hold Biggest Celebration." *Altoona Mirror,* February 29, 1940.

"Writes Message in Appreciation of Gable Store." *Altoona Mirror,* February 29, 1940.

"Founder's Day." Advertisement. *Altoona Mirror,* March 8, 1940.

"The Big Store." *Altoona Mirror,* March 13, 1940.

"Gable's Store Is Noted For Its Features." *Altoona Mirror,* March 28, 1941.

"Gable's Store To End Sale Marking 57th Anniversary." *Altoona Mirror,* March 28, 1941.

"Store Originates Newer Enterprise in Merchandising." *Altoona Mirror,* March 28, 1941.

"Gable's Concern Is Observing 58th Birthday." *Altoona Mirror,* February 27, 1942.

Hamilton, S.A. "First Customer's Glowing Tribute To Store Founder." *Altoona Mirror,* February 27, 1942.

"Gable Firm Observes Its 59th Anniversary." *Altoona Mirror,* March 1, 1943.

"Point Ration System Opens; Buying Light." *Altoona Mirror,* March 1, 1943.

"Founder Planned Future Expansion of Gable's Store." *Altoona Mirror,* March 1, 1943.

"County's Quota For Books Has Been Attained." *Altoona Mirror,* March 3, 1943.

"Rationing Information." *Altoona Mirror,* March 3, 1943.

"Tribute Is Paid J. George Anspach By Gable Forces." *Altoona Mirror,* March 26, 1943.

"George Gable Accorded High Honor, Tribute." *Altoona Mirror,* November 23, 1943.

"Gable's To Observe 60th Anniversary." *Altoona Mirror,* February 28, 1944.

"Growth Is Phenomenal For Concern." *Altoona Mirror,* February 28, 1944.

Hamilton, S.A. "Voices Tribute To Founder of Gable Company." *Altoona Mirror,* February 29, 1944.

"Head of Gable Firm Is Host to Newsmen." *Altoona Mirror*, March 2, 1944.

"Friendship Week at Gable's." Advertisement. *Altoona Mirror*, July 29, 1944.

Hamilton, S.A. "Wm. F. Gable Man of Many Varied Traits." *Altoona Mirror*, February 28, 1945.

"All Blair County Towns Are Represented at Gable Function." *Altoona Mirror*, February 27, 1946.

"Journalists Are Guests at Gable Store." *Altoona Mirror*, March 2, 1946.

"J. G. Anspach, Gable Official, Dies Suddenly." *Altoona Mirror*, May 21, 1946.

"J. George Anspach." *Altoona Mirror*, May 21, 1946.

"Last Tribute Is Paid Late J. Geo. Anspach." *Altoona Mirror*, May 23, 1946.

"Many Attend Last Rites for J. G. Anspach." *Altoona Mirror*, May 24, 1946.

"Resolution Is Tendered on J. G. Anspach." *Altoona Mirror*, May 27, 1946.

"Gable Company Appointments Are Announced." *Altoona Mirror*, June 21, 1946.

"Gable Company Fetes Newsmen On Anniversary." *Altoona Mirror*, March 1, 1948.

"Gable's Celebrates." *Altoona Mirror*, March 1, 1949.

"Gable Store Fetes Altoona Newspapermen With Banquet." *Altoona Mirror*, March 2, 1949.

"Gable Store Host to City Newspapermen." *Altoona Mirror*, March 2, 1950.

"First Program of WFBG-TV Slated Sunday." *Altoona Mirror*, February 28, 1953.

"'Going Up!' Is Good Word At WFBG-TV." *Altoona Mirror*, February 28, 1953.

"Altoona's New Television Station." *Altoona Mirror*, February 28, 1953.

"Host of Technical 'Angles' Absorb WFBG-TV Technicians." *Altoona Mirror*, February 28, 1953.

"WFBG-TV To Join In Many Network Ties." *Altoona Mirror*, February 28, 1953.

"WFBG-TV Came to City After Long, Patient Negotiations." *Altoona Mirror*, February 28, 1953.

"WFBG-TV Has 'Ideal' Spot For Telecasts." *Altoona Mirror*, February 28, 1953.

"TeeVee Studio Set to Handle Live Programs." *Altoona Mirror*, February 28, 1953.

"Important Event In History Of WFBG-TV." *Altoona Mirror*, February 28, 1953.

"George P. Gable Pioneered With Plans for TV Station." *Altoona Mirror*, February 28, 1953.

"New TV Station." *Altoona Mirror*, February 28, 1953.

"Bell Plans $2,524,000 Program Here." *Altoona Mirror*, February 16, 1956.

"Sale of Local WFBG Stations Is Completed." *Altoona Mirror*, February 20, 1956.

"Bell Opens New Business Office In Gable Block." *Altoona Mirror*, October 15, 1956.

"Gable's Store To Celebrate 73rd Birthday." *Altoona Mirror*, February 28, 1957.

"It's Gable's 73rd." *Altoona Mirror*, March 1, 1957.

"Hustle, Bustle Mark Telephone Installing Job." *Altoona Mirror*, September 5, 1957.

"Improvements to Front of Gable Store Explained." *Altoona Mirror*, September 17, 1959.

"Gable's Store To Celebrate 76th Birthday." *Altoona Mirror*, February 27, 1960.

"Gable's Store To Celebrate 77th Birthday." *Altoona Mirror*, February 28, 1961.

"Truby Succeeds Founder's Son As Gable's Head." *Altoona Mirror*, March 22, 1961.

"Gable's Hosts Representatives of News Media." *Altoona Mirror*, March 2, 1962.

"Gable's to Mark 82nd Birthday." *Altoona Mirror*, February 26, 1966.

"George Gable Dies After Long Illness." *Altoona Mirror*, February 13, 1967.

"Happy 83rd Anniversary to Gable's." *Altoona Mirror*, February 27, 1967.

"Gable's Honors Local Newsmen At 83rd Dinner." *Altoona Mirror*, March 2, 1967.

Grover, Pat Hinton. "Highlights." *Altoona Mirror*, August 23, 1967.

Polito, Frank. "Tipton Woman Works at Local Store for 50 Years." *Altoona Mirror*, January 26, 1968.

"Gable's to Hold Two-Day 84th Birthday Sale." *Altoona Mirror*, February 29, 1968.

"Press Luncheon Held as Kickoff For Gable Sale." *Altoona Mirror*, May 31, 1968.

"12th Street Section Designated 1-Way." *Altoona Mirror*, October 29, 1968.

"Robert S. Powers New President of Gable's." *Altoona Mirror*, February 1, 1969.

"Gable Store Front To Get 'New Look'." *Altoona Mirror*, August 13, 1969.

"Gable and the Downtown." *Altoona Mirror*, August 14, 1969.

"City Gives Okay To $500,000 Gable Project." *Altoona Mirror*, April 15, 1971.

"Gable's Set Half-Million Renovations." *Altoona Mirror*, May 28, 1971.

"$500,000 Downtown Project." *Altoona Mirror*, June 15, 1971.

"Gable's to Mark David A. Little Day on Saturday." *Altoona Mirror*, August 20, 1971.

"Eleventh Avenue Façade Nearing Completion." *Altoona Mirror*, September 22, 1971.

"Robert B. Gable Dies; Former Store President." *Altoona Mirror*, December 30, 1971.

"Gable's Sale to Feature 'New World of Values.'" *Altoona Mirror*, August 13, 1975.

"American Heritage Week." Advertisement, *Altoona Mirror*, May 8, 1976.

"Gable's Sale to Feature 'New World of Values.'" *Altoona Mirror*, August 11, 1976.

Helsel, Bets E. "Happy 25th Anniversary, WTAJ-TV 10." *Altoona Mirror*, March 4, 1978.

"Gable's to Mark Its 94th Year." *Altoona Mirror*, August 19, 1978.

Ray, Phil. "L.S. Good Sells Gable's." *Altoona Mirror*, March 10, 1979.

"Gable's Not Sold, Just the Building." *Altoona Mirror*, March 12, 1979.

Gibb, Tom. "Previews Launch Hess's Into Area's Retail Battlefield." *Altoona Mirror*, September 18, 1979.

Gibb, Tom. "Ribbon Cut, Mall Addition Draws Crowd." *Altoona Mirror*, September 19, 1979.

"Some Open Sunday." *Altoona Mirror*, September 19, 1979.

Gibb, Tom. "Onlookers 'Amazed' at Fight Over Sunday Openings in Blair." *Altoona Mirror*, September 26, 1979.

Gibb, Tom. "Some Downtown Stores Stay Open Sunday." *Altoona Mirror*, December 10, 1979.

Gibb, Tom. "Five Major Retailers To Stay Open Sundays." *Altoona Mirror*, January 4, 1980.

Gibb, Tom. "Gable's May Open New Store." *Altoona Mirror*, January 4, 1980.

"Ferguson Mall Decision Affects Gable's Proposal." *Altoona Mirror*, May 16, 1980.

Gibb, Tom. "Gable's Parent Firm Seeks Protection From Creditors." *Altoona Mirror*, May 29, 1980.

Gibb, Tom. "Gable's Going Out of Business—Final Sale Set." *Altoona Mirror*, June 20, 1980.

Gibb, Tom. "Attorney Says Downtown Store Closing Because It's 'Not Profitable'." *Altoona Mirror*, June 21, 1980.

Gibb, Tom. "Attorney Says Downtown Store Closing Because It's 'Not Profitable'." *Altoona Mirror*, June 21, 1980.

Hopey, Don. "Plan Formed to Aid Downtown, Gable's." *Altoona Mirror*, June 25, 1980.

Gibb, Tom. "Local Merchants See 'Outside' Influence." *Altoona Mirror*, June 25, 1980.

Cogan, Barbara. Letter to the Editor. "Tribute to Gable's." *Altoona Mirror*, June 27, 1980.

"Gable's Veteran Optimistic About Future of Downtown." *Altoona Mirror*, June 27, 1980.

Barry, Ralph F. and Don Hopey. "Gable's Sale Held Despite City 'Ban.'" *Altoona Mirror*, July 1, 1980.

Gibb, Tom. "Gable's Top 10 Creditors Seek More Than $750,000." *Altoona Mirror*, July 1, 1980.

Gibb, Tom. "Final Fling Under Way at Store." *Altoona Mirror*, July 1, 1980.

Hopey, Don. "Mayor Holds Firm, Gable's Must Pay Daily Fine for Sale." *Altoona Mirror*, July 2, 1980.

Gibb, Tom and Don Hopey. "City, Gable's Officials Brawl Over Daily Fine." *Altoona Mirror*, July 3, 1980.

Gibb, Tom. "Showdown on Gable's Closing Slated Monday." *Altoona Mirror*, July 5, 1980.

McGough, Hugh. "Judge to Issue Verdict Friday On Gable's Closing, City Fines." *Altoona Mirror*, July 8, 1980.

Gibb, Tom. "Gable's: Ruling Expected Tuesday." *Altoona Mirror*, July 14, 1980.

McGough, Hugh. "Judge to Rule on Gable's Sale by July 31." *Altoona Mirror*, July 16, 1980.

Stephens, Kay. "For Many Employees, Gable's Store Was Home and Family." *Altoona Mirror*, July 23, 1980.

Stephens, Kay. "Tillie Wolf of Gable's." *Altoona Mirror*, July 25, 1980.

Gibb, Tom. "Decision on Gable's Closing in Limbo, Sale Goes On." *Altoona Mirror*, July 31, 1980.

Gibb, Tom. "Retailers, Developer Eye Gable's Buildings." *Altoona Mirror*, August 1, 1980.

Gibb, Tom. "Gable's Still Open, Sale Nearing End." *Altoona Mirror*, August 20, 1980.

Gibb, Tom. "A City Sleeping: Retailing Expert Says Altoona Needs Highways, 'Fairy Prince.'" *Altoona Mirror*, August 23, 1980.

Gibb, Tom. "Pact 'Near' On Gable's." *Altoona Mirror*, September 8, 1980.

McGough, Hugh. "Bank Seeks to Halt L.S. Good Reorganization." *Altoona Mirror*, September 12, 1980.

Gibb, Tom and Rebecca Bennett. "Gable Store Hopes Fade, Lawyer Says." *Altoona Mirror*, September 13, 1980.

"Land Rezoned To Residential, Owner Unhappy." *Altoona Mirror*, October 1, 1980.

"Value City Not Involved in Gable's 'Situation.'" *Altoona Mirror*, October 7, 1980.

Gibb, Tom. "Gable's: No Reopening in '80." *Altoona Mirror*, October 25, 1980.

McGough, Hugh. "Court Wants Fast L.S. Good Liquidation." *Altoona Mirror*, October 29, 1980.

Gibb, Tom. "Gable's Reports Denied." *Altoona Mirror*, February 11, 1981.

"Gable's 100th Anniversary Reunion." Advertisement, *Altoona Mirror*, March 24, 1984.

Gracey, L.T. "Gable's store would have been 100." *Altoona Mirror*, May 21, 1984.

Gable's: An Exhibit Commemorating the 100th Anniversary of the Store's Founding. Booklet. Blair County Historical Society, 1984.

Chalmers, Mike. "Sweet memories: Gable's last employee says he'll retire—eventually." *Altoona Mirror*, June 24, 1990.

"Former Gable's worker." *Altoona Mirror*, February 21, 1992.

"Robert Southwick Powers." Obituary, *Altoona Mirror,* January 8, 2003.

Bookhamer, Larry. Phone interview by Robert Jeschonek. Digital recording. April 19, 2016.

Brantner, Virginia Parsons. Phone interview by Robert Jeschonek. Digital recording. February 8, 2016.

Conrad, Maxine. Phone interview by Robert Jeschonek. Digital recording. July 5, 2016.

Dixon, Anne. Phone interview by Robert Jeschonek. Digital recording. February 21, 2016.

Hildebrand, Helen. Phone interview by Robert Jeschonek. Digital recording. September 13, 2016.

Parsons, Georgia. Phone interview by Robert Jeschonek. Digital recording. March 13, 2016.

Powers, Jamie. Phone interviews by Robert Jeschonek. Digital recordings. February 8 & 10, 2016.

Shade, Nadine. Phone interview by Robert Jeschonek. Digital recording. March 30, 2016.

Shannon, Jim. Phone interview by Robert Jeschonek. Digital recording. April 5, 2016.

Sheedy, George. Phone interview by Robert Jeschonek. Digital recording. March 26, 2016.

Winstead, Dave. Phone interview by Robert Jeschonek. Digital recording. March 24, 2016.

Image Notes

All photos credited to Gelon V. Smith are from the collection of Jeffery D. Holland and William Burket unless otherwise indicated.

Some photos credited courtesy Frank Barry or Anne Dixon might also be the work of photographer Gelon V. Smith.

All photos credited to photographer Fred Deichert are courtesy the collection of Pam Toroian.

Other photos are credited "Courtesy of" without a photographer credit because the photographer of such images was unknown at the time of publication. We hope to provide additional details regarding these images in future editions of this book.

Images from Gable's 50th Anniversary edition of the *Altoona Mirror,* credited to the *Mirror,* are also courtesy Matthew Germann.

Image Courtesy Frank Barry

THE "BIG STORE"—William F. Gable & Co.

THE HOME OF THE GABLE & CO. MILL AND FACTORY SALE

Some Facts About The Big Store

It contains over 50,000 square feet of floor space.

There are thirty different departments, each one a store in itself.

From 250 to 350 employes, according to the season, are required to serve its patrons properly.

A modern cable cash carrier, operated by electricity, carries cash from fifty odd stations.

It requires six wagons to deliver the goods that are sold each day, to the homes of its customers.

It is heated by hot water and a perfect system of ventilation is secured from 26 ventilating flues leading from the salesrooms to the roof.

It is just one and one-half blocks from the Pennsylvania railroad station and is easy of access from all trolley lines.

Goods are bought at the lowest market prices and are sold accordingly— the principal reason why this store has grown so rapidly.

The One Price System was inaugurated when the store was opened, 22 years ago, and has been steadfastly lived up to ever since. It's a system that enables you to buy at Gable & Co.'s as cheaply as does your neighbor, as it means One Price to All.

It is abundantly lighted by daylight during the day and by electricity at night.

It is a homelike place throughout and we invite you to visit it often. You are welcome to make it your headquarters while in the city.

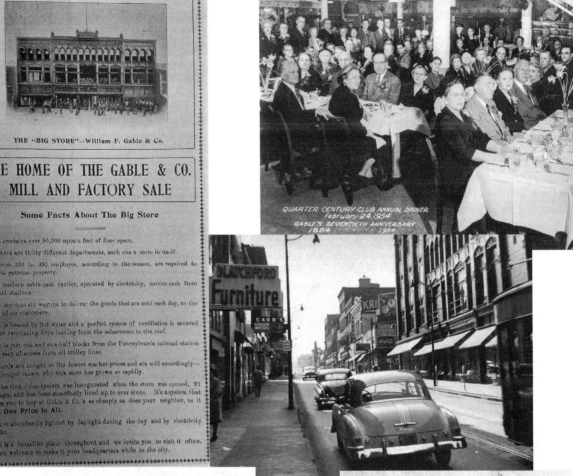

QUARTER CENTURY CLUB ANNUAL DINNER
February 24, 1954
GABLE'S SEVENTIETH ANNIVERSARY
1884   1954

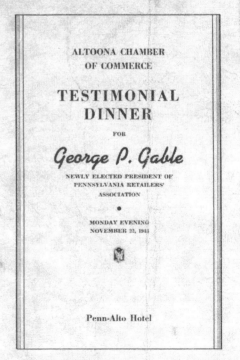

ALTOONA CHAMBER
OF COMMERCE

TESTIMONIAL
DINNER

FOR

George P. Gable

NEWLY ELECTED PRESIDENT OF
PENNSYLVANIA RETAILERS'
ASSOCIATION

•

MONDAY EVENING
NOVEMBER 22, 1943

Penn-Alto Hotel

Courtesy Frank Barry, Matthew Germann, Georgia Parsons, and David Seidel

Bonus Gallery

For Mother's Day ---
A
Singing
Canary
$6.95

One of these lovely Canary Birds would make a pleasing gift for Mother. They are specially priced for tomorrow.

All Birds Are Guaranteed Singers

Gable's

PET SHOP—11th AVENUE BUILDING—BASEMENT

Black and White Interior Photos by Gelon V. Smith   *Other photos courtesy Frank Barry, Jim Shannon, and Georgia Parsons*

Photos by Philip Balko, Frank Barry, Jim Shannon, and Gelon V. Smith

Courtesy Jeffery Holland

In Honor of Our Nation's Bicentennial

Gable's "AMERICAN HERITAGE" BICENTENNIAL WEEK

Photo by Gelon V. Smith

Courtesy Altoona Mirror

Can you smell the roasting peanuts?

The Glosser Bros. Department Store has reopened, just for you, just in the pages of this one-of-a-kind book. For the first time, the whole true story of Glosser's has been told, on the 25th anniversary of the fabled department store's closing. Step through the famous doors on the corner of Franklin and Locust Streets and grab a brown-and-white-striped shopping bag. You're about to embark on a journey from the humble beginnings of Glosser Bros. to its glory days as a local institution and multi-million dollar company…and the thrilling battle to save it on the eve of its grand finale. Read the stories of the executives, the employees, and the loyal shoppers who made Glosser Bros. a legend and kept it alive in the hearts and minds of Glosser Nation. Hundreds of photos, never before gathered together in one place, will take you back in time to the places and people that made Glosser's great. Experience the things you loved best about the classic department store, from the roasted nuts to the Shaffer twins to the Halloween windows and the amazing sales. Discover secrets and surprises that have never been revealed to the general public until now. Relive the story of a lifetime in a magical tour straight out of your memories and dreams, a grand reopening of a store that never really closed in your heart and will open its doors every time we shout…

Long Live Glosser's

BOLD BRIGHTS

Penn Traffic

PENN TRAFFIC COMPANY
QUALITY
SIGN OF QUALITY
FOR EVERY KIND OF MERCHANDISE
MERCHANDISE
JOHNSTOWN'S GREATEST STORE

Penn Traffic VIP

SAMUEL H. HECKMAN
PRESIDENT AND GENERAL MANAGER
YEARS OF SERVICE 57
1901-1958

Meet you on the mezzanine...

The Penn Traffic Department Store is back in business in the pages of this one-of-a-kind book. Now's your chance to revisit this Johnstown, Pennsylvania landmark or experience its magic for the very first time. The whole true story of the legendary store, its employees, and the shoppers who loved it is right here, complete with all your favorite treats and traditions. Help yourself to Penn Way candies...have a burger and fries in the Penn Traffic restaurant...relax on the mezzanine...and wait on the sidewalk on a cold winter's night for the grand unveiling of the most spectacular Christmas window in town. You'll never forget this trip through history, from the store's pre-Civil War beginnings to its dramatic finale 123 years later, with three devastating floods, an epic fire, and a high-stakes robbery in between. Hundreds of photos, never before gathered in one place, will whisk you back in time to the people and events that made Penn Traffic great...and carry you forward for a special tour of the Penn Traffic building as it stands today, complete with traces and treasures from the store's glory days. You'll feel like you've returned to the store of your dreams, especially when you cook up the authentic goodies in the Penn Traffic recipe section, handed down from the store's own bakery and candy kitchen all-stars. If you've ever longed to go back to the magical department store where you always felt at home, or you just long for a simpler, sweeter place where the air smells like baking bread and the customer is always right, step inside. Welcome to the grand reopening of the store that comes to life every time we shout the magic words...

Penn Traffic
Forever

Other Western Pennsylvania Books
By Robert Jeschonek

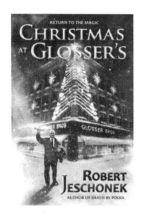

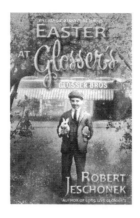

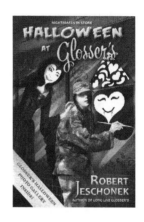

(A Johnstown Flood Story)   (A Johnstown Mystery)   (A Cambria County Adventure)

Order from Amazon, Barnes and Noble, Books-A-Million,
or any bookstore or online bookseller.

Ask your book dealer to search by title at Ingram or Baker and Taylor.

Also available from Pie Press at www.piepresspublishing.com
or call (814) 525-4783

pie press publishing

63698694R00170

Made in the USA
Charleston, SC
12 November 2016